PAT BROWN, MBA

Financial Literacy For Professors

"A Professor's Guide to Money, Retirement, and Wealth Beyond the Classroom"

ABRAM 47 BROWN

First edition

ISBN: 978-1-967737-47-5

This book was professionally typeset on Reedsy.
Find out more at reedsy.com

Contents

Preface vi
How to use this book viii
Why This Book Exists xii
Meet Pat Brown, MBA — Financial Advocate for the Academic... xiv
Part I: Starting the Journey — From First Offer to First... 1
Chapter 1: Welcome to Academia Understanding Your Employment... 2
Chapter 2: Salary vs. Stipend Reading Paychecks, Pay... 10
Chapter 3: Relocation & Start-Up Packages: Negotiating... 16
Chapter 4: Budgeting on an Assistant Professor's Income,... 22
Chapter 5: Your First 403(b), 457(b), or 401(a): How... 28
Chapter 6: State Pension vs. Defined Contribution:... 33
Chapter 7: Health, Dental, Vision & FSAs: Picking the Right... 38
Chapter 8: Campus Credit Unions & Banking: Leveraging... 44
Part II: Building Tenure & Financial Stability 50
Chapter 9: The Tenure Clock, Milestones, Money Mindset, and... 51
Chapter 10: Publishing, Grants, and Pay Bumps, Turning... 56
Chapter 11: Sabbaticals & Leaves, Planning Finances Around... 62
Chapter 12: Buying a Home in a College Town, Mortgage Math,... 67
Chapter 13: Campus Child-Care, 529s, and Education Perks,... 73
Chapter 14: Upgrading Insurance, Life, Disability, Umbrella,... 79
Chapter 15: Mid-Career Burnout, Recognizing Signs and... 88
Chapter 16: Negotiating a Counter-Offer, Using Competing... 93
Chapter 17: Saying "No" at Mid-Career, Guarding Time,... 98
Part III · Diversifying Income — Consulting, Side Gigs & IP 104
Chapter 18: Consulting 101, Structuring Engagements, Hourly... 105

Chapter 19: Expert Witness Work, Setting Rates, Retainers,... 115
Chapter 20: Speaking, Workshops, and MOOCs, Monetizing Your... 122
Chapter 21: Royalties & Book Deals, Negotiating Advances,... 127
Chapter 22: Patents, Licensing, and Start-Ups, Turning... 134
Chapter 23: Board Service & Advisory Roles: Compensation... 139
Chapter 24: Summer Salary Strategies: Grant Funding,... 148
Chapter 25: Creating an LLC or S-Corp, When, Why, and How... 156
Chapter 26: Travel Reimbursements & Per Diem, Keeping... 166
Chapter 27: IRS Red Flags for Faculty, Common Audit Triggers... 175
Part IV · Growing & Protecting Wealth Through the Career Arc 182
Chapter 28: Investment Basics for Scholars, Asset... 183
Chapter 29: Tax-Efficient Investing, Backdoor Roths, HSAs,... 190
Chapter 30: Real Estate Beyond the Primary Home, Rental... 198
Chapter 31: Caring for Aging Parents, Financial Support,... 204
Chapter 32: Family & Friends Asking for Money, Scripts,... 212
Chapter 33: Charitable Giving & Donor-Advised Funds,... 217
Chapter 34: Estate Planning for Academics, Wills, Trusts,... 223
Chapter 35: Managing Lifestyle Inflation, Keeping Up with... 230
Chapter 36: Insurance Tune-Ups at Every Decade, Coverage... 236
Part V · Late Career, Transitions, and Life After the Last... 244
Chapter 37: Full Professor Pay & Perks, Merit Raises, Named... 245
Chapter 38: Phased Retirement Programs, Gradual Exits,... 252
Chapter 39: Don't Roll It Yet, When State Retirement Plans... 257
Chapter 40: Leaving for Administration, Financial Trade-Offs... 262
Chapter 41: Changing Universities Mid-Career, Vesting Rules,... 269
Chapter 42: Bridge Jobs & Encore Careers, Consulting Firms,... 275
Chapter 43: Social Security & Medicare Timing for... 282
Chapter 44: Annuities, TIAA, and Lifetime Income, Converting... 288
Chapter 45: Legacy on Campus, Endowments, Scholarships, and... 294

Chapter 46: Downsizing, Second Homes, and Global... 299
Chapter 47: Retirement Rehearsal & Final Exit, Psychological... 304
Chapter 48: The Next Chapter Is Yours, Closing Reflections... 310
Disclaimer 313
Learn More and Stay Connected 316
Important Dates 319
Questions to Ask a Financial Advisor (For Professors and... 324
Wealth Manager's Coordination 330
Final Word 334

Preface

This book was born from a simple but persistent question I kept hearing from my colleagues, clients, and friends in higher education: *Why didn't anyone teach us this sooner?* Despite their intelligence, advanced degrees, and deep expertise in their disciplines, many professors, researchers, and academic professionals told me they felt underprepared—or worse, embarrassed—when it came to their personal finances. It wasn't for lack of ability. It was because no one ever explained the rules of the money game in a way that felt tailored to the academic life.

The truth is, managing money as a professor isn't as straightforward as it sounds. Your salary might be stable—or it might fluctuate with summer funding or grants. Your benefits might be generous—but hard to understand. You might have tenure, but also student loans. Maybe you're balancing a dual-academic household. Maybe you're moving across the country for a postdoc or weighing whether to become department chair. Maybe you're wondering how your 403(b) actually works, or how to help your kids without derailing your own retirement. The academic career path is unique. Your financial guidance should be too.

This book is my attempt to offer that guidance—not in the form of one-size-fits-all advice, but through clear explanations, relatable examples, and actionable steps that meet you wherever you are on your academic journey. Whether you're just starting out, in mid-career, or planning your transition into retirement, I wrote this book to feel like a conversation, not a lecture. My goal is to arm you with the context, clarity, and confidence to make smart financial decisions—without shame, fear, or jargon.

You won't find gimmicks here. You will find chapters on everything from budgeting with a nine-month salary to understanding phased retirement, from helping aging parents to protecting your intellectual property. Some chapters will feel immediately relevant; others may become more valuable as your career evolves. That's the point. This book is meant to grow with you. Use it as a reference, a guide, a conversation starter, and a quiet companion when financial questions feel loud in your mind.

If you've ever felt like the financial world wasn't built for people like you—too busy, too thoughtful, too specialized—I hope this book proves otherwise. You don't need to become a financial expert. You just need the right map, a little courage, and a reminder that your future is worth planning for.

Welcome. Let's begin.

How to use this book

Let's start with a truth that may surprise you: this book wasn't written for you to read cover to cover in one sitting. In fact, it was designed to meet you where you are, not where someone else thinks you should be. Whether you're a brand-new assistant professor, a mid-career faculty member managing multiple income streams, or nearing retirement and wondering how best to draw down your assets, this book was built as your toolkit. It's more like a guidebook than a novel—something you can revisit, flip through, and engage with over time. The chapters are intentionally modular so you can skip around based on your current questions and needs.

One of the best ways to use this book is to think of it as a collection of coffee chats with someone who's been around the academic and financial block a few times. You won't find lectures or intimidating jargon here, but you will find straight talk and real-world examples that reflect the actual lives of professors, researchers, and educators. If you see a chapter title that feels relevant—say, something about summer salary, phased retirement, or helping your kids with college—you can jump right in without worrying about reading the rest first. That flexibility is intentional, because your financial questions won't follow a linear path. Life has its own sequence of surprises, and your reading of this book can mirror that same non-linear rhythm.

Don't be afraid to write in the margins, highlight sections, or leave sticky notes on pages you want to revisit. Just like your teaching notes or journal articles, this book should be a living, evolving document that interacts with your professional and personal life. Your financial life isn't static, and neither is how this book can serve you. A chapter that doesn't seem relevant today might be exactly what you need a year from now, when your role shifts, your family changes, or a new opportunity comes your way. Think of this book as your financial companion throughout your academic journey—not just a reference, but a sounding board.

The best time to use this book is when you feel a little uncertain but also curious. For example, if your university HR sends out an open enrollment email and you suddenly realize you don't fully understand your health insurance options, that's a perfect time to flip to a chapter that touches on benefits and gaps in coverage. If a colleague starts talking about deferred comp plans, and you nod along but don't really get what that means, it's time to sit down and read that section slowly. This book can act as a translator between complex systems and everyday decision-making, helping you stay in the driver's seat.

It's okay if some chapters feel a little too advanced or too simple at the moment. The goal isn't to master everything right away—it's to keep learning in context. One reader might use this book to figure out how to manage variable summer income, while another is trying to sort out what to do with a 403(b) from a former institution. The beauty is that it can do both, at your pace. Some sections are for now. Others are for next semester. Others still are for when you start imagining what life might look like after your last lecture.

You'll notice that this book isn't filled with formulas or complicated charts. That's intentional. Financial literacy doesn't require you to be a math whiz. What it does require is a mindset shift—moving from reactivity to intentionality, from avoidance to awareness. This book focuses on helping you think through trade-offs, set realistic expectations, and prepare for transitions with eyes wide open. It gives you tools to reduce stress, minimize mistakes, and amplify what's already working in your life.

Another way to use this book is to spark conversations. Maybe you and a colleague have both been talking about estate planning, but neither of you has taken action. Why not read that chapter together, then meet for coffee to compare notes? Or perhaps your partner has questions about Social Security timing, and you want to explore it as a team. This book can be a bridge—not just between you and your finances, but between you and the people you care about. Talking about money can feel awkward, especially in academia where we often pretend everyone is making the same amount or share the same goals. But this book invites honesty, reflection, and dialogue.

If you're a planner, you might decide to make a reading calendar—one chapter per week, with time to reflect or take action on each topic. That's a great approach if structure helps you move forward. On the other hand, if you're a spontaneous type who likes to learn just-in-time, that's fine too. The index and table of contents are your best friends in that case. Look up what you need, when you need it, and go straight to the heart of the matter. There's no wrong way to use a resource that respects your time and intelligence.

When things in your life shift—maybe you take on a new role, inherit money, or become responsible for aging parents—this book will be here. It's built for the long haul. You might find that certain chapters hit differently depending on the season of life you're in. A section on insurance might seem dull now, but suddenly become urgent after a health scare. A chapter on real estate might have seemed out of reach, until you start daydreaming about downsizing or buying a second home. Don't be surprised if you find new meaning in familiar pages. That's a sign you're growing.

There's also something powerful about revisiting a chapter after taking action. Let's say you finally set up your estate documents, or move your old 403(b) into a low-cost IRA. Reading the chapter again can reinforce what you've done right—and offer insight into your next steps. It's like rereading a novel after a few years and catching details you missed the first time. Your evolving experience will keep reshaping what this book means to you.

This book is also a great check-in tool during your financial reviews. Whether you do a formal review once a year or a quick gut check each semester, flipping through the chapters can help you identify what's changed. Maybe a tax law has shifted. Maybe your institution updated its retirement plan rules. Maybe you're just ready for a new money goal. Whatever the case, this book can anchor your reflections and keep you from drifting off-course.

If something in the book feels overwhelming, pause. Don't let it stop your momentum. Take a breath, reread it slowly, or talk it through with someone. Many financial concepts are unfamiliar the first time we hear them—but they get easier with repetition and context. You're not expected to become an expert overnight. Progress is more important than perfection.

Use the real-life examples and analogies as jumping-off points. Picture yourself in those scenarios. Ask, "What would I do in that situation?" That kind of personal application helps the information stick. It turns abstract advice into lived wisdom. Even if the example doesn't mirror your exact life, there's usually a universal truth buried inside.

One of the most important takeaways from this book is that your financial decisions should reflect your values—not someone else's checklist. The goal isn't to "win" at money. It's to align your financial life with your academic, personal, and family priorities. That alignment creates clarity, confidence, and peace of mind. You'll find that kind of framing throughout the chapters, nudging you to think deeply and act intentionally.

This book won't give you all the answers—but it will help you ask better questions. That's where your power lies. Better questions lead to better conversations, better research, and better decisions. Just like your academic work, your financial life is a living, breathing process of discovery. Let this book be a steady companion as you navigate it all.

So when should you pick up this book again? Any time you feel stuck, curious, anxious, or ready to plan. Any time you want to reflect, regroup, or recommit to a financial goal. Any time someone drops a term like "backdoor Roth" in a meeting and you want to understand it before tomorrow. That's what this book is for. It's your financial anchor in an unpredictable world.

Keep this book close. Put a sticky note on your favorite chapter. Revisit it during office hours, late at night, or on a quiet Sunday morning with coffee in hand. Your future self will thank you for making time to learn, reflect, and act today. And if you ever wonder whether the effort is worth it—remember this: financial literacy is freedom. Freedom to say yes. Freedom to say no. Freedom to live life on your own terms. This book is your key.

Why This Book Exists

Let's get something straight: most financial advice wasn't written with you in mind.

If you're a professor, researcher, or academic professional, you already know your career doesn't follow a conventional path. Nine-month salaries. Grant cycles. Sabbaticals. Department politics. Retirement systems that sound like alphabet soup—TIAA, 403(b), 457(b), ORP, TRS. Add in student loans, delayed home buying, kids' college costs, and maybe a side consulting gig, and it's easy to feel like personal finance just isn't built for the faculty life. You're not alone. Most financial advice assumes a standard career path with steady raises, straightforward benefits, and retirement at 65. That's not your story—and pretending it is won't help you plan better.

This book was created because the academic path requires its own financial blueprint. Whether you're adjunct or tenured, early-career or emeritus, the money you earn—and the way it moves—needs context. You may have done everything "right": earned advanced degrees, secured a stable job, contributed to your retirement plan. But that doesn't mean you were ever taught how to read your pay stub, how vesting schedules work, or how to avoid overpaying in taxes when a summer grant kicks in. And let's be honest: talking about money in academic circles often feels taboo. But staying quiet about it doesn't protect you from confusion—or from costly mistakes.

Financial stress shows up in different ways. Maybe you've delayed buying a home. Maybe you're unsure if you can afford to take a sabbatical. Maybe you're helping your kids with tuition and your parents with long-term care—while wondering if your own retirement plan is on track. Maybe you're earning well but unsure how to turn income into long-term wealth.

Whatever stage of your academic career you're in, one thing is clear: financial literacy is no longer optional. It's essential.

This book isn't here to shame you for what you don't know. It's here to give you tools. Practical tools. Actionable strategies. And a little bit of peace of mind. You don't need to become a financial planner—you just need someone to explain how the pieces fit together. How to protect what you've earned, grow what you're saving, and make decisions you won't regret five or ten years from now. Because there are very real consequences for waiting too long to figure this stuff out.

You'll find chapters in this book that address your full career arc—from negotiating your first offer to navigating phased retirement. From understanding your university's retirement options to deciding whether to roll over funds or keep them in place. From insurance blind spots to tax traps. From funding your kids' education to planning your own legacy. It's not meant to be read in one sitting. It's meant to sit on your desk, ready when you are—when you finally decide to open your benefits packet or when you receive a consulting opportunity and want to know how to structure it wisely.

The goal is to give you clarity. To make the invisible visible. To teach you how to think about money with the same critical lens you bring to your discipline. And to remind you that wealth-building isn't just for other professions. You've spent years helping students think deeper and reach higher. Now it's time to do that for yourself—financially.

This isn't about becoming rich. It's about becoming resourced. Confident. Equipped. And free to make choices based on values—not fear or financial guesswork.

Let's begin.

Meet Pat Brown, MBA — Financial Advocate for the Academic Community

My name is Pat Brown, MBA, and I'm the founder of *Financial Literacy for Professors*. Over the past 20+ years, I've worked with educators, researchers, and academic professionals across the country, helping them navigate the often-overlooked financial complexities of university life. From nine-month pay structures and grant-funded summer income to retirement planning across multiple institutions, I've seen just how unique—and underserved—professors are when it comes to financial education.

My background spans financial advising, retirement planning, insurance, tax strategy, and real-world money conversations that impact your daily life and long-term future. But more than titles or certifications, what qualifies me to serve you is this: I listen. I pay attention to the blind spots, the unasked questions, and the institutional red tape that too often leaves professors confused or underserved. Whether you're tenure-track, adjunct, department chair, or stepping into an administrative role, I help you see your financial picture clearly, and take confident steps forward.

My approach is grounded in education and practicality. I'm not here to sell products—I'm here to empower you with the knowledge and tools you didn't get in your Ph.D. program. Together, we build a financial plan that reflects your values, protects your time, and helps you optimize your university benefits. We'll walk through real decisions—whether to roll over that 403(b), how to coordinate Social Security with your pension, how to plan for sabbaticals, or how to support your kids through college without derailing your own retirement.

If you'd like to connect, ask questions, or work together, I invite you to reach out. You can email me directly at **info@financialliteracyforprofessors.com**, or connect with me on LinkedIn: www.linkedin.com/in/patrickbrownmba. I regularly share free content, tools, and ideas for professors who want to take control of their financial future without needing to become full-time experts in investing, taxes, or retirement law.

This book is a reflection of the conversations I've had with professors just like you—conversations about money, yes, but also about freedom, stress, legacy, and choice. My goal is to make sure that all the years you've spent building knowledge, mentoring others, and doing work that matters are supported by financial decisions that serve *you*. I'm honored to be in your corner.

Let's get to work—together.

Part I: Starting the Journey — From First Offer to First Lecture

Part I sets the stage for life as a professor by walking readers through the pivotal transition from receiving their first academic job offer to stepping into the lecture hall for the very first time. This section focuses on demystifying the employment offer, helping new faculty understand that their compensation includes much more than just salary. It covers the nuances of nine-month vs. twelve-month pay structures, explains the difference between tenure-track, adjunct, and visiting positions, and offers practical guidance for negotiating salary, start-up packages, and moving allowances with confidence and clarity.

Readers will learn how to evaluate university-sponsored benefits—such as health insurance, retirement plans like 403(b) and 457(b), and tuition assistance—as part of their total compensation. This part also addresses the logistics and costs of relocation, how to avoid early-career financial pitfalls, and the importance of building a realistic budget around academic pay cycles. With real-life examples, simple analogies, and friendly advice, Part I equips new professors with the financial literacy they need to enter academia informed, prepared, and empowered. Whether you're stepping into your first classroom or still weighing offers, this section ensures you're starting your career on strong financial footing.

Chapter 1: Welcome to Academia Understanding Your Employment Offer and Total Compensation

Welcome to your first faculty desk, the place where coffee rings and chalk dust mingle with your ambition, and where the letter offering you the position suddenly feels both exhilarating and overwhelming. In that stack of pages, your dreams of shaping young minds meet the very real math of making rent, paying off loans, and planning for a future that still seems a little blurry. The salary figure in bold may jump out first, but slow down and notice the fine print: is it spread evenly over nine months or twelve, does it scale annually with merit or cost-of-living adjustments, and how does it compare to peer institutions in your field? Picture your paycheck as the trunk of a mighty oak; sturdy, yes, yet only part of the entire tree that feeds your financial ecosystem. Fringe benefits—health coverage, retirement matches, tuition waivers—are the roots, often hidden yet essential for growth. Understanding every nutrient in that soil early on is the difference between a sapling that flourishes and one that strains in rocky ground.

Even seasoned scholars can stumble on the concept of nine-month versus twelve-month pay, so here's a quick illustration: think of nine-month pay like teaching a summer-intensive course—compressed, denser, and gone before the sunburn fades. If your contract states nine months at $81,000, divide by nine to see $9,000 a month rolling in during the academic year, but nothing in June, July, and August unless you elect to stretch those dollars across all twelve pages of your calendar. Some universities let payroll "annualize" those checks so your budget doesn't dry up midsummer, but that also means a slightly leaner monthly amount. Whatever the setup, map it onto your real-life bills just like matching puzzle pieces, ensuring the picture looks whole even when class is out and the beach is calling. Because there's nothing quite like realizing mid-July that your mortgage is punctual but your paycheck is on sabbatical.

Next comes the subtle art of valuing health benefits, which often feel as abstract as quantum physics until you need an MRI on a sprained knee from campus pickup basketball. University plans can be surprisingly generous, especially if the institution self-insures and negotiates favorable group rates, yet premiums, deductibles, and out-of-pocket maximums differ more than dialects across regions. Ask for the summary of benefits and coverage, then run a simple thought experiment: if you broke your leg tomorrow, how much would leave your wallet before insurance took over? Multiply that risk by family members, sprinkle in dental and vision, and you have a clearer picture of whether Option A's higher monthly premium is actually cheaper protection than Option B's lower upfront cost but higher deductible. This mental exercise may seem unromantic compared with planning your first lecture, but it means safeguarding your capacity to stand in front of that lecture hall in the first place. Treat your body and mind as your primary instruments; insuring them properly is like tuning a Stradivarius before the concert.

Retirement contributions often hide in plain sight, buried under acronyms that resemble secret societies—403(b), 457(b), 401(a), and the grand old TIAA annuity. Imagine them as differently shaped jars lining your future pantry, each with its own lid, label, and rules on how and when you can eat the cookies inside. A 403(b) generally looks like a corporate 401(k) twin raised inside campus gates: pre-tax deposits, investment choices from index funds to annuities, and potential employer matching that is effectively free money you'd never leave on the table at a dinner party. A 457(b), if offered, adds another jar you can fill without stepping on the 403(b)'s toes, usually sporting fewer withdrawal penalties for early retirement. Then there's the sometimes-mandatory 401(a) or state pension alternative, whose fixed contribution rates feel like autopilot—comforting for some flyers, restrictive for others who crave manual control. Your task is to calculate how these jars can align with long-term goals, balancing risk, tax deferral, and liquidity like a chemist titrating a complex solution.

Before the ink dries on your contract, consider start-up funds, research allowances, and equipment budgets the way a chef eyes the quality of knives and pans in a new kitchen. Are you receiving a lump sum to equip a lab, a timeline for spending it, and clarity on whether leftover dollars roll over or evaporate? Likewise, conference travel money might sound lush until you price flights to that annual meeting in Singapore. Universities often reimburse only after proof of travel, turning you into your own short-term lender unless you plan ahead with a designated savings buffer or a credit card that earns points without burying you in interest. A well-negotiated start-up package is not greed; it's fuel for the scholarly engine your institution just invested in. Think of it as seeds for research productivity—skimping now only slows the harvest that benefits both you and the university.

If you are joining as an adjunct, the rules change like moving from full-course dining to à la carte. Per-course pay can appear robust until insurance, retirement matches, and job security vanish like footnotes in a draft. You may teach at multiple campuses, making scheduling a logistical jigsaw and healthcare coverage a patchwork quilt. To survive and thrive, adjuncts often form limited liability companies for consulting work, stash cash in individual retirement accounts, and lean heavily on networking to secure consistent gigs. The upside is agility: you can walk away from toxic departments faster than a tenure-track counterpart. But the downside—financial volatility—requires meticulous budgeting and a relentless focus on building portable skills the market will pay for, from instructional design to corporate training.

Negotiation may sound like adversarial chess, yet done well it resembles collaborative jazz—each party riffing until the tune satisfies both. Salary bands can be narrow, but you can often secure additional perks such as course releases, graduate assistant support, or higher moving allowances just by asking with data in hand. Show comparable offers, cost-of-living adjustments, and evidence of publications or grants, and you transform from hopeful candidate to informed partner. Remember that search committees and deans are still human; they respond to respectful, well-structured requests that demonstrate you value the institution's constraints while advocating for your worth. Even a modest bump early in your career compounds across raises and retirement contributions, turning hundreds into tens of thousands over decades. Approach the conversation like prepping students for a final: do your homework, anticipate questions, and lead with confidence rooted in preparation.

Relocation can be more expensive than a first-edition textbook, especially if your move crosses oceans rather than state lines. University reimbursements may cap movers, flights, and temporary housing, leaving hidden costs such as utility deposits, license fees, or increases in everyday expenses like groceries. Picture relocation like a marathon with sprint sections—you burst through packing and travel but still face months of settling in before the finish line. Pad your cash reserve to absorb surprises without resorting to high-interest credit. If the institution offers a zero-interest relocation loan, weigh the repayment schedule carefully, ensuring it doesn't choke your monthly budget once real paychecks start landing.

Onboarding paperwork will introduce tax withholding elections, and here's where a quick chat with a tax professional or sophisticated online calculator pays dividends. Under-withholding feels like a gift every payday until April reveals an unexpected bill, while over-withholding grants the IRS an interest-free loan. Aim for Goldilocks territory, adjusting allowances so your refund or balance due hovers in that sweet few-hundred-dollar zone. If you have summer ninths—extra course income or grant stipends—remember they spike your annual earnings and can catapult you into a higher marginal bracket. Set aside a portion in a high-yield savings account so quarterly estimated taxes don't ambush you like pop quizzes.

Campus perks extend beyond paycheck and benefits, sometimes saving you thousands if you know where to look. Free public transport passes, subsidized gym memberships, library borrowing privileges that include specialty databases, even discounted theater tickets—these are fringe benefits people outside academia might never see. View them as hidden coupons tucked in your wallet, stretching your salary without adding taxable income. Parking permits, though, lurk like pesky footnotes—cheap at rural colleges, painfully pricey in city campuses—so factor them into your commuting budget. By consciously tallying these costs and savings, you turn vague perks into line-item advantages, boosting your real purchasing power.

Assistant professors often fret about student loan balances that still feel mountainous. Income-Driven Repayment plans tether monthly payments to earnings, leaving room to breathe, but interest often lingers like background noise in a café. Investigate Public Service Loan Forgiveness if you're at a qualifying public or nonprofit university, ensuring you file annual employment certification so ten years of payments actually count. Even if forgiveness seems distant, automatic payroll deductions toward retirement can offset the emotional weight of loans by demonstrating forward progress in building assets. It's like hiking with a backpack: the pack may be heavy, but the view improves each mile you climb.

Your first syllabus probably includes office hours, and you need personal finance office hours too, even if just a biweekly appointment with yourself and a spreadsheet. Track fixed costs—rent, utilities, insurance—and variable ones like dining out or impulse Amazon orders that arrive faster than you can say "peer-reviewed." A zero-based budget forces every dollar to audition for a role, reducing the chance that extracurricular spending sabotages long-term aspirations such as buying a home or hitting retirement savings targets. And don't underestimate the thrill of small wins: paying off a high-interest credit card or establishing a $1,000 emergency fund releases mental bandwidth for research and teaching creativity. Your budget isn't a straightjacket; it's a tailored suit that helps you move confidently on the professional catwalk.

Dual-academic couples juggle two tenure clocks like synchronized swimmers performing intricate choreography under water. Departmental politics, geographic limitations, and child-care logistics add layers of complexity, but financially, you gain the advantage of dual benefit options. Compare health plans side by side, choose the richer coverage, and waive the lesser one if allowed, channeling saved premiums into a shared travel fund or Roth IRA contributions. Decide whose retirement match is most generous and prioritize maxing that out first, effectively capturing free investment capital. Treat your partnership like a mini board of directors: regular meetings, transparency, and clear roles prevent miscommunication that could erode trust faster than ungraded finals pile up on your desk.

Mid-career professors often earn supplementary "summer salary" from grants or administrative roles, leading to a cash infusion that can tempt extravagant vacations or kitchen remodels. Channel at least a portion into retirement or a brokerage account before lifestyle creep expands to swallow each dollar. Think of extra salary as a limited-edition research grant for your future self—invest it wisely or watch it vanish like sabbatical savings at an airport lounge. Automating transfers the day pay hits your account beats relying on willpower after a long teaching semester. Over time, these infusions compound in tax-advantaged accounts, turning seasonal opportunity into perennial wealth.

Consulting offers intellectual thrill and lucrative paychecks, but you must master the balancing act between institutional rules and entrepreneurial drive. Universities often require disclosure forms or caps on consulting days, and violating them can jeopardize credibility and employment security. Create a separate bank account for consulting revenue; it simplifies quarterly tax estimates and paints a clear financial portrait for audits. Adopt a time-tracking habit—just like logging lab hours—to ensure outside work doesn't erode the excellence you're paid to deliver on campus. Consulting income is spicy seasoning; use enough to flavor your career, but not so much that it masks the dish you were hired to cook.

Saying "no" to family and friends who perceive academia as a land of lavish grants can strain relationships, yet boundaries protect both wallets and affections. Practice compassionate honesty: explain that much of your salary is earmarked for retirement savings, tuition funds, or the mortgage because your job security depends on competitive performance, not guaranteed raises. Offer non-financial help—résumé reviews, mentorship, or networking introductions—demonstrating support without opening your checkbook. Frame each "no" as a "yes" to long-term stability, just as you decline to overextend your syllabus so students receive quality education instead of diluted attention. Honest conversations early prevent resentment and preserve the relationships you value more than any paycheck.

Burnout whispers at the door when grading stacks reach skyscraper height and committee meetings stretch into the dinner hour. Financial autonomy provides the cushion to say "enough" by funding mini-sabbaticals, professional coaching, or even a strategic job change. Build a "freedom fund"—six to twelve months of essential expenses—so you can pivot without panic if your mental health or family life demands it. Think of the fund like a tenure clock extension for your well-being: it buys time to recover, reassess, and re-ignite passion before cynicism sets in. Proactive self-care saves more careers than the fiercest ambition ever will.

Faculty housing options sometimes include university-owned properties with reduced rent or mortgage programs, yet the value depends on local real-estate dynamics. Analyze whether tying your residence to your employer's fortunes is wise or whether buying off-campus diversifies risk by decoupling home value from institutional health. If you do purchase, weigh fixed-rate mortgages against adjustable ones; the stability of tenure pairs well with the predictability of fixed payments, while shorter commitments like visiting appointments might favor flexibility. Plan to stay at least five years to offset closing costs and market volatility, and never underestimate the intangible benefit of a home that doubles as a writing retreat.

By the time you reach dossier season for promotion, your investment portfolio should look more diversified than your publication list: domestic and international equity funds, bonds, maybe a REIT or two. Rebalance annually, selling winners and buying laggards to maintain target asset allocations the way you curate a balanced course syllabus. This disciplined rhythm minimizes risk and maximizes long-term returns, even if headlines tempt you to chase hot sectors like a conference intrigue. Diversification embodies the scholarly virtue of considering multiple perspectives; in finance, that means spreading bets so one faulty thesis doesn't derail the entire argument. Your future self will thank you during retirement seminars when steady growth has done the heavy lifting.

When the retirement horizon finally comes into focus, run projections with both university pension estimates and Social Security statements in hand, noting how taxes and healthcare costs evolve post-employment. Consider annuitizing a portion of your 403(b) to guarantee income, but keep enough liquid assets for emergencies and bucket-list travel. Discuss phased retirement options allowing part-time teaching that maintains benefits while easing into new rhythms. Just as you guided freshmen through unfamiliar territory, you now mentor yourself across this exciting threshold. A thoughtfully planned exit transforms nostalgia into gratitude and frees you to pursue encore interests without financial fear.

Your career began with an offer letter, but it culminates in the legacy you leave through students, research, and perhaps a scholarship bearing your name. Financial literacy is the engine that powers every stage of that journey, from reading your first paycheck to designing a tax-efficient estate plan that funds young scholars long after your final lecture fades. Treat money as both a tool and a teacher; steward it wisely and it will grant freedom, resilience, and the ability to amplify your impact on generations you may never meet. The day you walk across campus for the last time, sun glinting off familiar red-brick walls, you'll feel the satisfaction of a mission fulfilled and a future secured, ready to cheer others on as they embark upon the path you once traveled with equal parts wonder and determination.

Chapter 2: Salary vs. Stipend Reading Paychecks, Pay Schedules, and Withholding Options

You've just landed your first academic job or maybe a new fellowship, and the offer letter is sitting in your inbox with a dollar amount that looks promising. But before you mentally divide that number into monthly spending plans, pause and dig a little deeper. The academic world doesn't always speak in plain terms when it comes to money. Words like "salary" and "stipend" might seem interchangeable at first glance, but they carry different meanings, expectations, and financial implications. Understanding those differences early on can prevent a lot of confusion and help you make smarter financial decisions right out of the gate.

When you hear the word "salary," think of a formal job with a fixed annual pay and accompanying benefits. That's what most tenure-track or full-time professors receive, and it's usually divided over a nine-month or twelve-month schedule. A salary implies not just a steady paycheck, but also deductions for health insurance, retirement contributions, taxes, and other benefits. A "stipend," on the other hand, often refers to compensation for temporary or less formal work, such as graduate assistantships, postdoctoral fellowships, or summer research appointments. It can be a set dollar amount paid in chunks or even as a lump sum, and it's not always subject to the same deductions or benefits. This is where the waters can get murky—some stipends are taxable, some aren't, and many don't come with things like retirement contributions or healthcare coverage.

Imagine you're on a university campus and two colleagues each say they're earning $30,000 this year. One is a new assistant professor on a salaried contract; the other is a doctoral candidate on a graduate stipend. Even though the number is the same, what's happening behind the scenes financially is very different. The assistant professor likely has income taxes withheld automatically, receives health insurance and retirement options, and is paying into Social Security and Medicare. The grad student, however, might be responsible for saving for their own taxes, may not receive any benefits, and isn't paying into Social Security. So even though they're both receiving "money," the infrastructure surrounding that money changes how much they actually take home and what protections or perks come with it.

Pay schedules can also create headaches if you don't know what to expect. Most salaried faculty are paid monthly or bi-weekly, but whether that salary is stretched across nine or twelve months makes a huge difference in how you budget. If you're paid over nine months, your paycheck stops in May even though your bills don't. This might catch you off guard the first summer unless you plan ahead or request to "annualize" your salary. Annualizing spreads your nine-month pay across twelve months, reducing each paycheck slightly but giving you income during the summer months. It's a great option for people who like consistent income, but it may not be available at every institution or for every type of appointment.

Summer pay introduces a whole new layer of complexity. For example, if you're teaching a summer class or working on a funded research project, you might be offered additional compensation, but it likely comes in the form of a stipend. This type of payment might be processed separately from your regular paycheck, may not have the same tax withholding setup, and sometimes gets paid on a different schedule altogether. That means you could end up with a larger-than-usual check with no taxes taken out—tempting to spend, but dangerous if you don't set aside money for tax season. A good rule of thumb is to squirrel away 20% to 30% of any untaxed stipend into a high-yield savings account until you know exactly what you'll owe. That way, you don't get blindsided come April.

Understanding the difference between gross and net pay can also help you avoid disappointment. Your offer letter may state you're earning $70,000, but that's your gross income—what you make before deductions. Your net pay, or take-home pay, is what actually hits your bank account after taxes, retirement contributions, insurance premiums, and other deductions. The difference can be thousands of dollars a year. This is why someone earning $70,000 might only see $4,200 or $4,500 a month in their bank account, depending on their withholding choices. Knowing this can help you build a more accurate budget, especially when planning rent, student loan payments, or big purchases.

Withholding options can feel like a choose-your-own-adventure story, especially if you're filling out a W-4 form for the first time or haven't touched one in years. The W-4 is what tells your employer how much federal income tax to withhold from each paycheck. If you claim too many allowances, you might take home more now but owe money at tax time. Claim too few, and you'll get a refund—but you also gave the IRS an interest-free loan for the year. Most people are better off aiming to break even. Using an online tax estimator or talking to a CPA during your first year can help you strike the right balance without stressing out next spring.

Some positions—particularly fellowships—don't withhold taxes at all. This can feel like a bonus in the short term but comes back to haunt you when it's time to file. For instance, if you're receiving a $24,000 postdoctoral stipend with no taxes withheld, you could owe several thousand dollars depending on your other income and deductions. Filing quarterly estimated taxes can prevent penalties and smooth out your cash flow. It's like paying a little at a time rather than one big painful check. This might not sound fun, but it's part of learning how to live well in the academic world, where pay structures don't always follow corporate norms.

In addition to federal income taxes, you'll likely see deductions for Social Security and Medicare—called FICA taxes—if you're on a regular payroll. But here's the kicker: if you're being paid via a fellowship or stipend that's not classified as "earned income," you may not pay into these systems at all, and that could affect your eligibility for future benefits. While skipping those deductions might feel like a financial win now, it could lower your future Social Security payout or delay your eligibility. It's worth checking how your position is categorized and asking your HR department if you're unsure. Understanding the long game helps you make better short-term decisions.

Another paycheck wrinkle involves state and local taxes. Depending on where your university is located, you might have additional withholdings for state income tax, city tax, or even school district tax. Moving to a new state for a job can mean not just new weather and new students but also a new tax structure. For example, someone working in New York City pays more in combined state and city tax than someone teaching in Florida, which has no state income tax at all. Even if salaries appear equal on paper, the amount that lands in your account can differ widely based on where you teach. So before you accept an offer, run a quick cost-of-living and after-tax income comparison to make sure you're seeing the full picture.

Retirement contributions are another piece of the paycheck puzzle that often gets overlooked. Many universities automatically contribute a percentage of your salary to a retirement plan like a 403(b) or 401(a), and some match your contributions up to a certain percentage. This is essentially free money for your future. But it also means slightly less in your take-home pay now, which can be jarring if you weren't expecting it. Take a moment to log into your payroll system and look at what's being deducted, what the university is contributing, and how that money is being invested. You might even have options for traditional (pre-tax) vs. Roth (after-tax) contributions, which affect your current and future taxes differently.

Don't overlook insurance premiums—another big reason your take-home pay is smaller than your gross salary suggests. Universities often offer a range of health insurance plans with varying costs. Some plans are free for individuals but cost extra if you want to add a spouse or children. Dental and vision are usually separate and come with their own premiums. While you may be tempted to skip coverage to save money, especially if you're healthy, one emergency room visit can cost more than a year's worth of premiums. Think of insurance like an umbrella—it might not be fun to carry around, but you'll be glad you have it when it rains.

Some academic appointments, especially adjunct roles, may not come with any benefits at all. In these cases, your gross pay is often all you get, and you'll need to manage everything else—health insurance, retirement, taxes—on your own. This can be intimidating, but it's doable with the right planning. Independent health insurance is available through marketplaces, and you can open your own Individual Retirement Account (IRA) or Solo 401(k) if you have other self-employed income. The key is to think of yourself as a one-person institution—responsible not just for teaching but also for HR, payroll, and long-term planning. Taking ownership of your finances is one of the most empowering things you can do in a career known for its unpredictability.

The emotional impact of your first few paychecks shouldn't be ignored either. It's common to feel a letdown when your take-home pay doesn't match your expectations or when you realize how much of your paycheck goes to taxes and deductions. This isn't a sign that you made a mistake—it's a sign that you're learning how the system works. Instead of frustration, use that energy to build a system that works for you. Set up direct deposit into both a checking account and a savings account, automate bill payments, and check in with your budget once a month. These habits help you stay in control even when your income fluctuates or your job title changes.

For international scholars, understanding paychecks can be even more complicated due to visa status, tax treaties, and different classifications of work. Some types of visas exempt you from certain taxes temporarily, while others don't. And your stipend may be subject to different reporting requirements than a U.S. citizen's salary. In these situations, it's especially important to talk with a university payroll representative who understands international payroll. Otherwise, you might end up paying taxes you don't owe—or worse, not paying ones you do.

There's also the matter of how your paycheck reflects your identity and values. For many academics, income isn't just about consumption—it's about contribution. You want your money to align with your mission, whether that means supporting causes, helping family, or investing in your own learning and travel. When you understand how your paycheck is built, you can allocate funds in a way that reflects who you are and what matters to you. It's not about having more; it's about using what you have more meaningfully.

Once you've decoded your paycheck and built a basic budget, you can start thinking more strategically. Are there flexible spending accounts you can use to save on medical or childcare costs? Are you eligible for loan forgiveness programs or state-level tax credits? These questions might not seem urgent now, but they're the kind of long-term plays that add up to financial security. Being proactive now means less scrambling later.

At the end of the day, your paycheck is more than a number—it's a snapshot of how your institution values your work and how you choose to steward that value. Whether you're salaried or stipend-based, whether you're full-time or part-time, your compensation has a story to tell. Learning to read that story clearly allows you to make decisions with confidence, reduce stress, and create a life where your finances support your academic goals, not limit them. This isn't just about understanding money—it's about owning your career, your worth, and your future.

Chapter 3: Relocation & Start-Up Packages: Negotiating Moving Costs, Lab Funds, and Course Releases

You've probably seen the job listings: one says "adjunct faculty," another says "visiting professor," and yet another touts a "tenure-track position." On the surface, they all suggest that someone's going to be teaching students, attending meetings, and possibly drinking a lot of coffee in the faculty lounge. But beneath the shared responsibilities lies a world of differences—differences that impact your income, your job security, your health insurance, and even your ability to plan for the future. Choosing one of these roles (or falling into one because of the market) isn't just a professional decision; it's a financial one too. Understanding what each role means—financially, emotionally, and logistically—is essential to navigating the landscape of higher education with your eyes wide open.

Let's start with the tenure-track position, the golden ring of academia. These jobs are competitive and come with a multi-year plan that—if all goes well—leads to tenure, which is essentially a permanent appointment. The pay is usually the highest of the three categories, and more importantly, it comes with benefits: health insurance, retirement contributions, paid leave, and eligibility for sabbaticals. Think of it like being offered a long-term lease with the option to buy the building—if you show you can publish, teach, and contribute to the university, you're in. But getting on this track often means moving for the job, facing intense scrutiny during the tenure review period, and balancing teaching, research, and service in a way that can feel overwhelming in the early years. It's not a walk in the park, but it is the most stable foundation you can build in the academic world.

Now compare that to a visiting professor position, which is often limited to one or two years. These roles are usually full-time but temporary, intended to fill a gap while a department does a tenure-track search or covers for someone on leave. Pay can be similar to an entry-level tenure-track job, and you might even get access to health insurance and other benefits, depending on the institution. But don't let that fool you into thinking you're on a permanent track—visiting roles rarely, if ever, lead to tenure unless you're invited to apply and compete for a new position. It's like house-sitting a fully furnished home that someone else owns; you're welcome there, but it's not really yours. If you're using a visiting role to gain experience or wait out a better opportunity, just be sure you're saving enough and networking aggressively during your time there.

Adjuncting, on the other hand, is the most flexible but also the most precarious role of the three. Adjunct professors are typically hired by the course, often teaching at multiple institutions to piece together a livable income. The pay is significantly lower—sometimes as little as $2,000 to $4,000 per course—and benefits are usually nonexistent. This is the gig economy of higher education, and while it allows for some autonomy and variety, it offers almost no financial security. Adjuncts are the substitute teachers of the college world: critical, underpaid, and often invisible in the long-term planning of the department. It's a tough way to build a stable life, and many adjuncts find themselves needing a second job, whether in tutoring, retail, or freelance work, to make ends meet.

What makes all this more complicated is that many people don't choose these roles as much as they're forced into them by the job market. You might have a freshly minted PhD and dreams of a tenure-track job, only to find that the only thing available is a visiting position in a town you've never heard of. Or you might live in a region where adjuncting at three different schools is the only way to stay in academia without uprooting your family. These aren't necessarily bad decisions—they're often the only decisions. But they do have consequences, especially when it comes to long-term financial health, so it's important to go into them with a plan and not just a passion for teaching.

Let's talk numbers. A tenure-track assistant professor might earn anywhere from $55,000 to $90,000, depending on discipline and location, with full benefits and annual raises. A visiting professor might make a similar salary, but the contract expires in a year or two, with no guarantee of renewal. An adjunct teaching four courses per semester might earn $16,000 to $25,000 annually, often with no benefits and no paid time off. That's a massive difference, and it doesn't just affect your bank account—it affects your ability to save, invest, buy a home, or even afford health care. It's the difference between building equity in your life and just keeping the lights on.

Health insurance is a huge factor in the quality-of-life equation, and it's one of the most significant benefits that comes with full-time positions. Tenure-track and many visiting roles include access to group health plans, sometimes even with family coverage. Adjuncts usually don't get this, which means paying out of pocket or going without, neither of which is a great option. If you're adjuncting and under 30, you might still qualify to be on a parent's health insurance plan. Others rely on the Affordable Care Act marketplaces, which can work well if you qualify for subsidies, but the costs add up quickly if you don't.

Retirement contributions are another invisible benefit that too many new professors overlook. In tenure-track roles, universities often contribute a generous percentage of your salary to a retirement plan, such as a 403(b) or 401(a). Over time, that adds up to tens or even hundreds of thousands of dollars. Visiting professors may get similar access, depending on the school, but adjuncts usually do not. That means an adjunct needs to create their own savings strategy, perhaps through an IRA or Solo 401(k), which requires more financial literacy and discipline. It's hard to think about retirement when you're just trying to pay rent, but the earlier you start—even with small amounts—the better your long-term outlook will be.

Job security is another major dividing line. Tenure-track faculty have a built-in timeline for promotion and long-term employment, while adjuncts are hired on a semester-by-semester basis and can be let go without notice. Visiting professors fall somewhere in between: you know the job ends soon, but you're not in constant fear of being canceled mid-semester. That psychological weight matters more than people admit. It's hard to do your best teaching, writing, or mentoring when you're worried about how you'll afford groceries next month. Stability isn't just a financial asset—it's a mental and emotional one too.

Your ability to plan your life also changes depending on the role. Tenure-track professors often feel comfortable buying a home, starting a family, or taking out loans because they have reliable income. Visiting professors may hesitate to make those big commitments without knowing what comes next. Adjuncts are often stuck in a holding pattern, postponing major life events because everything feels so temporary. That's not just frustrating—it's exhausting. The mental toll of constant uncertainty can be just as damaging as the financial strain, and it often leads to burnout or leaving academia altogether.

On the flip side, adjuncting can offer freedom and flexibility that tenure-track roles don't. You might have more time for creative work, side gigs, or caring for family. If you have another source of income—say, a partner with a stable job, or freelance work you enjoy—then adjuncting can be part of a larger, intentional lifestyle. But that only works if you go into it with clear eyes and a financial plan. Too many people take on adjunct roles thinking it's just a temporary stopgap, only to find themselves stuck in a cycle of low pay and few options years later. That's not failure—it's the system—but it's something to be aware of from day one.

Visiting positions can serve as a strategic stepping stone. They allow you to build your CV, get teaching experience, and stay visible in your field while applying for permanent jobs. But don't get too comfortable. Use that time wisely—publish, attend conferences, build relationships, and keep applying. Because when the contract ends, you don't want to be caught off guard. It's like running a timed race: you have a set window to hit your goals before the clock runs out.

If you're lucky enough to land a tenure-track position, congratulations—

but know that the work is just beginning. You'll likely face heavy expectations around publishing, committee work, and course development, all while learning to manage your time and energy. Financially, though, it's a great place to be. You can start building wealth through retirement contributions, home ownership, and long-term investing. You can also afford to turn down opportunities that don't serve your goals, which is a powerful kind of freedom. Use your early years to lay a strong foundation that supports both your career and your well-being.

Many professors shift between roles over time. You might start as an adjunct, move into a visiting role, and then land a tenure-track job. Or you might step off the tenure track for personal reasons and later return. These transitions are common, and they don't mean you're doing anything wrong. The key is to understand the financial implications at each stage so you can adapt accordingly. Treat each phase like a different financial season—each with its own needs, challenges, and opportunities.

It's also worth thinking about side income. Adjuncts often supplement their teaching with freelance writing, tutoring, or part-time work in other sectors. Visiting professors may do consulting or summer teaching. Tenure-track faculty might write books, lead workshops, or pursue paid speaking engagements. Each of these streams comes with its own tax and time considerations, but they can also provide much-needed financial breathing room. In a field where pay is often limited, diversification can make all the difference.

At the end of the day, there's no single right path—just the one that works best for your goals, values, and circumstances. Some people thrive as adjuncts, enjoying the flexibility and lower pressure. Others find fulfillment in visiting roles, using them as launch pads for bigger things. And for many, the tenure track offers the ideal balance of security and growth. What matters most is that you understand what each role means not just professionally, but financially. Because your career isn't just about what you do—it's about how you live while doing it.

So take the time to learn the landscape, ask questions, and make intentional choices. Talk to mentors, look up benefits policies, and don't be afraid to negotiate or ask for clarity. You're not just teaching students—you're building a life. And the more informed you are, the more freedom you'll have to shape that life on your terms. Whether you're an adjunct crafting syllabi in coffee shops, a visiting professor juggling job applications, or a tenure-track faculty member balancing research and grading, you deserve a financial future that honors your work, your time, and your potential.

Chapter 4: Budgeting on an Assistant Professor's Income, Living Below the Ivory Tower Means

So you made it through grad school, landed your first job, and now you're officially part of academia. You've got the title, the office (maybe shared, maybe windowless), and hopefully some stability. But as the student loan deferment period ends and the first real paycheck hits your bank account, you might also feel a wave of financial pressure. Welcome to the Debt Check-In—where idealism meets interest rates. It's completely normal to still have student loans hanging over your head early in your academic career. The good news? You're not alone, and you don't have to feel paralyzed by them. The key is to face your debt head-on, make a plan, and let that plan become a background hum—not a blaring siren.

Let's begin with something most of us skip: looking at the actual numbers. Not just a ballpark figure or what you think you owe, but the full picture. Log into your loan servicer's website, print or screenshot the balance sheet, and make peace with the total. For many early-career professors, the number is somewhere between $30,000 and $120,000 depending on the path you took to get your degree. That can feel overwhelming, but seeing it clearly is the first step toward taking back control. It's like mapping out a road trip—before you plan the route, you need to know exactly where you're starting.

Once you've got your total, break it down: how many loans do you have, what types, and what interest rates are attached to each? Federal loans, like Direct Subsidized or Unsubsidized, come with flexible repayment options and potential forgiveness programs. Private loans, on the other hand, usually have fewer options and higher interest rates. Knowing which is which can help you prioritize your repayment strategy. Think of your loans like a room full of houseplants—some need more attention, some are just fine with occasional water, and one or two might be slowly dying in the corner because they were forgotten. Paying extra attention to the ones with high interest can save you hundreds or thousands over the life of the loan.

Now let's talk about cash flow—your day-to-day money reality. When that first paycheck lands, it can be tempting to celebrate. You've waited a long time for this moment, and you deserve to enjoy it. But if you're not careful, a few celebratory dinners or new gadgets can set off a cycle of overspending that makes debt management harder. Start by tracking your monthly expenses, even just for a few weeks. Use an app or an old-school spreadsheet to see what's really going on with your money. You might be surprised by how much is going to subscriptions, takeout, or random Amazon orders. Knowing where your money goes is crucial when you're juggling debt payments and trying to build financial momentum.

Once you have a handle on your expenses, it's time to choose a repayment strategy that fits your goals. There's no one-size-fits-all approach, but there are two main methods to consider: the avalanche method and the snowball method. The avalanche method focuses on paying off the highest interest loans first, which saves the most money over time. The snowball method, on the other hand, prioritizes the smallest balance loans, giving you psychological wins and motivation as you knock them out. Both work, and neither is wrong. Choose the one that keeps you consistent and emotionally engaged. Personal finance isn't just about math—it's also about mindset.

Income-Driven Repayment plans can be a lifesaver for early-career professors, especially if your student loan burden is high relative to your starting salary. These plans base your monthly payments on your income and family size, sometimes reducing them to manageable levels—even as low as zero. But remember: these payments often don't cover the interest, which means your balance can grow over time. That's not ideal, but it can be a smart trade-off if it gives you breathing room in your budget while you're building your career. Just be sure to recertify your income annually and understand how forgiveness works after 20 or 25 years on the plan.

If you work for a public university or a qualifying nonprofit, you may be eligible for Public Service Loan Forgiveness (PSLF). This program forgives your remaining federal student loan balance after 120 qualifying payments—usually over 10 years. But to stay eligible, you must be on an income-driven repayment plan and employed full-time at a qualifying institution. It's not a magic wand, and the process involves meticulous documentation, but for many academics, it's one of the best tools available. Think of PSLF like a long hike up a mountain: the climb takes time and effort, but the view at the top is worth it if you stay the course.

Let's talk lifestyle inflation. Once that paycheck starts coming in, you might feel the urge to upgrade everything—your apartment, your car, your wardrobe. After years of scraping by, who wouldn't want to live a little? But be careful. Just because you earn more doesn't mean you should spend more. In fact, the early years of your career are the best time to live below your means and throw extra money toward your loans or savings. Keep your fixed expenses low while you're still building, and you'll have far more freedom down the line. Every dollar you don't spend now is a dollar that can work for you later, whether in reducing interest, investing for the future, or creating a cushion for unexpected life events.

Don't underestimate the psychological impact of student debt. Even if your payments are manageable, just knowing the debt is there can feel like a weight on your shoulders. It's easy to internalize that burden and think of yourself as "behind" or "financially delayed." But here's the truth: education debt is different from consumer debt. It's an investment in your earning power, your personal growth, and your life's work. That doesn't mean you should ignore it, but it does mean you should carry it with context—not shame. You pursued something meaningful, and now you're building a future that reflects that choice.

Creating an emergency fund should happen alongside paying off debt—

not afterward. A good rule of thumb is to save at least $1,000 initially, then aim for three to six months of essential expenses. This money isn't for vacations or furniture—it's for when your car breaks down or a medical bill catches you off guard. Having even a small cushion can keep you from turning to credit cards when life surprises you. Think of it like an umbrella: you hope you don't need it, but when the storm comes, you'll be glad you planned ahead.

Some people consider refinancing their student loans to get a lower interest rate, especially if they have private loans or high-rate federal ones. This can make sense if your credit is solid and your income is stable. But be cautious—refinancing federal loans means losing access to benefits like PSLF and income-driven plans. It's like trading in your flexible hiking boots for a pair of sleek dress shoes—they might look better, but they don't handle rough terrain nearly as well. Make sure you're not sacrificing flexibility for a small savings on interest unless your long-term plan justifies it.

One trick that helps many people is automating their payments. Set up automatic transfers for your minimum loan payments, and if you can, add an extra payment each month toward your highest-interest loan. Even an extra $50 or $100 a month can cut months—or even years—off your repayment timeline. Automation reduces the mental effort needed to stay on track, and it helps you build consistency without constantly thinking about it. And over time, that consistency builds real momentum.

If you receive a windfall—like a tax refund, grant, or honorarium—consider putting at least part of it toward your student loans. These "bonus" dollars can make a huge difference when applied strategically. You could also split them between debt repayment and fun spending, giving yourself a reward while also making progress. This balanced approach helps you avoid burnout while staying focused on your goals. Financial health isn't just about deprivation—it's about alignment.

Don't ignore your retirement savings while paying off loans. It might feel counterintuitive to invest while still in debt, but if your university offers a retirement match, take full advantage. That match is free money, and no loan interest rate can compete with that kind of guaranteed return.

Contributing even a small amount to your retirement while managing debt can set you up for long-term financial security. It's like planting a tree while still fixing the roof—you need both shade and shelter for the future.

Talk openly about your debt with trusted friends, mentors, or financial advisors. There's still a lot of stigma around student loans, but the more we share strategies and stories, the more we all benefit. Someone might know about a loan forgiveness program you've never heard of or recommend a budgeting app that makes your life easier. You're not the only one navigating this path, and there's no shame in asking for guidance. Community can be a powerful antidote to debt anxiety.

It's okay to adjust your plan as your life changes. Maybe you get a fellowship that boosts your income, or maybe your expenses increase because of a move or family responsibility. Financial planning isn't about rigid rules—it's about adapting with purpose. Revisit your budget and debt strategy every six months to make sure it still fits your reality. Think of it like revising a syllabus: what worked at the beginning of the semester might need tweaking now that the students—or circumstances—have changed.

Don't forget to celebrate your wins. Paying off a loan, hitting a savings milestone, or even just sticking to your budget for a month deserves acknowledgment. These small victories build confidence and make the larger journey feel doable. Mark your progress with whatever feels meaningful—whether it's a nice meal, a new book, or just a quiet moment of pride. Momentum is built not just through progress, but through reflection.

If you're married or in a partnership, talk openly with your partner about your student loans and repayment strategy. Financial alignment can reduce stress and strengthen your relationship, while secrecy or miscommunication can lead to conflict. Share your goals, your worries, and your progress. Build a plan together that supports both of your dreams. Money conversations aren't always easy, but they're worth having early and often.

Above all, be kind to yourself. Debt doesn't define you, and it doesn't diminish your accomplishments. You pursued a challenging path because you believed in education, inquiry, and service—and that commitment has value beyond any balance sheet. The road to financial freedom isn't always straight, but every step you take builds resilience and clarity. With a thoughtful plan, consistent effort, and a few well-timed breaks, you can manage your debt without letting it manage you.

Early-career finances are about more than just student loans—they're about setting the tone for how you'll handle money for the rest of your life. Now's the time to build habits, mindset, and confidence that will carry you through every stage of your academic journey. Whether you're teaching intro classes or publishing your first book, let your financial decisions support your values, not hinder them. That's the real goal: freedom, flexibility, and the ability to pursue your work with clarity and purpose. You've already done the hard part—earning your degree. Now let's build a financial life that honors the effort it took to get here.

Chapter 5: Your First 403(b), 457(b), or 401(a): How University Plans Work and Why Eligibility Matters

So you finally landed that faculty job—maybe it's your first assistant professor appointment, a visiting role with benefits, or a long-awaited tenure-track position. Either way, you've probably heard that your university offers some type of retirement plan. You might've glanced at your benefits packet and seen names like 403(b), 457(b), or 401(a) and immediately felt like you were reading a bowl of alphabet soup. These codes can look intimidating, but they're actually just labels for the buckets you can use to save money for your future. And if you understand how they work, those buckets can fill faster than you'd expect—especially with some help from your university along the way.

A 403(b) plan is probably the most common option you'll encounter in higher education. Think of it as the academic world's version of a 401(k), which is what private-sector employees typically use. You contribute money directly from your paycheck, either pre-tax (meaning it lowers your taxable income today) or after-tax through a Roth option (which grows tax-free and isn't taxed when you withdraw it later in retirement). Most universities offer a menu of investment choices—usually mutual funds, index funds, or annuities—so you can decide how aggressively or conservatively you want to invest. And the best part? Some universities will match a portion of what you contribute. That's free money added to your retirement fund just for participating.

A 457(b) plan may also be on the table, especially if you work for a public university. It looks similar to a 403(b) on the surface—same contribution limits, same investment options—but it comes with some unique perks. The biggest one is flexibility. If you withdraw money from a 457(b) before age 59½, you usually don't pay the 10% early withdrawal penalty that applies to 403(b) or 401(k) accounts. That makes it a valuable tool if you think you might retire early, change careers, or just want more freedom with your money later. It's like having a second suitcase packed just in case your travel plans change.

Then there's the 401(a), which is often a mandatory retirement plan. If your university offers this, it might not be optional. You contribute a fixed percentage of your salary—often between 5% and 10%—and the university contributes too, sometimes even more than you. You usually don't get to choose the percentage, and you might have fewer investment choices, but the contribution amount can be significant. Think of the 401(a) like a base salary supplement that gets invested on your behalf. You don't see it in your paycheck, but it's quietly growing in the background every month.

Eligibility is where things start to matter a lot. Not everyone gets access to these plans immediately. Some schools have a one-year waiting period for employer contributions, meaning you can start saving your own money right away, but you won't see any matching funds until your anniversary date. Others give you access from day one. If you're a visiting faculty member or part-time lecturer, you might not be eligible at all—or only for limited versions. It's like being invited to a dinner party but not being told which courses you're allowed to eat. That's why reading the fine print on eligibility rules is so important.

Vesting is another crucial detail that's often overlooked. Vesting refers to how much of the employer's contributions you're allowed to keep if you leave the university before a certain amount of time. Your contributions are always yours, but the employer's money might be subject to a vesting schedule. Some universities vest immediately—you get 100% of what they contribute from day one. Others require you to stay two, three, or even five years before you can take all of it with you. It's like a loyalty program: the longer you stay, the more perks you get to keep. Knowing your vesting timeline can help you make better decisions if you're thinking about switching jobs or leaving academia altogether.

One of the smartest things you can do early in your career is contribute at least enough to get the full employer match—if it's offered. Let's say your university offers a 100% match on the first 5% of your salary that you contribute. If you make $60,000 and contribute 5%, that's $3,000 from you and $3,000 from the university, adding up to $6,000 a year. Over ten years, with modest investment growth, that could become $80,000 or more. Not bad for money you never had to negotiate for or earn through extra labor. Skipping that match is like saying no to a raise you didn't have to ask for.

You may wonder how much you *should* be contributing to your retirement plan beyond the match. A good starting point is 10% to 15% of your salary, including any employer contributions. If that feels like too much right now, don't worry—start small and increase gradually. Even 3% or 5% is better than nothing, especially if you're also paying off student loans or adjusting to a new cost of living. The important thing is to build the habit early. Retirement might feel like it's a million miles away, but the earlier you start saving, the more time compound interest has to work in your favor.

Let's not forget the investments inside these accounts, which are just as important as the contributions going in. Most university plans offer a menu of mutual funds, typically grouped into categories like stocks, bonds, target-date funds, and annuities. A target-date fund is often the easiest choice for beginners—it automatically adjusts its mix of investments based on the year you plan to retire. If you want more control, you can build your own portfolio using a mix of stock and bond funds. Just be sure to check the fees. Lower-cost index funds often outperform actively managed funds over time, especially when fees are factored in. Think of investing like grocery shopping: you want good quality, but you don't need to buy the fanciest label to get the best nutrition.

Tax treatment is another benefit of these plans that often gets overlooked. Traditional 403(b), 457(b), and 401(a) contributions are made with pre-tax dollars, which lowers your taxable income today. That can mean a smaller tax bill each year you contribute. Roth options—if your plan offers them—are funded with after-tax dollars but grow tax-free, and you won't pay taxes when you withdraw them in retirement. Each approach has its pros and cons, and the best choice depends on your current tax bracket and where you expect it to be in the future. It's a bit of a balancing act, but even a basic understanding of these choices can make a big difference down the road.

If you're juggling multiple offers or university positions, don't forget to compare retirement plans. One school might offer a higher salary but no match, while another offers a lower salary with a generous 10% employer contribution. Over time, that difference can outweigh a slightly smaller paycheck. You'll also want to consider whether your contributions are portable—meaning whether you can roll them into another retirement account if you change jobs. Most plans allow this, but it's worth double-checking. It's like moving your stuff from one apartment to another—you want to make sure you can take your furniture with you.

While these plans are great, they shouldn't be your only form of retirement savings. Supplementing with an IRA (Individual Retirement Account) or even a taxable brokerage account can provide more flexibility. Some people also use 457(b) plans as a bridge to early retirement, since they can often be tapped without penalties before age 59½. Building a layered retirement strategy gives you options, which means less stress and more freedom as your career and personal life evolve. Flexibility is the name of the game in both academia and finances.

The earlier you engage with your retirement plan, the better your chances of building lasting wealth. Every dollar saved in your 20s and 30s has decades to grow. If you wait until your 40s or 50s to start, you'll have to contribute much more to reach the same goal. And if that feels unfair, you're right—it is. But you're not powerless. Taking small steps now puts you on the path toward financial security and lets your money work while you're working hard in the classroom or the lab.

It's okay to feel overwhelmed at first. No one teaches this stuff in grad school, and your HR packet probably reads like a foreign language. But you don't have to understand everything right away. Start by logging into your retirement portal, looking at your balance, and reviewing the fund options. Make sure you're contributing at least enough to get any employer match. Then set a calendar reminder to revisit your selections in six months and adjust as needed.

Talking to a financial advisor can also be helpful, especially one who understands the academic world. Some universities even offer free financial consultations through their HR departments or retirement plan providers. A good advisor can help you evaluate your risk tolerance, set retirement goals, and choose investments that align with your timeline and lifestyle. You don't need to be a finance expert—you just need to be willing to ask questions and take action.

It's also worth talking to older colleagues to see how they've handled their retirement planning. You might hear some cautionary tales—like people who didn't start early enough or didn't understand the vesting rules—but you'll also hear about strategies that worked. These conversations can be eye-opening and reassuring. After all, the academic journey is long, and the people who've walked it ahead of you often have wisdom to share, especially when it comes to financial survival.

One final note: don't make perfect the enemy of good. You don't need to maximize every account or optimize every fund right away. The most important thing is to start. Even small contributions add up. And the sooner you make retirement savings a habit, the easier it becomes to keep going. Over time, those small decisions compound into big results.

So if this is your first 403(b), 457(b), or 401(a), welcome to the club. You're not behind—you're beginning. And now that you understand what these plans are and why they matter, you can make choices that serve both your present and your future. Retirement might feel far off, but planning for it now is one of the smartest moves you can make. It's not about giving up today's joys—it's about making sure you can enjoy life long after the lecture halls fade into memory.

Chapter 6: State Pension vs. Defined Contribution: Understanding TRS, ORP, and Hybrid Systems

If you've landed a faculty job at a public university, chances are you've come across something called a state pension plan or a defined contribution plan. And if you're like most new hires, your eyes probably glazed over at the mention of acronyms like TRS, ORP, or "hybrid system." These aren't just random letters or red tape—they're the foundation of your long-term financial security. Understanding the difference between these retirement systems is one of the smartest moves you can make early in your academic career. It's not glamorous, and no one's going to throw you a parade for learning about pension options, but choosing the right plan now can impact how comfortably you live decades from today.

Let's start with the state pension, often known as a defined benefit plan. The Teacher Retirement System, or TRS in many states, is a common example. In this system, you and your employer both contribute a percentage of your salary to a pool that promises you a specific benefit when you retire. That benefit is calculated using a formula based on your years of service and your salary—usually your highest three or five years of earnings. It's like planting a tree early in your career and knowing that, if you stay long enough, it will provide guaranteed shade no matter how hot the economy gets. There's security in that promise, but also limitations.

With TRS and similar defined benefit plans, you trade flexibility for predictability. The longer you stay in the system, the better the payout. But if you leave your job after a few years—or switch states—you might walk away with much less than you expected. For example, if you only stay in the system for five years and leave before you're vested, you may only get your contributions back, sometimes without interest. That can feel like renting a home and only getting your deposit back after years of paying into it. You're helping others build equity, but you're not taking much of it with you unless you stick around.

Now let's talk about defined contribution plans, which you'll often see labeled as Optional Retirement Plans or ORPs. These work more like a 401(k), where you and your employer both put money into an individual account that belongs to you. You get to choose how it's invested—stocks, bonds, index funds—and you carry that account with you if you change jobs, as long as it's vested. There's no guarantee of how much you'll have at retirement, but the account is portable, and you're in the driver's seat. It's like buying your own home instead of renting—your equity depends on how much you invest and how wisely you manage it.

The key difference between TRS and ORP comes down to who carries the risk. With TRS, the state assumes the investment risk. Your benefit is guaranteed by a formula regardless of how the market performs. With ORP, you assume the risk. If the market soars, you benefit. If it crashes, your retirement account could take a hit. It's a bit like choosing between a fixed paycheck for life or a commission-based job with no cap. Neither is inherently better—it depends on your personality, goals, and how long you plan to stay in the system.

Hybrid systems add another layer to the decision. Some states offer a mix of defined benefit and defined contribution plans. You might have a small guaranteed pension along with a 401(k)-style account that grows based on contributions and market returns. This structure aims to balance the best of both worlds: a little security and a little flexibility. Hybrid plans can be great for people who want some stability but also appreciate control over their investments. Think of it as splitting your money between a reliable savings account and a growth-oriented investment portfolio.

Choosing between TRS and ORP is one of the most important financial decisions you'll make early in your academic life—and here's the catch: it's often irrevocable. In many states, you have just 30 to 90 days to choose, and once you pick, you're locked in for life. That means you need to think long term, even if you're still trying to figure out what you'll teach next semester. If you know you'll stay in public education in the same state for most of your career, TRS might make more sense. But if you think you'll move, change sectors, or want more control, ORP could be a better fit.

To make the decision clearer, it helps to think about vesting. Vesting refers to how long you have to work before you're entitled to your employer's contributions. In TRS, you often need five years to be vested. In ORP, it might be one or two years, depending on your state. If you're not sure you'll be around long enough to vest in TRS, you could be better off with ORP, where your account is truly yours after a shorter period. It's like dating someone who won't split the tab unless you've been together for five years—you might not want to take that risk unless you're sure about the relationship.

The contribution rates also matter. With TRS, you might contribute 7% of your salary, and your university contributes around 7% as well, all going into a collective fund. With ORP, the contribution percentages are similar, but the money goes directly into your personal account. Over time, that account grows based on investment performance. If you're savvy about investing—or willing to learn—this can be a powerful way to build wealth. But if the idea of choosing funds stresses you out, you'll need to be intentional about getting advice or selecting a target-date fund that manages risk for you automatically.

Another factor to weigh is your risk tolerance. TRS offers the comfort of knowing exactly how much you'll get every month in retirement if you meet the eligibility requirements. It doesn't matter if the market tanks—you still get your payout. ORP, by contrast, doesn't promise a dollar amount. It only promises contributions. Your future balance will depend on market returns, fees, and how consistently you save. Some people find this exciting, others find it terrifying. You need to know which camp you fall into.

One common misconception is that pensions are "old school" and no longer relevant. In truth, a pension can be incredibly valuable—especially if you live a long time and maintain a modest lifestyle. It's steady, predictable income that can pair well with Social Security and personal savings. But pensions also come with a trade-off: less flexibility. You can't access your money early without penalties, and you can't change your investment options. It's more like a subscription service—you pay in, and you get what they offer.

With ORP and defined contribution plans, you have more control, but also more responsibility. You can start withdrawing your money at 59½, and in some cases, roll it into an IRA if you leave the university. You can also leave it where it is and continue to let it grow. This kind of flexibility is appealing to people who like choices and want to manage their own financial future. But it requires discipline. You'll need to review your investments regularly, make sure your asset allocation matches your age and goals, and avoid the temptation to pull the money out too early.

One of the overlooked benefits of defined contribution plans is how they can align with early retirement goals. If you're someone who dreams of leaving academia at 55 to write books, consult, or travel, ORP offers more options to access your funds before the traditional retirement age. With careful planning, you can structure withdrawals in a way that supports your lifestyle without penalties. TRS, on the other hand, is designed to reward longevity. If you don't stay until your full retirement age, the payouts are often much lower.

Of course, all of this is harder if you don't understand how your own state's system works. Each state has its own version of TRS, ORP, and hybrids, with slightly different rules and benefits. Texas is not the same as Georgia, which is not the same as New York. You have to read the plan documents, ask HR for clarification, and—if needed—talk to someone who can explain it in plain English. It's your money and your future, so don't be shy about asking what each acronym really means.

Some professors find that their colleagues are the best resource for understanding these systems. Talk to someone who's been there a while and ask which plan they chose and why. You'll probably hear a mix of stories—some full of confidence, others tinged with regret. The important thing is to gather a variety of perspectives and then make the decision that fits your own goals. You don't need to copy someone else's path—you just need to understand what you're signing up for.

It's also worth thinking about what retirement really means to you. Do you want to stop working completely at 65, or do you envision a phased retirement with part-time teaching or consulting? Your answer can influence which plan makes more sense. TRS is great for people who want to punch out and live on a stable income. ORP is better for people who want to continue earning and want their money to keep growing alongside them.

Remember, your retirement plan is just one piece of the financial puzzle. You'll still want to save in a Roth IRA, build an emergency fund, and perhaps invest outside of your workplace accounts. But getting this piece right early can take a lot of pressure off later. It's like building the foundation of a house—you want it solid, even if it's not the part anyone sees.

Whether you choose TRS, ORP, or a hybrid option, the most important thing is that you're thinking about it now—not ten years from now. Early attention leads to long-term success. Take the time to read the options, ask questions, and imagine your future self looking back. Will they thank you for locking in a stable pension, or for giving them the freedom to manage a growing portfolio? Either way, your future self will thank you for caring enough to decide. That's the first step toward building a life and career that isn't just meaningful—but also financially secure.

Chapter 7: Health, Dental, Vision & FSAs: Picking the Right Mix of Campus Benefits

One of the most overlooked parts of your new academic job might be your benefits package. After focusing so hard on landing the position—prepping for interviews, polishing your CV, securing letters of recommendation—it's easy to skim through the HR documents and assume your health, dental, and vision insurance will take care of themselves. But campus benefit plans aren't one-size-fits-all, and they don't always make it easy to understand what you're signing up for. That's why it's important to slow down, read the fine print, and ask yourself what you really need from your health coverage—not just for emergencies, but for everyday life.

Health insurance is typically the biggest piece of your benefits puzzle, and for good reason. A single trip to the emergency room or a surgery out of network can leave you with thousands of dollars in bills if you're not careful. Most universities offer a few different plans—usually a high-deductible health plan with a lower monthly premium, a traditional PPO (preferred provider organization), and sometimes an HMO (health maintenance organization). The differences come down to how much you pay each month versus how much you'll pay when you actually need care. A lower premium might look good on paper, but it usually means higher out-of-pocket costs when you go to the doctor or need tests. It's a little like picking between a cheaper phone plan that charges per text versus an unlimited one that costs more upfront but saves you stress later.

When choosing your health insurance plan, consider how often you go to the doctor, whether you have any chronic conditions, and if you're covering anyone else—like a spouse or child. If you're young and generally healthy, you might think a high-deductible plan is the best way to save money. But even the healthiest people get surprised by unexpected events: a car accident, appendicitis, or a weird lump that needs a biopsy. That's when insurance really earns its keep. The peace of mind that comes from knowing you can get care without draining your savings is worth every premium dollar you pay. And in a profession where stress and burnout are common, keeping your health in check isn't just self-care—it's career preservation.

Dental and vision coverage might feel optional, but they play a bigger role in your overall well-being than many people realize. Dental insurance helps with preventive care—cleanings, X-rays, basic fillings—and sometimes more involved procedures like crowns or root canals, though those often come with higher copays. Vision insurance is great if you wear glasses or contacts, but even if you don't, it usually covers an annual eye exam that can catch health issues you wouldn't spot otherwise, like high blood pressure or diabetes. Skipping these benefits might seem like a good way to save money, but neglecting your teeth or eyes can lead to more expensive problems down the line. Think of them as low-cost investments in staying sharp and avoiding costly surprises.

Universities sometimes bundle benefits into tiers—basic, mid-level, or premium. The premium tier might have a higher payroll deduction, but it usually comes with lower copays, deductibles, and better coverage for prescriptions or specialists. That might be worthwhile if you or a dependent has an ongoing medical condition or needs regular care. The basic plan might be just fine for someone who rarely sees a doctor. The trick is not to pick the cheapest or the most expensive option by default, but to match the plan to your real-life habits and needs. It's like buying shoes—not the fanciest pair in the store, and not the cheapest either, but the one that fits your feet and supports your stride.

Another key part of campus benefits is the Flexible Spending Account, or

FSA. This is a tax-advantaged account that lets you set aside pre-tax dollars for medical expenses. You decide how much to contribute—up to an annual limit—and the money can be used for things like copays, prescriptions, glasses, dental work, and even over-the-counter items like pain relievers or allergy medicine. The big catch with an FSA is the "use-it-or-lose-it" rule. If you don't spend the money by the end of the year (or by a short grace period after), it disappears. That makes FSAs best for people who can predict their medical expenses fairly accurately. They're fantastic tools if used wisely, but they require a little planning.

Some employers offer a dependent care FSA as well, which lets you set aside pre-tax dollars to pay for childcare expenses like daycare, preschool, or after-school programs. If you're a parent working full-time on campus, this can be a big help. Just like the medical FSA, it's a use-it-or-lose-it account, so you need to plan carefully. But it's one of the few ways the tax code helps working parents directly. In higher education, where salaries don't always match the hours worked, saving on taxes through an FSA is one way to stretch your paycheck a little further.

Health Savings Accounts, or HSAs, are different from FSAs but often confused with them. You can only use an HSA if you're enrolled in a high-deductible health plan, but the advantage is that the money rolls over year to year and stays with you if you change jobs. HSA funds grow tax-free and can even be invested like a retirement account. They're especially powerful if you can afford to pay out-of-pocket for minor medical expenses now and let the HSA grow for future use. For young faculty with fewer health expenses today, this can be a strategic long-term play. But it only works if you're okay with higher deductibles and more upfront costs.

Understanding in-network versus out-of-network providers is another must. Insurance companies negotiate lower rates with in-network doctors and hospitals. If you go out of network, you could be responsible for the full bill or a much higher portion of it. Always check whether your current doctors—or any specialists you might need—are covered under your plan. Some university towns have limited networks, especially in rural areas, so finding a plan that includes local care is essential. It's like having a gift card to a store that doesn't exist in your area—technically helpful, but useless in practice.

Prescription coverage is often a big differentiator between plans. If you or a family member takes medication regularly, look at each plan's drug formulary—a list of covered medications and what tier they fall under. Tier 1 drugs are usually generics with low copays, while Tier 3 drugs can be brand names with higher costs. Some plans require you to try a cheaper medication first—a practice called step therapy—before approving a more expensive option. Understanding how your plan handles prescriptions can save you time, money, and frustration at the pharmacy counter. No one likes arguing with their insurance company while sick or in pain.

Mental health coverage has improved significantly in recent years, but it's still worth checking what your plan includes. Many universities partner with employee assistance programs that offer a few free therapy sessions, access to counseling, or mental health hotlines. Some health plans include behavioral health services, but not all providers are in-network or accepting new patients. If mental health care is important to you—which, let's be honest, it should be—make sure your chosen plan makes it accessible and affordable. Your emotional well-being is just as important as your physical health, especially in a job that demands so much intellectual and emotional energy.

Preventive care is another area where insurance can help you stay ahead of major problems. Most health plans cover annual checkups, vaccinations, and basic screenings at no additional cost. Taking advantage of these services helps you stay healthy and can catch issues before they become expensive or life-altering. Don't wait until something feels wrong to go to the doctor. Think of preventive care like regular maintenance on your car—it might seem unnecessary when everything's running fine, but it can prevent major breakdowns later.

Some plans also include wellness incentives—rewards for getting your annual physical, completing a health assessment, or participating in a campus wellness challenge. These might include gift cards, premium discounts, or contributions to your FSA or HSA. While these perks won't make or break your financial future, they're a nice bonus and a subtle reminder that taking care of yourself is part of your job. After all, you're not just a professor—you're also the CEO of your own well-being.

It's important to remember that your benefits may change from year to year. Premiums can rise, coverage can shift, and plans can be added or removed depending on what the university negotiates with insurance providers. That's why open enrollment—usually held once a year—is a critical time to review your choices, update your information, and make any changes. Even if you're happy with your current plan, take ten minutes to make sure nothing significant has changed. It's your money, your health, and your responsibility.

If you're married or have a domestic partner, compare their employer's benefits to yours. Sometimes it's cheaper to cover each person individually through their own employer. Other times, one person's plan is so good that it makes sense to put the whole family on it. Don't assume that combining coverage is always the smartest move—it depends on the premiums, deductibles, and network of each plan. Sit down and do the math together like a team. Financial intimacy builds trust, and health decisions often bring up deeper conversations about values, priorities, and long-term plans.

For single faculty members, benefits still matter. You may not be juggling kids' doctor visits or family prescriptions, but you'll still want protection for yourself. Many young professionals put off doctor visits, skip dental care, or ignore eye strain until something goes wrong. Having access to preventive care, checkups, and affordable treatment keeps you working, writing, and living your life without the added stress of unexpected medical bills. Your body and mind are your most important professional assets—treat them accordingly.

Keep in mind that you can usually change your benefits midyear only if you have a qualifying life event. These include things like marriage, divorce, the birth of a child, or losing coverage elsewhere. Otherwise, your choices during open enrollment are locked in for the year. Plan ahead and make selections based on what you expect—not what you hope will happen. No one wants to pay for coverage they never use, but it's far worse to need coverage and not have it. Insurance is one of those things you hope to never use, but you're incredibly grateful for when you do.

At the end of the day, campus benefits are part of your compensation package, just like your salary and retirement contributions. Don't treat them as an afterthought. Choosing the right mix of health, dental, vision, and supplemental accounts can help you stay healthy, reduce stress, and save money over the long haul. It might take a few hours to research your options, but the payoff lasts all year—or longer. And when life throws you a curveball, you'll be glad you took the time to plan ahead.

Whether you're new to academia or just new to this institution, making smart benefit choices is one of the easiest ways to set yourself up for success. Your health is the foundation for everything else—teaching, research, writing, mentoring, and showing up for the people who matter. So take a deep breath, pour another cup of coffee, and give your benefits packet the attention it deserves. You're not just choosing an insurance plan—you're investing in your well-being, your future, and your peace of mind. And that's a benefit you can't put a price on.

Chapter 8: Campus Credit Unions & Banking: Leveraging Faculty-Friendly Financial Services

One of the unexpected perks of joining a university isn't found in your classroom, your office, or even your benefits package—it's often sitting just a few blocks from campus in the form of a credit union. Campus-based credit unions and university-affiliated banks are quiet gems in the financial landscape. They don't market themselves with flashy Super Bowl ads or celebrity endorsements, but they quietly offer some of the best, most faculty-friendly banking options around. If you've only ever banked with a national chain, you might not realize how much more personal and affordable your finances could be by switching. For professors and campus employees, especially those early in their careers, credit unions can offer more support, better rates, and a stronger sense of community.

At their core, credit unions are not-for-profit cooperatives. That means they're owned by their members—people like you who have accounts there—and any profits are reinvested into better services or returned to members as lower fees and higher interest on savings. It's like being part of a neighborhood potluck where everyone brings something to the table and everyone benefits. Unlike big banks, credit unions aren't focused on maximizing shareholder value. Their goal is to serve members, which often leads to more favorable terms on loans, fewer fees, and customer service that feels human rather than robotic.

One of the best reasons to consider a campus credit union is that they understand the rhythms and realities of academic life. They know you might be on a nine-month pay schedule, that your income might dip over the summer, or that you're balancing student loans, a mortgage, and your first sabbatical. Many of these institutions have been serving faculty, staff, and students for decades, and they've built products with those unique needs in mind. This might include flexible auto loans, mortgage programs with lower down payments, or personal lines of credit for those who need to bridge a funding gap between semesters or grants.

Let's say you're buying your first home near campus. A credit union affiliated with the university might offer a mortgage program specifically designed for faculty and staff. This could mean lower rates, reduced closing costs, or more lenient approval terms if you're still early in your career and don't have decades of financial history behind you. They understand that being an assistant professor with great earning potential but lots of student debt is different than being a retail employee with the same credit score. They'll often take a more holistic view of your situation, which can make all the difference when trying to qualify for a loan.

For everyday banking needs, credit unions tend to offer checking and savings accounts that are simpler and more generous than those at big-name banks. You might find no monthly maintenance fees, lower minimum balance requirements, and better interest rates on savings. While that difference might only be a few dollars a month, it adds up over time—especially if you're just getting started with budgeting and saving. And when you call with a question, you're more likely to get a friendly voice who knows your name and your department than a call center in another time zone.

Credit unions also tend to be more forgiving when you need a small personal loan. Maybe your car's transmission goes out right before the semester starts, or your laptop dies during finals week. Traditional banks might run you through a bureaucratic maze, but a campus credit union often has fast-approval personal loans with reasonable interest rates that don't feel predatory. It's not charity—it's just what happens when a financial institution is mission-driven rather than profit-driven. They recognize that helping members stay afloat isn't just good business—it's part of their purpose.

Another often-overlooked benefit is access to financial education. Many credit unions offer free workshops, lunch-and-learns, or one-on-one consultations about credit scores, homebuying, retirement planning, and debt reduction. These sessions aren't sales pitches—they're practical resources designed to help you build financial literacy, often tailored to the campus community. A workshop titled "Budgeting on a Nine-Month Salary" or "How to Maximize Your Retirement Contributions as Faculty" can be far more useful than anything you'd hear from a generic online advisor. This is the kind of knowledge that helps you go from just surviving your early years in academia to building a solid foundation for long-term wealth.

Technology has come a long way in credit unions, too. If you're worried they won't have the mobile app or online features you're used to, think again. Most campus credit unions have robust digital platforms that let you deposit checks via your phone, transfer money between accounts, pay bills, and even set up alerts and savings goals. And because they're smaller and more agile than big banks, they often respond faster to feedback and suggestions. If something isn't working for you, they actually listen and sometimes make changes based on member input—something you almost never see in national institutions.

One unique feature of some credit unions is that they allow membership based on your university affiliation, and you can keep that membership for life—even if you change schools or retire. That means the benefits don't stop when you take a sabbatical or accept a position at another university. It's a little like being an alumnus—you stay part of the family even after you leave. This continuity can be especially helpful if you've set up automatic payments, have a mortgage, or are building a long-term banking relationship.

It's also worth considering credit unions when thinking about your kids or spouse. Many credit unions allow family members of account holders to join, and they often have youth accounts, student loans, or first-time credit cards with low limits and educational features. Teaching your teenager or college student how to manage money with a friendly credit union can be far less intimidating than throwing them into the deep end with a big bank. And if you're supporting elderly parents, a credit union may offer tools to help you manage or monitor their accounts without a complicated legal process.

One area where credit unions consistently shine is auto financing. If you're looking to buy or refinance a car, it's worth getting a quote from your credit union before you go to the dealership. Credit unions tend to offer lower interest rates and more flexible terms than car dealers or national lenders. Plus, they usually don't try to upsell you on unnecessary warranties or insurance add-ons. You walk in knowing the numbers, and you walk out with a better deal. That peace of mind is valuable, especially when you're trying to make smart choices with a limited budget.

Security is another strong suit. Credit unions are federally insured by the National Credit Union Administration (NCUA), which is the credit union equivalent of the FDIC for banks. Your money is protected up to $250,000 per account holder, per institution. So while they may feel smaller or more local, they're just as safe as any major bank when it comes to protecting your deposits. And because they tend to have fewer data breaches and scandals, many people feel more confident trusting their savings to a credit union.

One question people often ask is whether credit unions have enough ATMs or physical branches. The truth is, while your campus credit union might only have a few branches, they're often part of a shared branching network. This allows you to use thousands of ATMs and credit union branches nationwide without fees. So whether you're traveling for a conference, visiting family, or moving across the country, your access to cash and services doesn't disappear. It's like having a hometown bank with nationwide reach.

When it comes to credit cards, campus credit unions typically offer lower interest rates and fewer gimmicks than big banks. You might not get flashy airline miles, but you'll likely get a straightforward card with a fair APR and reasonable fees. For someone looking to build or rebuild credit, this can be an ideal option. And if you ever run into trouble making a payment or need to adjust your limit, you'll be dealing with people who actually want to help, not a collections department reading from a script.

Faculty sometimes overlook the potential of using a credit union for business or professional expenses. Some credit unions offer small business checking, equipment loans, or expense tracking tools that can be helpful if you run a side consulting gig, publish books, or lead workshops. Keeping your professional and personal finances separate is smart for both tax and clarity reasons, and your campus credit union might have tools to help you do it in a way that's easy to manage. They understand the academic hustle and often cater to those hybrid career paths that blend scholarship and entrepreneurship.

If you're transferring to a new university, it's worth checking whether your new institution has a credit union and comparing it with your current bank. Even if you don't switch everything right away, opening a secondary account can help you test the waters. You might find it easier to manage your local expenses, set up direct deposit, or take advantage of on-campus perks by having a nearby credit union account. And over time, that relationship can evolve into your primary banking connection.

Finally, building a strong relationship with your campus credit union is about more than convenience—it's about trust. In a world where banking can feel impersonal, complicated, or even predatory, having a financial institution that knows you, respects your profession, and actively supports your goals is incredibly valuable. It's not just about saving a few bucks on fees or getting a slightly better loan rate—it's about being seen and served as a whole person, not just a number. That's something worth investing in, no matter where you are in your academic journey.

So if you haven't yet walked into your campus credit union or logged onto their website, consider this your friendly nudge. Open an account, ask questions, and explore what they offer. You might find that your best financial ally has been on campus all along—quiet, practical, and ready to help you succeed. Whether you're managing your first real paycheck, planning for retirement, or saving for your kid's education, having the right

Chapter 9: The Tenure Clock, Milestones, Money Mindset, and Emergency Funds for Uncertainty

The moment you accept a tenure-track position, an invisible clock starts ticking. That's the tenure clock. It's usually five to seven years long, depending on the institution, and it sets the timeline for proving that you deserve a permanent place at your university. It's academic probation at the highest level—an extended, high-stakes job interview with set milestones, but often unclear expectations. From the outside, it might look like you've "made it," but inside, you're juggling teaching, research, publishing, committee work, mentoring, grant applications, and possibly family life, all under the pressure of looming review deadlines. It's not just a professional challenge; it's a financial and emotional one too.

The tenure clock isn't just about building your CV—it's about building your financial infrastructure while you do it. During these years, you may see your income rise gradually, receive start-up funds, or pick up summer teaching gigs. But there's also a great deal of financial uncertainty. Will your contract be renewed annually until tenure? What if your department undergoes leadership changes, funding cuts, or a shift in institutional priorities? These unknowns make it essential to develop a money mindset that's both cautious and strategic. Think of it as planting seeds while the weather is unpredictable—you hope for sunshine, but you pack an umbrella, just in case.

One of the smartest things you can do during your pre-tenure years is build an emergency fund. This is your financial safety net, designed to keep you afloat in case of job loss, health issues, or any life event that derails your income. A good target is three to six months of living expenses, though in academia, closer to six is ideal given the slow hiring cycles. This fund doesn't have to be huge right away—start with $1,000 and grow it steadily. Even small monthly deposits build confidence and security. Your emergency fund isn't a sign you expect to fail—it's a sign you're preparing to navigate whatever twists the tenure journey throws your way.

Milestones along the tenure path usually include annual reviews, mid-tenure reviews (typically in year three or four), and the final tenure application. Each one is a checkpoint not only for your professional progress but for your financial planning too. After each milestone, revisit your finances. Are you saving enough? Can you afford to increase your retirement contributions? Did you receive a merit raise or research stipend that could boost your emergency fund or knock down debt? These review moments are also great times to assess whether your spending and saving habits match the direction your career is going.

Early on, you may be tempted to treat your job like it's already permanent, buying a house or committing to major expenses. While homeownership can be a good investment, it's important to be cautious before tenure is secured. If you need to relocate after a negative tenure decision, a house can become a financial and logistical burden. Renting or choosing a smaller home can keep you flexible. It's not about living in fear—it's about giving yourself room to maneuver in case your path changes. Remember, mobility is power, especially in a field where jobs are geographically scattered and competitive.

Another challenge of the tenure clock is the time crunch. You're being pulled in multiple directions, and it's easy to put financial planning on the back burner. But ignoring money doesn't make the stress go away—it often makes it worse. Even dedicating one hour a month to review your accounts, adjust your budget, or learn about investing can give you more peace of mind. Treat that time like office hours with your financial future—show up consistently, ask good questions, and take notes. It's not about perfection.

It's about presence.

For many academics, publishing is the make-or-break element of tenure. But the process is slow, uncertain, and often unpaid. That means you may pour months or years into research without seeing a financial return. Meanwhile, your living costs don't pause. That's why it's crucial to make sure your regular paycheck is working as hard as you are. Automate savings, avoid lifestyle creep, and use your start-up funds wisely. Don't let the pressure to "look successful" push you into financial decisions that don't align with your long-term goals.

Grants and fellowships can be a lifeline during the tenure years, both professionally and financially. If you land one, it might come with summer salary, course releases, or travel funding. But grants also require careful planning. Some provide lump sums without tax withholding, which can lead to big surprises in April if you're not prepared. Others might limit how funds are used, meaning you can't rely on them for basic living expenses. Before you accept any award, make sure you understand the tax implications and build a spending plan. A windfall is only helpful if you manage it well.

Your department may offer faculty development funds—modest grants for conference travel, books, or professional memberships. These funds are incredibly useful, but they don't replace a personal financial plan. If your research takes you overseas or to expensive conferences, plan for those costs ahead of time. Save a little from each paycheck into a dedicated travel account. This way, you're not scrambling when it's time to book flights or register. Investing in your academic visibility is important, but doing so without accruing credit card debt is even smarter.

Student loans often still linger during the early faculty years. While you may not be able to pay them off aggressively, make sure you're on the best repayment plan for your income and goals. If you work for a public university, explore Public Service Loan Forgiveness (PSLF). Keep meticulous records of payments and employment certifications. And even if you're not pursuing forgiveness, set up automatic payments and review your interest rates annually. Just because you're juggling teaching and publishing doesn't mean your debt should be ignored. Keep it manageable so it doesn't become a source of anxiety during an already demanding time.

Insurance coverage also deserves a tenure-track check-in. Make sure you have adequate health insurance, especially if you're relying on university plans. Consider disability insurance—many faculty overlook it, but your income depends on your ability to work. If your school offers group coverage, it's often affordable and worth taking. Life insurance is also worth considering, especially if you have dependents or financial obligations that someone else would need to cover if something happened to you. These aren't fun topics, but addressing them gives you and your loved ones peace of mind.

The tenure clock is also a mental health challenge. Anxiety, imposter syndrome, burnout—all are common during these years. And while these aren't strictly financial issues, they have financial consequences. Therapy, coaching, and mental health resources may be covered under your benefits. Use them. The cost of support is often much lower than the cost of burnout. If you're not sure what's available, reach out to your HR rep confidentially. Taking care of your mind is just as important as taking care of your CV.

Networking can have financial ripple effects too. Building relationships with colleagues across campus can lead to extra teaching opportunities, grants, or interdisciplinary projects that offer stipends. Stay open to collaborative work, but don't overcommit. Time is your most valuable currency during the tenure clock. Spend it wisely. Every "yes" should support your tenure case, your well-being, or your wallet. If it doesn't check at least one of those boxes, think twice.

If you're in a dual-academic household, coordinate your tenure timelines and financial planning. Two people on the tenure clock at once can be a blessing or a logistical circus. Share calendars, plan for dual review years, and consider staggering major purchases. Dual incomes can be a financial advantage, but only if you're aligned on goals. If one of you gets tenure and the other doesn't, what's the plan? Talk through those "what if" scenarios now. Clarity makes crisis management easier if you ever need it.

Faculty with children face unique tenure-clock challenges. From child-care expenses to school schedules to sick days, parenting adds another layer of unpredictability. Budget for help where you can—whether that's after-school care, babysitters, or meal services during crunch time. Use your dependent care FSA if offered. And remember, your kids don't need a Pinterest-perfect parent—they need a healthy, present one. Financial flexibility helps make that possible.

At some point, you might consider buying out a course release—paying for time rather than just relying on grants or institutional funding. This is a big decision. Buying time can make room for writing, but it also means giving up income or using precious start-up funds. Think of it like investing in yourself. Will this time lead to a publication that boosts your tenure file or secures future funding? If yes, the return might be worth it. If no, reconsider. Time is money—but only if used well.

As you get closer to your tenure review, don't let fear paralyze your financial planning. It's easy to think, "I'll wait to save more or invest until I know I have tenure." But money grows with time, not certainty. Start where you are. Save something. Contribute to your retirement plan. Pay off a credit card. Build a buffer. These actions don't just improve your finances—they give you a sense of control during an unpredictable process.

When the final tenure decision comes, it will affect your finances one way or another. If you're approved, congratulations. You can now plan long-term with more confidence—maybe consider a bigger home, college savings for your kids, or more aggressive investing. If the answer is no, it's not the end of the world, even if it feels like it. Use your emergency fund, lean on your network, and start planning your next chapter. Many brilliant, successful academics have found fulfilling careers after tenure denials—some even happier than if they'd stayed.

The tenure clock is a pressure cooker, but it's also an opportunity to build habits, systems, and awareness that will serve you for decades. If you use this time to build your financial resilience alongside your academic record, you'll emerge stronger no matter what the outcome. Your career is important, but so is your financial peace of mind. Don't let uncertainty paralyze you. Instead, let it motivate you to prepare with intention, act with clarity, and plan with purpose.

Chapter 10: Publishing, Grants, and Pay Bumps, Turning Scholarly Output into Income Opportunities

Publishing a book, landing a major grant, or securing a mid-career merit raise can feel like winning three different lotteries; yet each "win" is more skill than luck when you understand how universities convert scholarly output into dollars and cents. Your first goal is visibility: journals, presses, and grant agencies cannot reward work they never see, so treat submission deadlines like fixed departure gates at an airport—arrive prepared and on time. Early in your career, that preparation means knowing which journals weigh heaviest in your tenure file, which university presses have a track record in your niche, and which funding agencies align with your methodology. Too many faculty spray manuscripts everywhere or chase every call for proposals, wasting precious writing hours on mismatched outlets. Instead, create a short list of tier-one targets for both articles and grants, then reverse-engineer your project timelines so that each submission feeds both your scholarly narrative and your financial story.

Next comes the art of stacking outputs so one project yields many forms of currency—academic, reputational, and literal. Picture a single research study as a tree: the main trunk might become a flagship journal article worth tenure points, while branch data sets can sprout conference papers, invited talks, and perhaps a public-facing op-ed that raises your profile for future consulting gigs. When reviewers or grant panels see that you squeeze every drop of insight from your funding, they feel more confident investing in you again; likewise, department chairs become more generous at merit-raise time when they witness a steady stream of citations and press mentions originating from one seed grant. Efficiency not only saves time but multiplies payoffs, so build reuse and repurposing into your research design from day one.

External grants are the most obvious route to new money, yet many faculty overlook how internal mini-grants prime the pump. Winning a $5,000 seed fund from your college may not pay the mortgage, but it buys course releases, travel funds, or research assistants who accelerate the pilot data you need for a six-figure national-science-foundation proposal. Funders love momentum stories; show that small dollars already produced preliminary results, and larger agencies feel safer writing bigger checks. Meanwhile, your institution often lets you take a percentage of grant overhead—or "indirects"—as discretionary money, which can underwrite future projects or even supplement summer salary. Track those indirect distributions carefully, as they are one of the few revenue streams you control directly once awarded.

Summer salary itself is a game-changer for cash flow when nine-month contracts leave three blank pay periods. Most federal agencies allow investigators to budget up to two months of summer pay at their institutional rate; calculate that figure early and include it in every grant budget justification. If you land overlapping awards, be mindful of caps on cumulative summer salary—overages can jeopardize compliance—yet you can often shift excess funds to graduate assistants or equipment, freeing department resources that later translate into merit raises or start-up top-ups. Always coordinate with your grants office so you maximize allowable compensation without triggering audit flags.

Royalties from scholarly books rarely make you rich, but structured wisely they become passive income that funds conference travel or sabbatical airfare. Negotiate higher advance payments if the press is small and the royalty percentage low; for larger presses that push print-on-demand and e-book versions, fight instead for a tiered royalty schedule where your percentage jumps after certain sales thresholds. Deposit royalty checks straight into a dedicated savings sub-account labeled "research freedom" so the money doesn't dissolve into daily expenses. Over a decade, even modest annual royalties can finance a qualitative study abroad or cushion a semester of unpaid leave to finish the next manuscript.

Open-access fees often scare authors, yet some departments reimburse them because publicly accessible articles raise citation counts and institutional rankings. If your university has an open-access fund, apply early in the fiscal year when dollars are plentiful. That single reimbursement works like a micro-grant, turning a sunk publication cost into free marketing for your ideas. Higher downloads attract media interviews, and journalists often pay honoraria for expert commentary, adding small but meaningful deposits to your consulting income.

Speaking of consulting, every polished keynote builds directly on published scholarship. When a civic organization or corporate board cites your article in its white paper, follow up with an email offering a tailored workshop. Price your time based on value delivered, not campus hourly rates; industry clients expect to pay four-figure day rates for niche expertise. Funnel consulting fees into a solo 401(k) or SEP-IRA to convert self-employment spikes into retirement assets while lowering your taxable income. This maneuver turns a one-off talk into long-term wealth and demonstrates to promotion committees that your research impacts stakeholders beyond the ivory tower.

Department merit raises frequently hinge on performance rubrics that weight publication counts, impact factors, teaching scores, and service. Read your college's annual evaluation policy the way attorneys study contracts, highlighting verbs like "shall result" versus "may result" in salary bumps. If service counts minimally toward pay but heavily toward goodwill, volunteer strategically—chair a short-term task force that ends before manuscript deadlines rather than a standing committee that swallows weekly writing sessions. Align every hour of labor with the line items that move your salary needle; when review season arrives, quantify accomplishments in the policy's exact language so evaluators check the highest boxes.

Don't underestimate the power of retention offers. If another institution invites you to interview, that signal alone can prompt your current employer to sweeten your package with research funding, lab space, or an immediate salary boost. Never bluff with phantom offers, but cultivate genuine networking so that occasional inquiries arrive organically. Before negotiations, calculate what matters most—cash, teaching relief, spousal hire—then let the dean choose among options; administrators prefer spending discretionary funds over recurring salary dollars, and a well-funded research account may ultimately outpace a modest raise through travel savings and grant leverage.

Publishing with students multiplies impact and can unlock co-author funding pools. Many universities reward faculty-student publications with stipends that go directly to research or summer pay. Mentoring undergraduates on a data project might feel altruistic, yet those collaborations often qualify for institutional showcases that come with monetary prizes or professional-development grants. Plus, future employers note your mentorship record, strengthening your candidacy for endowed chairs that carry prestige pay bumps.

In the realm of creative disciplines, juried exhibitions or performances sometimes yield honoraria smaller than travel costs. Counter this by bundling events: schedule workshops or guest lectures at nearby campuses during the same trip, collecting multiple stipends on a single airfare. Track every mile and per diem; many states allow you to deduct unreimbursed professional expenses, lowering your tax bill and effectively raising your net income. The key is stacking outputs—turning one gallery showing into three revenue streams.

Intellectual property from patents or software licenses offers the glitziest payouts but demands patience. Technology-transfer offices typically split royalties between inventors, departments, and the university. Ask upfront about percentages, patent-cost recoveries, and milestone payments. If your field leans theoretical, explore creative-commons licensing paired with paid consulting for implementation; sometimes open tools spread faster, generating workshops and training contracts that eclipse modest royalty checks.

Conference honoraria are rare, but travel grants abound. Even a $750 travel award frees departmental funds that can later justify a discretionary raise. Keep a spreadsheet of every external dollar brought in—grants, royalties, consulting, reimbursements—and share it during annual reviews. Administrators love faculty who "pay their own way," and visible self-funding strengthens your hand when requesting a salary equity adjustment.

Collaborative grants can feel like herding cats, yet large multi-PI awards often include a percentage for each investigator's effort—effectively adding to your base salary for the grant's duration. Before joining such teams, negotiate your percent effort in writing and verify that it buys out teaching rather than piling on top of existing duties. Protect your research days like office hours for your future income; without time to publish the grant's findings, you lose the downstream merit-pay and promotion benefits.

When a book contract arrives, resist the urge to sign immediately. Ask for escalator clauses that increase your royalty percentage if the publisher recoups the advance quickly. Request copies at author discount to resell at speaking events, turning each engagement into a micro-bookstore. Some presses cut checks for subsidiary rights—translations, audiobooks, film options—so carve out a clause giving you approval power and a higher split on those deals, which often happen years later and feel like surprise bonuses.

Small wins accumulate: a $1,200 keynote here, a $500 essay prize there, a $2,000 course development grant next semester. Funnel every unexpected dollar into a separate high-yield savings account labeled "Opportunity Fund." When larger chances arise—self-funded archival research, a short-notice residency—you'll have cash ready, avoiding credit-card interest and demonstrating fiscal responsibility to future funders who ask for proof of institutional or personal matching funds.

Finally, remember that scholarly income isn't just about getting more money; it's about buying freedom—time to write, resources to explore risky ideas, and flexibility to say no to draining commitments. Each article, grant, or pay bump is a lever that moves you closer to a sustainable, fulfilling academic life. Track your progress, celebrate incremental gains, and reinvest windfalls strategically. Over a career, these choices compound like interest, transforming scholarly passion into lasting financial resilience.

Chapter 11: Sabbaticals & Leaves, Planning Finances Around Paid and Unpaid Time Off

At some point in your academic journey, you may find yourself yearning for space to think, write, research, or simply recharge. That's where sabbaticals and other types of academic leave come in. These periods away from regular teaching duties are often built into the academic system as a reward for years of service and scholarly contribution. They're a chance to go deeper into your work, pursue a new project, or even switch directions entirely. But as refreshing as they sound, sabbaticals and leaves come with financial implications that are often misunderstood. If you don't plan carefully, the time meant to nourish your career can end up straining your budget instead.

Sabbaticals typically happen every seven years, though the timing can vary by institution and contract. Some universities offer a full year at half pay or a single semester at full pay. Others may allow more flexible options, like two semesters at three-quarters pay or short-term mini-leaves. These choices might sound interchangeable, but they affect your financial picture very differently. It's not just about the salary—it's also about what benefits continue, whether retirement contributions change, and how your department handles teaching loads in your absence. Before committing to a leave, you need a detailed understanding of what you're gaining and what you might be giving up.

One of the first things to check is your eligibility. Some universities require tenure before you can apply for a sabbatical, while others allow pre-tenure leaves under different titles like research leave or junior faculty leave. If you're planning to apply for a sabbatical down the line, keep track of service years and any interruptions, like time off for parental leave or administrative appointments, that might reset the clock. You'll also need to prepare a compelling proposal that outlines your goals, timeline, and expected outcomes. That proposal isn't just an academic exercise—it's a form of budgeting. You're asking your institution to invest in your work, and it's wise to think about how you'll make the most of that investment, both intellectually and financially.

Let's say you're approved for a one-semester sabbatical at full pay. That's the easiest option to manage financially. Your income and benefits continue uninterrupted, and you gain time to focus without the stress of replacing lost wages. But many faculty aim for the full-year sabbatical, which usually comes with a 50 percent pay cut. This is where the financial planning really kicks in. You'll need to look closely at your monthly budget, fixed costs like rent or mortgage, and discretionary spending. If you're already living paycheck to paycheck, a sabbatical at half salary could feel more like a financial emergency than a professional break.

To make a reduced-pay sabbatical viable, some faculty turn to grant funding, book advances, or fellowship stipends to supplement their income. This strategy works well, especially if the external funds are compatible with university leave policies. But timing is everything. You may need to apply for grants a year or more in advance, and many fellowships have deadlines that don't align neatly with your sabbatical schedule. That's why it's helpful to create a leave planning timeline that includes both your university's application process and the funding cycles of external organizations. You're essentially choreographing a dance between institutional permission and financial sustainability.

If no grant or fellowship funding is available, you'll need to create your own income cushion. Start by calculating the gap between your regular salary and your sabbatical pay. Then work backward to figure out how much you need to save each month leading up to your leave. Treat it like preparing for parental leave or a big move—you're trying to build a short-term fund that keeps your life running smoothly while your income dips. Some faculty set up a separate savings account labeled "sabbatical fund" and make regular transfers into it. Even small contributions add up, especially if you start early. This approach gives you a sense of control and avoids last-minute panic when the sabbatical finally arrives.

Another option is to negotiate with your department for additional support, such as summer teaching assignments or course releases in the years leading up to your sabbatical. These strategies can help you front-load your work or spread the impact of a leave more evenly. Some departments may also allow you to bank professional development funds or unused travel grants to support your sabbatical expenses. These aren't guaranteed, so you'll need to advocate for yourself and keep communication open with your chair or dean. Being proactive here is not selfish—it's strategic. You're not just planning a break; you're investing in your scholarly productivity, which benefits the whole department.

Faculty with families often face added considerations when planning a sabbatical. Will you stay put or move for a fellowship? If you relocate, how will you cover moving costs, temporary housing, or differences in the cost of living? If your partner works, can they take time off or work remotely? If you have kids, what about school enrollment and childcare? All of these questions affect your budget and can make or break your sabbatical experience. It helps to make a detailed list of potential costs—both one-time and recurring—and to be honest about what level of disruption your household can tolerate. A glamorous year abroad sounds exciting, but not if it comes with financial strain and logistical headaches that make it impossible to write.

Health insurance is another big question, especially if your leave is unpaid or partially paid. At many universities, benefits continue during sabbaticals, but this isn't always the case with unpaid leaves. You may need to pay the full premium cost, which can be a shock if you're used to the university subsidizing a large portion. Make sure to confirm this with your HR department and factor those premiums into your sabbatical budget. Going without coverage is rarely a good idea—one medical emergency can wipe out years of savings. If you're covered through a partner's plan, check their policy's eligibility requirements before assuming you can hop on their benefits.

Taxes can also change during a sabbatical, especially if you receive income from multiple sources. For example, if part of your leave is funded by a grant or fellowship, that money might not have taxes withheld. That means you could owe a sizable amount come tax season unless you make estimated payments throughout the year. Consulting a tax professional or using a reliable tax calculator can help you plan ahead. Don't wait until the following April to figure it out. You'll have enough on your mind without scrambling to cover a surprise IRS bill just as you're coming off your leave.

Sabbaticals are also a good time to evaluate your long-term financial goals. Without the daily grind of teaching, you may finally have space to revisit your retirement plan, update your insurance policies, or explore new investment opportunities. Use some of your sabbatical bandwidth to meet with a financial advisor or simply audit your accounts. Are you on track to meet your savings goals? Are your expenses aligned with your values and future plans? This kind of financial check-in doesn't need to dominate your sabbatical, but even an afternoon spent rebalancing your portfolio or adjusting your contributions can make a meaningful difference.

If you're taking an unpaid leave—for research, caregiving, or personal reasons—the stakes are even higher. Without a paycheck, you'll need a more substantial savings cushion and a detailed spending plan. Prioritize your essential expenses and look for ways to cut back temporarily. Pause contributions to discretionary spending categories like dining out, subscriptions, or travel, and redirect that money toward fixed costs like housing and insurance. Consider whether you can defer student loan payments, negotiate lower bills, or apply for short-term assistance programs. Unpaid leave is not ideal, but with the right planning, it can still be financially survivable and even worthwhile.

Returning from a sabbatical or leave also requires financial transition planning. If you took a pay cut or used savings, it might take time to rebuild your reserves or adjust your cash flow. Resist the urge to immediately "reward" yourself with big purchases or new commitments. Instead, treat your re-entry like the end of a training program—ease back in, assess your progress, and course correct if needed. Revisit your monthly budget, reset your savings goals, and think about what worked well financially during your leave that you might want to carry forward. Sabbaticals can change your relationship with time and money in ways that extend far beyond the leave itself.

Not all leaves are voluntary, of course. Sometimes health issues, family emergencies, or burnout force you to step back unexpectedly. That's why having an emergency fund is so critical for academics. Unlike industry jobs with generous short-term disability plans or guaranteed paid leave, academia often leaves the burden on the individual to bridge financial gaps during time off. Building an emergency fund—even slowly—isn't just for worst-case scenarios. It's a way of buying yourself dignity and options when life throws you curveballs you didn't see coming.

Ultimately, sabbaticals and leaves are one of the greatest privileges of the academic life, but only if you plan them thoughtfully. Time is valuable, and so is money—and the best sabbaticals balance both. They give you room to think big, write deeply, and restore your energy without wrecking your bank account. So start planning early, ask the right questions, and don't be afraid to be strategic about the financial side of your time off. A well-planned sabbatical isn't just a break from work—it's a catalyst for what comes next. And when done right, it can be one of the smartest financial and professional moves of your entire career.

Chapter 12: Buying a Home in a College Town, Mortgage Math, Town-Gown Price Dynamics, and Tax Breaks

Being in a dual-academic household is a little like being in a tag-team match where both people are juggling the same chaos. You both understand the pressures of research deadlines, committee work, grading marathons, and tenure clocks. That can make for deep empathy—but it also creates some real complications when it comes to planning finances, benefits, and career moves together. Coordinating two academic lives isn't just about finding jobs in the same zip code. It's about making financial decisions that support both your careers without burning out or missing key opportunities. The better you plan, the less likely you'll find yourselves stuck in a pattern of sacrifice and resentment.

The first and often hardest hurdle is job placement. The academic job market isn't kind to couples. You might get offers in two different cities or one of you lands a position and the other is left scrambling. This is where some institutions offer dual-career hiring support, sometimes called spousal accommodation. It sounds good in theory, but in practice, it can be complicated. Not all departments want to take on an extra hire, even if the provost is pushing it. If you're in this situation, try to understand the political landscape, and make sure your request is seen as a partnership opportunity, not a favor.

Assuming you both land positions at the same or nearby institutions, the next challenge is choosing benefits. You might both be eligible for health insurance, retirement plans, and tuition waivers. But that doesn't mean you need to duplicate coverage. For example, it's often cheaper and more efficient for one partner to cover both under a single health plan. The catch is figuring out which one has the better network, lower premiums, or better prescription coverage. This is where sitting down during open enrollment with both your HR packets side-by-side becomes essential. Think of it like comparing cell phone plans—you're looking for value, not just what's "free."

Retirement planning in dual-academic households also has layers. Many universities offer 403(b), 457(b), or 401(a) plans, and some even provide pension-like defined benefit systems. If one of you has access to a generous employer match, it might make sense to prioritize that account while the other contributes to a Roth IRA or taxable brokerage account. It's about optimizing total household savings, not trying to match each other dollar-for-dollar. Remember, you're building one long-term financial life together. Just because the account names have different Social Security numbers doesn't mean the goals are separate.

Another often-overlooked area is life insurance and disability coverage. If both of you have employer-sponsored policies, do a side-by-side comparison. Look at the benefit amounts, premiums, and portability if one of you leaves your job. Also, ask yourself how financially vulnerable you'd be if one partner couldn't work for six months. Dual incomes can create a false sense of security, especially if you've built a lifestyle that requires both paychecks. A serious illness or sabbatical can quickly show the cracks in that plan. A small monthly premium for long-term disability insurance can save your finances from a much bigger disruption later.

Moving is another point of stress and opportunity. If one partner gets a great offer, it may come with relocation funds, spousal hiring help, or better long-term career growth. But uprooting also means financial and emotional costs: selling a house, breaking a lease, moving kids, and starting over socially. The academic world is notorious for placing its demands above personal convenience, so you have to be brutally honest about whose opportunity takes precedence—and why. Sometimes it's about following the money. Other times it's about tenure security, research resources, or quality of life. But don't let inertia or guilt make the decision for you.

When it comes to buying a home, two professor incomes can be a blessing or a trap. On paper, you qualify for more. But remember, academic salaries don't always come with job security, especially if one of you is in a non-tenure-track role. Be careful not to overextend based on a dual-income assumption that might not hold up during sabbatical years, grant gaps, or if one person decides to shift into administration or consulting. Many academic couples find peace of mind by basing major financial decisions on one income and treating the second as a buffer, not a necessity.

Childcare is another puzzle piece. While it's amazing to have two highly educated, committed parents, academic schedules don't always align with daycare hours or school pickups. Coordinating teaching schedules and office hours takes effort, and sometimes a sacrifice has to be made. Maybe one partner teaches online or accepts evening classes so the other can manage mornings. Maybe you alternate semesters of lighter service loads. Whatever the plan, the key is to talk openly and revisit your strategy often. As your kids grow and your responsibilities shift, what worked two years ago may not make sense now.

Some dual-academic couples find that running parallel tracks isn't sustainable. One partner may decide to step back temporarily, switching to adjunct work or taking on a more flexible role to support the other's career move. That can be a loving, strategic decision—but it needs to come with financial planning and mutual respect. If you're the one scaling back, make sure you're still contributing to retirement and maintaining your professional identity. If your partner is stepping back for you, acknowledge the value of that sacrifice and think ahead about how to rebalance things later. Resentment grows when one partner feels invisible or stuck while the other thrives.

Filing taxes as a dual-academic household also comes with quirks. You may both have W-2s, but if one of you does consulting, speaking, or publishing on the side, there may be 1099 income to report. That opens up the world of quarterly estimated tax payments, Schedule C filings, and business deductions. Keeping a shared spreadsheet of side income and expenses can reduce stress at tax time and also help you spot patterns. Maybe you both start seeing income spikes in summer when you're not teaching, or one of you earns honoraria that are inconsistent but meaningful. Recognizing those rhythms helps you budget and plan more effectively.

Professional development and travel are often negotiable and sometimes unequal. One partner might have access to more generous research funds or be in a more travel-heavy discipline. Instead of competing or feeling guilty, talk about how to support each other's professional growth across seasons. Maybe one year, you attend multiple conferences while your partner stays home with the kids, and the next year you swap roles. Building flexibility into your plans honors both careers without framing it as a zero-sum game.

As you move further into your careers, conversations about tenure, promotion, and leadership roles become more complex. It's not uncommon for one partner to advance faster than the other, and that can stir up insecurity or strain if you're not careful. Talk openly about your timelines, goals, and the pressures you're facing. Share wins, celebrate milestones, and resist the urge to compare titles or salaries. Academic success often comes in waves, and supporting each other through the ebb and flow builds a stronger foundation than any single achievement.

Sometimes, dual-academic couples face a more permanent imbalance—where one partner moves into a high-earning, secure role, and the other continues in contingent or adjunct positions. This can create tension, especially around power dynamics and financial control. If you're in this situation, clarity and communication are vital. Share access to financial accounts, make joint decisions about large purchases, and recognize each other's contributions beyond salary. The work of managing a household, raising children, or supporting a partner's career doesn't always show up in a paycheck—but it absolutely counts.

University benefits like tuition remission or dependent care FSAs can be maximized by planning ahead. If you have kids, coordinate who claims the childcare tax credit and who uses the FSA. If one partner's university offers tuition discounts for dependents, plan your timing around when your kids might enroll in college. Sometimes, one spouse's university benefit becomes the family's greatest financial asset—and it's easy to miss if you don't read the fine print. It's worth sitting down with HR or a benefits specialist at both institutions to walk through what's available to you as a household.

Retirement planning as a dual-academic household should include discussions about retirement dates, income bridges, and Social Security timing. Maybe one of you plans to retire at 62, while the other wants to keep going until 70. That affects everything from cash flow to health insurance to housing. The earlier you talk about those plans, the more likely you'll create a transition that feels intentional instead of reactive. Building a financial plan together that accounts for staggered retirements or part-time transitions can reduce stress and expand your options down the road.

Debt repayment strategies also benefit from collaboration. If one of you still has student loans and the other doesn't, consider targeting the higher-interest balance first. You can still keep things equitable in your household finances without pretending all debt is created equal. Likewise, if one of you has significant consumer debt, talk about why it happened and what systems you can build together to avoid future pitfalls. The academic life is already financially fragile in many ways—dealing with debt as a team, not in secret or shame, makes you both stronger.

If you're planning on big purchases or lifestyle upgrades—buying a home, adopting a child, starting a business—use both your academic calendars and your financial calendar to time things wisely. Maybe you wait until after a sabbatical, or you use a merit raise to cover increased costs. Smart timing can make a big difference, especially when both of you are working within rigid academic cycles. When you sync your financial goals with your professional ones, you start to build a rhythm that honors both.

Lastly, don't forget about joy. Dual-academic households can become so focused on logistics, calendars, and deadlines that they forget to celebrate what makes the partnership special. You've built a life together based on shared values, deep curiosity, and mutual respect. Set aside money and time for travel, hobbies, or just slow weekends. Financial planning is about more than spreadsheets and benefits—it's about crafting a life that feels balanced and meaningful for both of you. In the end, the strength of your academic careers will reflect the strength of the foundation you've built together.

Chapter 13: Campus Child-Care, 529s, and Education Perks, Maximizing University Family Benefits

One of the more unexpected joys of working in academia is discovering how many family-related perks universities quietly offer. From campus child-care centers to tuition discounts for your kids, these benefits can be real financial lifelines—if you know they exist and understand how to use them. Many faculty members are so focused on syllabi and research deadlines that they miss the chance to tap into programs that could ease both their parenting stress and their financial strain. Whether you're just starting a family or already juggling teenagers and tenure-track responsibilities, taking full advantage of your university's family benefits is a smart, often underutilized strategy for long-term peace of mind. It's about learning how to build a life that works alongside your academic career, not in spite of it.

Campus child-care centers are one of the first stops for many academic parents. These programs are usually run by the university itself or through a partnered organization, and they tend to be in high demand. The cost is often lower than private daycares in the area, and the convenience of having your child nearby can't be overstated. Imagine walking across campus to read a bedtime story during lunch or being able to nurse between office hours and a committee meeting. But there's a catch: waitlists. If you're expecting, it's not uncommon to put your name on the list before your baby is even born. Planning ahead and calling early can make a huge difference in getting a spot.

Another advantage of campus child-care programs is the built-in academic culture. The teachers often understand faculty schedules and are more flexible during exam weeks or research crunches. Some centers even offer half-day or drop-in options during breaks or summer terms, which is a huge help if you're not teaching full-time or if your partner's schedule changes seasonally. Still, don't assume these programs are automatically affordable. Some charge tiered rates based on salary, which can surprise early-career professors who've just landed a tenure-track job. Take the time to budget for this expense and weigh it against nearby alternatives. What you gain in proximity and culture might cost a little more upfront, but the time and stress you save may well be worth it.

If your university doesn't offer on-campus child care—or if the waitlist is too long—it's worth asking about child-care subsidies. Some schools provide vouchers or reimbursements to offset daycare costs. These can be especially valuable for graduate students, adjuncts, and early-career faculty with modest incomes. Others allow pre-tax payroll deductions through dependent care flexible spending accounts (FSAs), which lower your taxable income. These accounts are use-it-or-lose-it within the year, though, so careful planning is essential. Think through your calendar: will you need full-time care, part-time, or just summer coverage? The more accurate your projections, the more effectively you can use the tax savings.

Speaking of tax strategies, don't forget about 529 plans—tax-advantaged savings accounts specifically designed for education costs. Many universities partner with state-sponsored 529 programs and may even offer automatic payroll contributions. The money in a 529 grows tax-free, and as long as it's used for qualified education expenses, withdrawals are also tax-free. That can include college tuition, of course, but also K–12 tuition, student loan repayments, and even some apprenticeship programs. Starting a 529 early—even with small monthly amounts—can make a big difference over time thanks to compound interest. If both you and your partner work for the university, you might even be able to double your efforts or earmark separate plans for each child.

There's also the magic of tuition remission, a benefit many university employees don't think about until their kids are older. Some schools offer partial or full tuition coverage for dependents who attend the same institution. Others participate in tuition exchange programs, where your child can apply to a network of affiliated colleges at a steep discount. This perk can translate into tens of thousands of dollars in savings over a college career. The catch? There are often strings attached—length of service requirements, competitive admissions, or restrictions on graduate programs. Still, it's worth researching well in advance so you can shape your long-term education strategy around the benefits you've earned through years of academic service.

Don't overlook employee tuition benefits for yourself, either. If you're considering another degree or certification, check whether your institution offers faculty discounts or fee waivers. These can apply to graduate-level coursework, continuing education, or even online programs. That's not just a nice-to-have—it can be a real career boost, particularly if you're pivoting into administration or adding a new area of expertise. In some cases, departments will even cover the cost of coursework if it aligns with your current teaching or research focus. Taking advantage of these opportunities shows initiative and helps you remain competitive in a constantly evolving academic landscape.

For those with school-age kids, some universities operate lab schools—elementary or secondary schools directly affiliated with the college of education. These schools often pilot innovative teaching methods and maintain small class sizes, making them attractive options for faculty families. Admission can be competitive, and sometimes there's a lottery, but it's worth exploring if you're looking for a school that understands your academic lifestyle. Lab schools often align their breaks with the university calendar, meaning fewer conflicts during holidays or finals season. Plus, your kids benefit from being part of a learning community that's surrounded by research, creativity, and a commitment to education.

Summer can be particularly tricky for academic parents, especially when university classes pause but research and service commitments continue.

Fortunately, many campuses offer summer camps, enrichment programs, and other seasonal childcare options. These programs are often subsidized and staffed by university students or staff, making them more affordable than off-campus alternatives. Whether it's a week-long robotics camp or a month of nature studies, these programs keep your kids engaged while you stay productive. And since they're on campus or nearby, you can check in between meetings or swing by for a quick lunch visit. Little moments like that can make a big difference during a hectic academic summer.

One unexpected area where universities shine is parental leave. Policies vary widely, but many schools now offer paid leave for faculty who are growing their families through birth, adoption, or foster care. These policies can include teaching releases, partial pay, or extensions on the tenure clock. Make sure you understand what's available to you—not just the formal policy, but how it's applied in your specific department or college. Sometimes unwritten norms matter just as much as what's on paper. Talking to recently tenured parents in your department can give you insight into how to request leave and how to plan your teaching and service load accordingly.

Budgeting around child-related expenses can be challenging, especially in an academic job with variable income, like summer teaching stipends or inconsistent grant funding. Building a family budget that includes regular child-care costs, future education savings, and healthcare expenses requires intentional planning. One useful strategy is to treat irregular income as "bonus" money and use it to pad your emergency fund, contribute to your child's 529, or pay down debt. Living primarily on your base salary—especially if it's steady during the nine-month academic year—creates predictability in your finances and builds in resilience when unexpected costs arise.

Don't be afraid to advocate for family-friendly policies on campus. If your institution doesn't yet offer certain benefits, consider joining a faculty senate committee or parent caucus to push for change. A well-organized group of faculty voices can often influence HR policies, especially when backed by data about retention, productivity, and employee satisfaction.

Universities are under pressure to attract and retain top talent, and family-friendly benefits play a big role in that equation. You don't have to wait for someone else to make things better—you can be part of the shift. Even small wins, like adding lactation spaces or improving parental leave transparency, make a difference.

Another resource many faculty don't realize exists is the Employee Assistance Program, or EAP. These programs offer counseling, legal support, and parenting resources—often free of charge. Whether you're navigating school placement, struggling with work-life balance, or facing a family crisis, an EAP counselor can help you find solutions. These programs are confidential and underused, making them a valuable tool for stressed-out academic parents. You might even find resources like college planning workshops or financial counseling sessions that tie directly into your family's educational goals.

When considering your overall compensation package, think about the non-monetary benefits just as seriously as your salary. Having access to reliable child care, quality education options, and financial tools like 529s can save you thousands of dollars a year. But they also reduce stress and help you show up fully at work and at home. A well-supported academic parent is more likely to meet research deadlines, teach with energy, and contribute meaningfully to campus life. Your kids benefit, too, from seeing a parent who is engaged, supported, and present.

As your kids grow, their needs change—and so should your financial strategies. What worked during preschool may not be ideal for middle school. Maybe you switch from daycare expenses to tutoring budgets or from summer camps to travel enrichment experiences. This evolution is normal, but it requires periodic financial check-ins to stay on track. You might rebalance your savings goals, adjust your FSA contributions, or change your 529 allocations to match your child's age and education goals. Treat your family finances like a syllabus: revise it regularly to reflect where you are now and where you hope to go.

If you're part of a dual-academic household, these decisions become even more nuanced. Coordinating benefits across two institutions, managing multiple academic calendars, and balancing time commitments all impact how you use family-related resources. Maybe one partner takes the lead on child-care decisions while the other focuses on 529 planning. Or perhaps you divide by semester, alternating who teaches summer classes and who manages summer camp pickups. However you split the load, communication is key. Regular check-ins about finances, scheduling, and long-term goals help keep your partnership strong and your family grounded.

It's easy to feel like you're barely keeping up as an academic parent. The schedule is unforgiving, the emotional demands are high, and the systems aren't always built with families in mind. But by using your university's family benefits to your advantage, you can buy back time, reduce financial pressure, and create space for joy. These programs aren't charity—they're part of your compensation, and you've earned them through your hard work and service. Whether it's a tuition discount that lightens the load during college or a summer camp that gives you two quiet weeks to finish your book manuscript, every benefit you use is a tool that supports your career and your kids.

In the end, academic life is often described as a marathon, not a sprint—and parenting is no different. The most successful academic parents aren't necessarily the ones who do everything perfectly; they're the ones who find ways to make the system work for their family. That means asking questions, seeking out hidden perks, and getting creative with what your university has to offer. With a little planning and a lot of communication, you can build a career and a family life that complement each other rather than compete. You don't have to choose between thriving at home and thriving on campus. With the right tools, you can do both.

Chapter 14: Upgrading Insurance, Life, Disability, Umbrella, and Professional Liability for Professors

Insurance is one of those adult responsibilities that rarely gets the attention it deserves, especially for professors who often have their minds occupied with lectures, research deadlines, and committee meetings. It's easy to think of insurance as just a check-the-box item during open enrollment, but it's actually one of the key pillars of a strong financial foundation. For professors—many of whom have irregular pay structures, multiple side gigs, or families counting on their income—it's essential to go beyond the basics. Upgrading your insurance coverage isn't about being paranoid. It's about being proactive so that one unexpected twist doesn't derail your long-term plans. And trust me, once you understand what you need and why, the peace of mind is worth every penny.

Let's start with life insurance, which often feels like a "someday" thing until life demands otherwise. Many universities offer a default life insurance policy, often one or two times your salary, which is fine for covering short-term expenses like funeral costs. But if you have a spouse, kids, a mortgage, or student loans, you'll likely need more coverage than your employer offers. Think about this: If your income disappeared tomorrow, how long would your family be okay financially? Would your partner be able to pay the mortgage, fund the kids' college, or even just take time off to grieve? That's the real purpose of life insurance—not to make anyone rich, but to buy them time and options when they need it most.

Term life insurance is usually the smartest move for faculty members who want affordable protection during their working years. You can lock in a level premium for 20 or 30 years, enough to cover the years when your kids are still at home or your retirement savings are growing. Whole life insurance sounds fancy but tends to be expensive and unnecessary for most people, especially those who are already investing through other vehicles like 403(b)s or IRAs. The goal isn't to over-insure—it's to right-size your policy based on your actual needs. Many people start with a million-dollar policy and adjust over time. That might sound like a lot, but when you factor in income replacement, debts, childcare, and tuition, it's not as excessive as it seems.

Now let's talk disability insurance, which may be the most underappreciated form of protection in higher ed. Professors don't always see themselves as people at risk for injury, but disability insurance is really about protecting your paycheck if illness or injury keeps you from working. Even a bout with long COVID, a serious back problem, or a mental health crisis could leave you unable to teach, write, or serve in your usual role for months. University policies vary widely—some offer short-term disability but not long-term, and others cap benefits at a percentage of your base salary, which might not include stipends or summer income. You need to understand what you're getting and whether you should supplement it with a private policy. Because here's the truth: your earning power is your biggest asset, and disability coverage is the insurance that protects it.

A good disability policy covers at least 60% of your income and uses an "own occupation" definition, which means it pays out if you can't do your specific job—not just any job. This matters for professors because your role is specialized. Teaching chemistry at a university is not the same as managing a retail store, and you don't want an insurance company saying you're not disabled just because you could theoretically do something else. Also, check if your university benefits are taxable. If they're employer-paid, you may owe income tax on any benefits received, which reduces your real take-home amount. A private, after-tax policy often pays tax-free benefits and gives you more control.

Umbrella insurance is another upgrade that smart faculty often overlook. This type of policy sits on top of your regular auto and homeowners insurance and kicks in if you're sued for an amount above those policies' limits. Say you're in a car accident and the other driver sues you for $750,000, but your auto policy only covers up to $300,000. Without umbrella coverage, you're on the hook for the difference—and that could mean draining your retirement savings, selling your home, or garnishing future wages. Umbrella insurance is surprisingly cheap—often less than $250 a year for a million dollars of coverage—and it protects against risks that aren't always your fault but could ruin your financial future.

Professional liability insurance, also called errors and omissions insurance, is something professors should consider if they're consulting, publishing, or offering expert advice outside of their university employment. While your university may provide coverage for your on-campus duties, that coverage doesn't always extend to your side gigs or freelance work. If you write a book, give paid talks, or work as an expert witness, a client could sue you for bad advice, and your employer's policy may not back you up. Having your own professional liability insurance helps you take on those roles with confidence, knowing that one miscommunication or disagreement won't turn into a personal financial crisis. It's like wearing a seatbelt when you get behind the wheel of your expertise.

It's also worth mentioning that professors are increasingly targets of public scrutiny, social media pile-ons, or even legal complaints, particularly in controversial fields. Some professional liability policies offer legal defense coverage for defamation or reputational harm, which is a growing concern in today's environment. While you don't want to live in fear, it's helpful to know that there are tools available to protect your livelihood if a public incident spirals out of control. The cost of a basic policy is usually a few hundred dollars a year—less than what many of us spend on conference travel or new textbooks. For the peace of mind it brings, it's a worthwhile investment in your future.

Another place where insurance often gets overlooked is during major life transitions. Getting married, buying a home, having kids, moving to a new state, or even landing a promotion can all shift your financial picture—and your insurance needs right along with it. Many professors make the mistake of setting their policies once and forgetting about them, but insurance should evolve as your life does. Think of it like updating your syllabus each semester. It might be fine to carry over last year's version, but checking for outdated material or gaps is just smart planning. Each transition is a cue to reevaluate your coverage and make sure you're still protected in the way your current life requires.

Another piece of this puzzle is beneficiary designations, especially on life insurance policies and retirement accounts. Many people forget to update these when they get married, divorced, have children, or experience loss. The scary part is that beneficiary forms usually override wills, so if your ex-spouse is still listed on that policy from ten years ago, they're getting the money—not your new partner or your kids. It's a simple thing to check, but it can save your family an enormous amount of stress and confusion later on. Just log into your HR portal or call your provider once a year to confirm everything is current. This five-minute check-in is one of the easiest and most impactful things you can do for your loved ones.

For professors who moonlight as consultants, workshop facilitators, or expert witnesses, having separate business insurance is another area worth exploring. If you're receiving income outside of your university paycheck—even just a few thousand dollars a year—you're operating as a small business in the eyes of the IRS and the legal system. That means you should think about general liability and errors and omissions coverage. One disgruntled client or a misinterpreted report could spark a lawsuit, and without proper protection, your personal finances could be dragged into the mess. Having a basic business insurance policy or forming a legal entity like an LLC can create a protective barrier between your work and your personal life.

Even within your primary academic job, it's good to ask your HR department about what kind of professional liability coverage the university provides. Some universities cover you fully for classroom instruction, advising, and committee service but exclude any activities that involve publishing, media appearances, or outside affiliations. If you're involved in research with human subjects, sensitive data, or public health, you may be more exposed to legal risk. Knowing where your coverage begins and ends helps you identify the gaps—and more importantly, it gives you time to fill them before something goes wrong. You don't want to be in a deposition finding out your university won't cover your legal fees.

Professors in clinical or counseling roles—like those in psychology, social work, or medicine—face unique risks that require more tailored insurance strategies. If you're working with patients or clients, malpractice insurance should be on your radar, even if you're based at a university. Most academic institutions offer some kind of malpractice coverage, but it may not be enough or may not extend to off-campus work. If you supervise students, provide therapy, or do any hands-on work with the public, it's critical to verify what's covered. You might need to purchase a "tail" policy or supplemental coverage to protect yourself after you leave a position. Skipping this step can leave you financially exposed years down the line, even after you've moved on.

When shopping for insurance, don't just rely on whatever policy pops up first online or through your university's benefits portal. It's worth taking time to compare quotes, read the fine print, and—when possible—work with an independent insurance broker who can explain your options in plain English. The cheapest policy isn't always the best, and sometimes the difference in cost is a result of huge differences in what's covered. Look at things like coverage limits, exclusions, and waiting periods. And be honest about your risk tolerance—some people sleep better with high coverage even if it costs a bit more, while others prefer a leaner policy with lower premiums.

One of the most practical ways to fit upgraded insurance into your budget is by timing your purchases alongside income increases. If you get a raise, summer teaching stipend, or consulting check, earmark part of that income for better coverage. It feels less like a sacrifice when it's tied to extra money you weren't counting on. Another trick is to ladder your policies. For example, if you expect your kids to be financially independent in 20 years, you might get a 20-year term life policy now and add a 10-year one later if needed. This strategy helps you adjust coverage without locking yourself into more than you'll need long-term.

It's also smart to think about bundling when you're reviewing your insurance plans. Many companies offer discounts if you combine auto, homeowners, and umbrella policies, and this bundling often makes managing your coverage easier too. One point of contact, one set of documents, and often one monthly payment can reduce stress and paperwork. Just make sure you're not sacrificing coverage for the sake of a discount—those savings should be a bonus, not the main driver of your decision. Also, check that the company has good customer service reviews. You don't want to deal with a difficult claims process during an already stressful event.

A good insurance plan is like a well-balanced syllabus—it's not about covering every possible contingency but about preparing for the most likely and most financially damaging events. Professors are often planners by nature, so apply that same thinking to your personal financial risk. Ask yourself: What would happen if I couldn't teach for six months? If someone sued me after a guest lecture? If my spouse or children needed to make ends meet without my salary? These aren't easy questions, but facing them now is far better than trying to figure things out in the middle of a crisis. Being proactive isn't pessimistic—it's pragmatic.

Estate planning and insurance are deeply connected, and it's important to understand how your policies fit into the broader picture of what happens if something happens to you. Life insurance, in particular, is a tool that can help your loved ones maintain stability after you're gone. But it only works if you've made a plan for how that money will be used. If your goal is to pay off a mortgage, send your kids to college, or support a spouse in retirement, you need to be clear about how much coverage is required and who is responsible for managing it. Don't let vague instructions or outdated documents create more stress for your family. Even a basic estate plan with a will, a healthcare proxy, and a list of account information can make an enormous difference.

Insurance can also be a quiet act of love. It's the kind of thing people don't notice until they need it—and when they need it, it speaks volumes. Having the right policies in place says, "I thought about this. I cared enough to prepare." That level of foresight is especially powerful in academic families where one or both partners may carry a lot of intellectual and emotional load. By handling the logistics of risk ahead of time, you're making room for healing and decision-making when your family needs it most. And in the meantime, you're buying the confidence to move forward with less fear.

If you've never worked with a financial advisor, this is one of the topics where a good one can really shine. Insurance isn't one-size-fits-all, and it touches every area of your financial life—from income to retirement to estate planning. An advisor can help you decide which policies to prioritize, how much coverage to get, and how to evaluate the tradeoffs between cost and benefit. They can also help you compare policies side-by-side and explain what all those terms mean so you're not just guessing. Think of them like a TA for your financial life: they help you master the material faster and with fewer mistakes.

Don't forget to review your insurance policies annually. Just like you might tweak your syllabus or rework a lecture slide every semester, insurance deserves that same level of attention. Life changes. Jobs change. Families grow. Expenses shift. That policy you set up five years ago might be under-serving you now, or maybe you're overpaying for coverage you no longer need. A quick yearly review can help you stay on top of things and avoid surprises when you need your insurance to perform.

It's also worth talking to your colleagues about what they've done—especially those further along in their careers. We don't often talk about insurance in faculty lounges or at conferences, but you'd be surprised how much insight people are willing to share once the conversation starts. Maybe someone found a great disability policy. Maybe they had a scare that changed their whole approach. Peer insights are powerful, especially in academia, where we're all trying to navigate the same institutional structures with wildly different life circumstances. Sometimes the best learning happens through casual conversation, not just HR handbooks.

One final note about professional liability insurance: if you work across multiple institutions—as an adjunct, visiting scholar, or consultant—you need to confirm who covers what. Coverage might apply only at your main campus or only during the academic year. If you're publishing in controversial fields or speaking on politically sensitive topics, you may also want to consider supplemental coverage that includes reputational risk. Again, none of this is about being fearful. It's about protecting the work you've spent years building so that one accusation or mistake doesn't wipe out your progress.

For younger professors or those just stepping into academia, the temptation is often to skip all of this and figure it out later. But the reality is, the earlier you build a solid insurance foundation, the easier and cheaper it usually is. Premiums tend to be lower when you're younger and healthier. And having basic protections in place allows you to take more professional and personal risks—like buying a home, starting a family, or taking on a side business—without putting everything on the line. Insurance doesn't just guard you against the bad stuff; it frees you to pursue the good stuff more confidently.

If you're feeling overwhelmed by all this, just start with one policy. Maybe it's term life. Maybe it's adding umbrella coverage to your home and auto. Maybe it's scheduling a disability insurance quote. Take it step by step, and each move will build your financial resilience. You don't have to do it all in one weekend. Think of it like building a course syllabus—you don't need all the reading materials and assignments on day one, but you do need a plan. And over time, each layer adds up to a secure, thoughtful structure.

Insurance may not be glamorous, but it's one of the most important tools you have to safeguard your academic journey and the people who count on you. The work you do as a professor is valuable. It's worth protecting. And so are you. These policies aren't just about worst-case scenarios—they're about best-case planning. A little effort now can save you and your loved ones a lot of trouble later, and that's the kind of wisdom that stands the test of time, whether you're in your first year of teaching or your final days before retirement.

So, take a breath. Open that HR packet. Make a checklist. Talk to your partner or your advisor. You're not expected to know it all—but you are capable of learning what you need to feel secure. Insurance, like education, is a long game. The sooner you engage with it, the more peace of mind you can carry with you through every semester of your career. And that's a kind of protection no policy can fully capture—but you'll be glad it's there when life shows up unannounced.

Chapter 15: Mid-Career Burnout, Recognizing Signs and Funding a Recharge Strategy

Mid-career burnout sneaks up like a slow leak in a bicycle tire—you can still move forward, but every mile feels harder than the last until you finally notice you're riding on rims. For professors, the trouble often starts after the sprint to tenure when the adrenaline ebbs and the committee invitations, graduate student crises, and family obligations expand to fill every free moment. You might catch yourself rereading the same sentence three times, sighing at calendar alerts that once excited you, or fantasizing about quitting to open a bakery even though you hate baking at 4a.m. None of these feelings make you weak or ungrateful; they simply signal that the fuel you burned so brightly in early career has dipped below reserve. Recognizing that depletion is the first step toward a sustainable recharge strategy rather than a dramatic exit.

Classic signs of academic burnout include emotional exhaustion, creeping cynicism, and a gnawing sense that your work no longer matters. Maybe you dismiss student emails without your usual patience or you dread conferences where you once thrived on lively debate. Physical symptoms can appear too—headaches, insomnia, or a constant low-grade cold you just can't shake. The tricky part is that academia normalizes overwork, so these warning lights often blend into the dashboard glow. Paying attention to changes in your mood, health, and motivation helps you spot trouble before it morphs into full-blown crisis.

Once you suspect burnout, resist self-blame and turn instead to diagnostics. Track how you spend time for two typical weeks: lectures, grading, emails, meetings, research, family care, and actual rest. Most professors discover hidden black holes—those two-hour committee preps that balloon into six, or grant applications tackled in midnight bursts because daylight is over-scheduled. The goal isn't to shame yourself but to gather data. Like any research project, good data clarifies problems and points toward solutions.

Financial stress often hides at burnout's core. Maybe your salary hasn't kept pace with childcare costs, elder-care responsibilities, or student-loan payments. Perhaps grants you counted on dried up, leaving you to self-fund research trips or buy lab supplies out of pocket. Money worries sap mental energy, sharpening every other frustration. Facing your finances head-on—listing debts, upcoming expenses, and income sources—can relieve some pressure, because uncertainty tends to amplify anxiety more than hard numbers do. Even if the figures aren't pretty, knowing them empowers planning.

Building a recharge fund is one practical antidote to burnout. Start by earmarking a separate savings account labeled "Sabbatical Lite" or "Recharge Reserve." Automate monthly transfers, even if they're small, treating that line item as non-negotiable as your mortgage. Over a year or two, this fund can underwrite a no-email vacation, pay a writing-retreat fee, or cover salary gaps during an unpaid research leave. Having cash set aside turns wishful thinking about rest into a feasible, scheduled event.

Next, audit your benefits for low-hanging relief. Many universities offer wellness stipends, mental-health counseling, or small internal grants for course releases that go untapped. HR portals are dense, so schedule a call with a benefits specialist and ask pointed questions: Is there a dependent-care FSA you've ignored? A faculty grant that pays a teaching assistant for one semester? Sometimes the infrastructure to lighten your load already exists—you just haven't had the bandwidth to notice.

If departmental politics make you hesitate to request time off, remember that burnout carries costs for students and colleagues too. A foggy, resentful professor grades inconsistently, declines mentorship, and drags down meeting morale. Framing your recharge plan as an investment in better teaching, sharper research, and healthier collegiality can win administrative allies. Draft a brief proposal outlining what you'll accomplish with reduced duties—perhaps a manuscript submission, curriculum overhaul, or grant application—and how the department ultimately benefits. Decision-makers respond well to specific timelines and outcomes, especially when paired with partial funding you secured independently.

Sometimes burnout stems less from quantity of work and more from sameness. Mid-career is ripe for a pivot—co-authoring in a new subfield, pursuing an administrative fellowship, or designing an interdisciplinary course. Novelty stimulates intellectual curiosity and can reignite motivation. Funding such exploration might involve small external grants, professional-development allowances, or strategic use of conference travel budgets to visit unfamiliar venues. Treat the financial piece like seed capital for a start-up: a modest investment can yield fresh energy and expanded networks.

Don't overlook micro-recharges: protected writing mornings, tech sabbaths, or walking office hours that blend exercise with mentorship. These tweaks cost little yet accumulate into meaningful relief. Pair them with boundary tactics—setting email auto-responses during evenings, capping committee service, and practicing the artful "no." Sometimes burnout fades not by subtracting everything but by pruning strategically so the essentials flourish again. A garden thrives when weeds are removed and soil is nourished; your schedule is no different.

If you share finances with a partner, especially another academic, coordinate recharge strategies together. Maybe you alternate lighter teaching loads across academic years, or pool travel grants so one can take the kids while the other attends a conference stress-free. Joint planning reduces guilt about stepping back and ensures neither partner carries the entire domestic or financial load during the other's recharge phase. Think of it as academic tag-teaming rather than solo survival.

Mental-health support is a legitimate budget line, not a luxury. Therapy copays, mindfulness apps, or stress-management workshops should reside alongside textbooks and journal subscriptions in your spending plan. Many insurance policies cover a set number of sessions; if yours doesn't, inquire about sliding-scale clinics or virtual counseling. The return on investment—improved focus, sleep, and resilience—pays dividends in both productivity and personal happiness. Academia trains us to starve distractions and feed disease; let's flip that script by funding our well-being.

Consider diversifying income to ease financial strain without inflating workload. Royalties from an open-educational-resources textbook, modest consulting gigs, or paid peer-review stipends can supplement salaries without long-term commitment. Funnel this extra income directly into your recharge fund or use it to outsource chores—house cleaning, grocery delivery, or grading assistance via trained graduate students. Buying back hours converts money into recovery, an exchange often overlooked in academic frugality narratives.

Sabbaticals remain the gold standard for deep restoration, yet many faculty defer applying because half-pay seems impossible. Bridge that gap by stacking revenue streams: a fellowship that covers part of your salary, savings from your recharge fund, and perhaps deferred expenses like pausing retirement over-contributions just for that year. Calculate the true cost after tax and benefit adjustments; it's often less daunting than the headline salary cut. Remember, a well-planned sabbatical can boost future earnings through publications and grants that burnout would have sabotaged.

Burnout can also whisper that your department, institution, or even academia itself is no longer right for you. Distinguish between temporary exhaustion and chronic misalignment. Talk with mentors outside your immediate circle, maybe at other universities or in adjacent industries, to gauge whether the spark can return in a new context. Having "walk-away" money—six to twelve months of living expenses—grants you the clarity to evaluate options without fear-driven bias. Sometimes the best recharge is a strategic relocation to a role that fits the scholar you've become.

While mapping financial solutions, keep an eye on physical health costs. Stress can trigger costly ailments, from hypertension to repetitive-strain injuries. Budget for preventive care: ergonomic office gear, regular checkups, or a gym membership you'll actually use. Universities sometimes reimburse wellness expenses up to a yearly cap; submit those receipts. Every dollar you spend avoiding illness now saves multiples in future medical bills and lost sabbatical opportunities.

Track progress like you would a research experiment. Set measurable indicators—hours slept, pages written, days with inbox under control—and review monthly. If burnout symptoms recede, double down on what's working. If not, revise hypotheses and interventions. This iterative mindset keeps you engaged as an active agent in your recovery rather than a passive victim of circumstance. It also generates data you can share with colleagues, normalizing conversations about faculty well-being.

Celebration is crucial. When you reclaim a weekend for hiking, finish a long-stalled article, or finally schedule that counseling session, acknowledge the victory. Small rewards—fancy coffee, an afternoon at a museum, a game night—train your brain to associate self-care with positive outcomes, reinforcing the habit loop. Over time, these micro-celebrations weave resilience into your academic identity, making burnout less likely to return.

Ultimately, mid-career burnout is neither a failure nor an endpoint. It's a signal that your inputs and outputs have drifted out of alignment. By diagnosing honestly, budgeting strategically, and investing in purposeful rest, you transform burnout from threat to turning point. Your scholarship, students, and loved ones benefit when you operate from replenished reserves. More importantly, you rediscover the curiosity and joy that drew you to academia in the first place—a gift no grant or promotion can match.

Chapter 16: Negotiating a Counter-Offer, Using Competing Offers Without Burning Bridges

Few things in an academic career stir up as much anxiety and opportunity as receiving a competing offer from another institution. On the one hand, it can feel validating—proof that your work is recognized and valued beyond the boundaries of your current university. On the other hand, the idea of using that offer to negotiate a better package can feel uncomfortable, even disloyal. Many professors weren't trained to think like negotiators, and some of us worry that bringing up a counter-offer might paint us as ungrateful, selfish, or even replaceable. But the truth is, the academic job market is dynamic, and learning to navigate it wisely is not only permissible—it's often essential for building a sustainable, financially stable career.

First, it's important to understand that the competing offer isn't just a salary number. It often comes with details around teaching load, startup funds, spousal accommodations, lab space, title, sabbatical eligibility, research support, and housing help. Think of it as a package deal, not a single lever to pull. When another university wants you, they're not just trying to win you over with cash—they're sending a signal that they see your potential and want to support your long-term success. That perspective can be empowering, especially if you've spent years feeling stuck or undervalued where you are.

Before you even mention the competing offer to anyone at your home institution, take time to clarify what you truly want. Are you hoping to stay but want better pay or support? Are you leaning toward leaving unless your current department makes a serious move? Are you using this offer as leverage, or are you genuinely curious about the change? These aren't just semantics. Knowing your own motivation will shape how you present the conversation—and how you respond if things don't go as planned. Self-awareness is the foundation of a negotiation that's both strategic and respectful.

Once you've done some internal reflection, gather your facts. Create a simple side-by-side comparison of your current compensation package and the one being offered elsewhere. Include the tangibles (salary, bonuses, retirement contributions, course load) and the intangibles (location, work culture, student demographics, research expectations). This isn't just for your own decision-making—it also prepares you to articulate clearly and respectfully what the competing offer includes, which lends credibility to your ask. Think of this like preparing your syllabus: the more organized and thoughtful your plan, the more likely others are to take you seriously.

When you're ready to approach your department chair or dean, set up a formal meeting rather than dropping it into a hallway conversation. This shows respect and signals that you're approaching the situation professionally. Be direct but warm. Something like, "I want to talk with you about a recent opportunity that's come up, and I'd like to discuss what it might mean for my role here," opens the door without throwing anyone on the defensive. Your tone matters just as much as your words—this is a conversation, not a confrontation.

During the meeting, avoid ultimatums. You're not walking in with a list of demands or threats; you're initiating a discussion. Frame your position as exploratory: "I've received an offer from another institution that includes some compelling components, and before making any decisions, I wanted to have an honest conversation about my future here." This invites your department to respond with curiosity rather than panic or resistance. And if your goal is truly to stay, say so. "I love this department and want to continue building my career here, but I also need to consider what's best for my family and professional growth." That kind of honesty builds goodwill.

What often surprises faculty is how common these conversations are behind the scenes. Department chairs negotiate all the time—they just may not advertise it. When you bring a competitive offer forward, you're giving them leverage to advocate for you internally. That might mean pushing for a raise, a lighter teaching load, better lab space, or funds to attend conferences. If they've been waiting for an excuse to upgrade your support, now they have one. It's not about favoritism—it's about retention, and any good chair understands that retaining strong faculty is cheaper and easier than starting a new search.

At the same time, it's smart to keep your expectations grounded. Not every institution has the budget or flexibility to match an outside offer. Sometimes they'll counter with non-monetary support—like allowing you to buy out a course to finish your book or offering a leadership role in a department initiative. Don't dismiss these just because they don't show up in your paycheck. Ask yourself whether the counter-offer helps you thrive where you are, even if it's not a perfect match to the external offer. Value isn't always measured in dollars, especially in academia.

If your current institution chooses not to make a counter-offer—or offers less than you hoped—you still have options. You can accept the new position, decline and stay put, or even use the experience to catalyze a longer-term plan to transition on your own timeline. What matters most is that you've done the work of assessing your value, advocating for yourself, and making a choice rooted in both professional growth and personal priorities. That's a win, no matter what you decide.

Now, let's talk about the bridge. You know, the one everyone's afraid of burning. In most cases, if you handle the process with respect, transparency, and grace, that bridge remains intact—even if you end up leaving. Send thank-you notes. Express appreciation. Make clear that your decision wasn't made lightly and that you value the relationships and opportunities you've had. The academic world is small. Today's colleague could be tomorrow's conference organizer, peer reviewer, or hiring committee member. Don't let a poorly managed exit sour years of goodwill.

Even if you stay, things may feel different afterward. Some colleagues might treat you with more respect, seeing you as someone who advocated for their worth. Others might bristle, especially if they feel unsupported or stuck in their own roles. These reactions often say more about them than you. Stick to your work, keep showing up with integrity, and avoid gossip or posturing. Eventually, things normalize. And the next time someone in your department receives an outside offer, they may come to you for advice on how to navigate it well.

Money is just one dimension of the negotiation. Timing, workload, support, autonomy, and recognition all matter too. If your new offer includes the chance to teach fewer classes, live closer to family, or join a more vibrant intellectual community, those elements might outweigh a bigger paycheck. Don't let prestige or peer pressure drown out your own values. This is your life, your energy, your contribution. Choose the path that allows you to flourish, not just survive.

Faculty often underestimate their market value, especially in fields where imposter syndrome runs deep. But if another university is willing to invest in you, it's worth asking why your current one wouldn't do the same. Negotiating isn't arrogance. It's stewardship—of your time, your talents, and your trajectory. And it doesn't just benefit you. When one person advocates successfully, it often sets a precedent that makes it easier for others to do the same. That's how departments evolve.

Some universities have formal policies about counter-offers, including salary caps or equity reviews. If you hear "we can't go higher because of HR rules," ask questions. What are the exceptions? When were they last used? What else can be offered—research funding, summer salary, or housing support? Don't assume the first no is final. Negotiation is often a multi-round process, not a one-shot conversation. Persistence with professionalism can uncover possibilities that weren't initially on the table.

Your department chair is not your enemy, even if they can't deliver everything you want. Most chairs are juggling tight budgets, political pressures, and competing priorities. If they see you as a thoughtful, committed faculty member trying to build a viable career, they'll often go to bat for you—even if they can't say that out loud. Treat them as collaborators, not adversaries. The best outcomes happen when both sides approach the table with mutual respect and a shared desire to find common ground.

Timing matters too. Spring is often peak season for these conversations because that's when job offers and budgets are in play. But don't rush. Take time to think, consult trusted mentors, and draft a clear, concise email or talking points for your meeting. A hasty ask can sound sloppy or panicked. A calm, confident tone—backed by facts—shows you're serious, professional, and worth investing in.

Finally, remember that you don't have to navigate this alone. Talk with mentors, union reps (if applicable), senior faculty, or even a career coach. Role-play your pitch, review your materials, and practice responding to pushback. The more you prepare, the more composed you'll feel—and the better your odds of walking away with a deal that reflects your real worth. In academia, we're trained to analyze everything but ourselves. This is your chance to turn that analytical lens inward and make strategic, empowering decisions about your career.

You've earned this moment. Whether you stay or go, negotiating from a place of clarity and self-respect is one of the most powerful moves you can make. It's not about playing games—it's about playing your long game.

Chapter 17: Saying "No" at Mid-Career, Guarding Time, Energy, and Wallet from Endless Requests

Sometime around the middle of your academic career, you wake up and realize that your days have become a patchwork quilt of everyone else's priorities. A colleague wants you on yet another committee, a journal begs for peer reviews, students crave extra office hours, the dean needs a strategic plan drafted by Friday, and a community group is convinced you'd be the perfect keynote speaker—for free, of course. You look at your calendar and see slivers of white space wedged between a kaleidoscope of colored blocks, none of which represent actual research or rest. That creeping exhaustion isn't just physical; it's financial and emotional, too, because every "yes" costs you time you could spend writing the grant that funds next summer's salary or the book that nabs the promotion. Learning to say "no" isn't selfish; it's a mid-career survival skill that protects your scholarship, your sanity, and your wallet.

The first step to mastering "no" is recognizing the hidden price tag attached to every request. When you agree to chair a new committee, you're not just donating an hour here or there; you're committing brain space, calendar space, and often incidental expenses like conference calls or travel. Those hours could be translated directly into journal pages produced, data analyzed, or even time billed for consulting. Picture each request as a debit card swipe on your personal energy account: small charges add up fast, and overdraft fees come in the form of fatigue and missed deadlines. Once you see the true cost, it becomes easier to weigh whether a request aligns with your long-term goals or drags you further from them.

Next, clarify your own priorities so you can measure new requests against them. Mid-career academics often juggle tenure or promotion dossiers, grant renewal cycles, and family responsibilities. Write down the top three professional goals you must hit in the next two years—maybe finishing a book, winning a major grant, and maintaining teaching excellence. Any invitation that doesn't directly advance those goals, or provide significant personal joy, starts with a default "no." This isn't closing doors; it's keeping essential ones open. A clear priority list acts like a campus map—without it, every hallway looks equally tempting and you lose time wandering.

A polite but firm refusal is an art, and like any craft, it improves with practice. Begin with genuine appreciation—"I'm honored you thought of me"—then insert a concise boundary—"my schedule is committed to existing projects through next spring." End with a brief alternative if you have one—"perhaps Professor X, whose work overlaps more closely, could help?" The key is brevity. Long explanations invite negotiation; short, respectful sentences communicate finality. Remember, you're declining the task, not diminishing the relationship.

Faculty often fear that saying "no" will brand them as uncooperative, but the opposite is true when done consistently and courteously. Colleagues quickly learn to approach you for roles that fit your expertise and availability, rather than peppering you with every stray request. Over time, your yes carries more weight because people trust you won't overcommit and underdeliver. Think of your reputation like a currency: spend it selectively, and its value appreciates; throw it at every passing offer, and it inflates into something less meaningful. Respect for your own limits teaches others to respect them, too.

Guarding your wallet means recognizing unpaid labor masquerading as prestige. Universities rely on free faculty work—editing journals, organizing symposia, mentoring beyond contract hours. Some of this service is essential for promotion, but plenty is optional. Before agreeing, ask yourself whether the role comes with tangible resources: course releases, stipend support, travel funding, or at least clear credit in your annual evaluation. If not, consider negotiating—"I'd be delighted to lead the seminar series if the department can fund a TA for my large intro course." Cash or workload offsets prove the institution values your time as much as your goodwill.

Mid-career is also prime time for external invitations—from keynote talks to media commentary—that flatter the ego but empty the calendar. Exposure has value, but so does compensation. If an organization can't pay an honorarium, request travel expenses or professional videography you can repurpose for teaching. Even a high-profile event should meet one of three criteria: pays you, advances your research agenda, or expands your network in concrete ways. Otherwise, it's a costumed distraction in academic glamour. Learn to ask, "What's the budget for speakers?" and practice silence while they answer.

Family and community requests deserve boundaries, too. You might be the go-to volunteer for the school science fair because you're "the professor," but multiple weekend commitments erode personal rest. Saying yes to your kid's classroom once a year feels meaningful; saying yes every month feels draining. Let loved ones know your schedule fills quickly and you may need advance notice. Offering limited, high-quality involvement signals commitment without perpetual availability. Remember, modeling healthy boundaries teaches children and students alike how professionals balance service and self-care.

One practical tactic is creating a "no script" document—pre-written, polite declines you can tweak and send quickly. Having text ready reduces decision fatigue and the temptation to procrastinate on uncomfortable emails. It also standardizes your language so emotional tone stays consistent even on busy days. Store these templates in a folder alongside acceptance templates, so each request meets a calibrated response rather than an impulse. Efficiency breeds confidence, and confidence makes future "no's" easier.

Consider instituting office hours for service requests, much like you do for students. Perhaps Friday afternoons are your window for short committee consultations or peer-review commitments. When someone asks for a favor, you can reply, "I handle new service inquiries on Fridays; please send details by Thursday." This micro-structure pushes requesters to clarify their needs and respects your focused research blocks the rest of the week. Small systems protect big chunks of time without sounding dismissive.

Financially, track the hours you decline as deliberately as the ones you accept. If you say no to reviewing a manuscript likely to take five hours, note that saved time in a spreadsheet. At semester's end, total the hours and imagine billing them at your consulting rate or converting them into pages written. Seeing saved value in concrete terms reinforces the power of "no" and curbs guilt. It's your personal ledger of reclaimed bandwidth, proof that restraint funds progress.

Saying no can also open doors to strategic yeses. If you decline a low-impact committee, you create room to accept a prestigious editorial board invitation that may come next month. Empty space invites opportunity; overcrowded calendars repel it. Think of yourself as an investor trimming low-yield stocks so you have capital for a blue-chip prospect. Selectivity isn't selfish—it's portfolio management for your career.

As you build confidence, practice proactive no-setting. Before service season begins, email your chair a concise list of roles you can realistically fulfill and state that you will need to decline others to protect research time. Chairs appreciate clarity; they hate last-minute back-outs caused by overextension. This approach positions you as responsible and self-aware rather than unavailable. You become a partner in departmental planning, not a wild card.

Mental rehearsal helps, too. Envision the next high-pressure request—a student asking you to sponsor three new clubs, a dean seeking an emergency task force. Picture yourself taking a breath, thanking them, stating you're at capacity, and perhaps suggesting another resource. Play the scene until it feels natural. Athletes visualize performance; professors can visualize boundaries. When the real moment arrives, muscle memory kicks in, and you speak calmly instead of defaulting to a frantic yes.

Technology can aid boundary enforcement. Use calendar sharing to show busy blocks labeled "research" or "writing retreat," deterring meeting invites during sacred hours. Email filters can route committee chatter to specific folders, so your main inbox remains research-centric. Auto-responses can outline your turnaround times—"I review external requests biweekly; expect a reply on the 15th." Digital barriers complement verbal ones, reinforcing that your availability is structured, not limitless.

Financial wellbeing improves alongside time management. Fewer unpaid obligations free weekends for consulting, writing, or true rest—all of which either boost income or reduce burnout expenses like takeout and late-night retail therapy. Over time, you'll notice tangible gains: a healthier grant pipeline, a clearer mind during lectures, maybe even lower healthcare costs as stress dips. Money saved is money earned, and disciplined no-saying is a cost-cutting measure disguised as self-care.

Inevitably, you'll still say yes to things that later feel draining. Mid-career wisdom includes graceful exit strategies. If a commitment balloons beyond expectation, schedule a check-in with the organizer: "When I agreed, we projected ten hours; it's trending past forty. How can we redistribute tasks?" Most people understand scope creep and will adjust rather than risk losing you entirely. You're not breaking a promise; you're renegotiating terms based on new data—something scholars do all the time.

Remember to celebrate successful no's. Each time you guard a weekend, finish a manuscript, or spend an evening with family instead of on an unnecessary Zoom call, acknowledge the win. Small rewards—an extra chapter of a novel, a walk, a fancy coffee—condition your brain to associate boundary-setting with positive outcomes. Over time, the reflex to protect your time becomes as natural as checking citations, and guilt fades into purposeful calm.

Finally, extend grace to yourself and others. The academic ecosystem thrives on collaboration, and sometimes you'll be the one making the ask. Approach colleagues with empathy, giving them space to decline without shame. When you model healthy boundaries, you contribute to a culture where everyone's time and energy are valued. Saying "no" at mid-career isn't a barricade; it's a gate you open and close with intention, ensuring that what enters enriches rather than depletes your professional and personal life.

Part III · Diversifying Income – Consulting, Side Gigs & IP

In Part III, we explore how professors can move beyond their base salary and unlock new streams of income using the skills, expertise, and intellectual capital they already have. As academic life becomes more demanding and traditional compensation often lags behind industry counterparts, this section provides practical, empowering guidance for building financial resilience and creative freedom. We begin by examining the fine print and gray areas of university policies around consulting, including what's allowed, what needs approval, and how to balance outside work with institutional expectations. We then move into the world of side gigs—everything from speaking engagements to writing, tutoring, expert witness work, and developing online courses—and how to turn those one-off opportunities into sustainable revenue streams. Intellectual property (IP) becomes a major theme, as we break down what happens when your research or inventions have commercial potential, how IP rights are often shared or negotiated with universities, and how to make sure you're fairly compensated when your ideas take off. Whether you're exploring a passion project, trying to fund your kid's college, or creating a financial runway for eventual career change, Part III offers realistic strategies and mindset shifts for monetizing your work ethically and effectively.

Chapter 18: Consulting 101, Structuring Engagements, Hourly vs. Project Fees, and Conflict-of-Interest Rules

At some point in your academic career, someone will reach out to ask if you'd be willing to consult. Maybe it's a nonprofit that wants help designing a program evaluation, a tech startup seeking subject-matter expertise, or a law firm asking for a written opinion in your field. The first time it happens, it feels flattering, even thrilling. You've spent years mastering your discipline, and now someone wants to pay for that knowledge beyond the confines of campus. But once the excitement settles, the practical questions roll in: How much should I charge? Do I need a contract? Will my university care—or worse, will they stop me? Consulting as a professor can be deeply rewarding, but only if you enter with a clear structure and a good understanding of your obligations.

The first thing to understand is that consulting isn't just "extra" work—it's professional work, and it requires the same level of care, clarity, and planning you'd bring to any formal academic role. Unlike internal service commitments, consulting relationships are governed by the expectations of your client, your institution, and potentially even the law. You'll want to define the scope of work in writing, determine whether you're billing by the hour or per project, and make sure there's no overlap with your university responsibilities that might trigger a conflict-of-interest review. This might sound intimidating, but think of it like developing a syllabus: you're laying out what you'll deliver, when, and how, so everyone's expectations are aligned from the start.

One of the most common mistakes early consultants make is undercharging. Many professors approach their first gig with an hourly rate that reflects their university salary—essentially dividing their paycheck by the number of hours they work. But academic compensation rarely captures your market value. If someone is seeking you out for your specific knowledge, that expertise has value far beyond your teaching load. Imagine if you're an expert in educational equity and a school district asks you to advise on a multi-million-dollar curriculum overhaul. That's not a casual favor—it's high-stakes guidance that deserves real compensation. As a starting point, research rates for consultants in your field, and don't be afraid to set a rate that reflects your time, training, and unique perspective.

When deciding between hourly and project-based fees, think about the nature of the work. Hourly billing makes sense when the scope is vague or open-ended—say, reviewing a new policy document, sitting in on strategy meetings, or providing feedback over time. It allows you to be flexible while ensuring you're paid for each chunk of time. Project fees, on the other hand, are better for well-defined deliverables: writing a report, conducting a training session, or evaluating a dataset. Project rates also reduce client anxiety about the final bill and give you the freedom to work more efficiently. Just be careful not to underbid—if you quote a flat fee and the project balloons, you may end up earning less than minimum wage for high-level work.

Setting boundaries is key to a healthy consulting relationship. Your time is limited, and if you're actively teaching, researching, or mentoring, consulting has to fit around those commitments. That means clearly stating your availability up front and resisting the urge to be constantly accessible. Create simple templates that outline your work hours, response time, and preferred communication methods. If the client wants access outside those parameters, that's a negotiation—often, one that justifies a higher fee. Remember, consulting is not a 24/7 hotline. It's a professional service, and the same boundaries you'd expect from a lawyer or accountant apply to you as well.

Now, here's where things get a little trickier: conflict-of-interest rules. Most universities allow faculty to consult, but they usually place limits on how much time you can spend and require disclosure. You might be capped at one day a week for outside work, or need to submit an annual report of consulting activities. This isn't about micromanagement—it's about ensuring that your university role isn't compromised. For example, if you're consulting for a textbook company and also assigning their materials in your class, that's a potential red flag. So is using university resources—grad students, labs, email lists—for private gain. Always review your institution's policies before signing any external agreement. It's better to get ahead of concerns than to explain them retroactively.

Some universities also distinguish between consulting and what they consider "outside employment," even though the two can look similar on the surface. Consulting generally involves offering your academic expertise in a limited, advisory capacity. Outside employment might include things like teaching at another institution, operating a side business, or holding a regular role with a company. The key difference often lies in whether the work is episodic and based on your scholarly knowledge, or ongoing and more like a second job. Understanding where your institution draws that line matters because the rules—and required disclosures—might differ. A misstep here, even if unintentional, can cause headaches when it's time for your annual review or if a promotion committee is combing through your professional activities.

Contracts are a must in consulting, even for small jobs. A verbal agreement might feel comfortable, especially if the client is someone you know, but it won't protect you if expectations shift. A good contract doesn't have to be complex—it just needs to clearly state what you're doing, how much you're getting paid, when payments are due, and what happens if the project is delayed or canceled. Think of it like a syllabus for your consulting work. It's not about mistrust; it's about making sure everyone's on the same page. If you're not comfortable drafting your own, there are templates online, or you might ask a trusted colleague for a sample they've used.

Another decision point is whether to consult under your own name or through a legal entity. For small, occasional engagements, operating as a sole proprietor (yourself, using your Social Security number) may be enough. But as your consulting expands, forming an LLC (Limited Liability Company) or S-Corp can offer liability protection and potential tax benefits. For example, an LLC separates your personal assets from any business risk, and you may be able to deduct expenses like software, subscriptions, and travel. Setting up a business bank account is another smart move—it makes it easier to track income, manage tax payments, and present yourself professionally. You don't need to be a business guru to do this; just think of it as organizing your professional side hustle like the real operation it is.

Taxes are another area where new consultants often stumble. Consulting income isn't taxed like your university paycheck—there's no automatic withholding. That means you'll need to set aside money for federal income tax, state taxes, and self-employment tax, which covers Social Security and Medicare. A good rule of thumb is to reserve 25–30% of your consulting earnings for taxes, and consider making quarterly estimated payments to the IRS if your income is steady. It may sound daunting, but plenty of professors have navigated this terrain successfully with the help of a CPA or tax preparer familiar with academic side work. The sooner you build this habit, the less stress you'll feel come tax season.

Don't underestimate the power of a polished invoice. Many professors slap together a quick email with the amount owed, but a professional-looking invoice with your name or company name, a description of services, payment terms, and a due date shows you mean business. Include your address, phone number, and how you prefer to be paid—check, ACH transfer, or even platforms like PayPal or Zelle if the client allows. Clients tend to pay faster when the invoice is clear and easy to process. It's also a document you'll need for your own records when tracking revenue, expenses, and client history over time. Again, think of it as a teaching tool for your client: here's what I delivered, and here's how to compensate me for it.

Sometimes, consulting offers come from unexpected sources. You might meet someone at a conference who later emails with a short-term opportunity, or your research gets cited in the media and sparks interest from the corporate world. These serendipitous gigs are often the most fun—and sometimes the most lucrative—but they still deserve thoughtful structure. A quick yes can turn into a long-term relationship, so treat the first engagement like the start of something bigger. Ask good questions: What's the deliverable? Who is my main contact? How will success be measured? You don't have to make it formal immediately, but writing down the answers will help you manage expectations and spot potential red flags early.

Universities also differ in whether you need prior approval for consulting work. Some expect you to report only if your earnings exceed a certain amount, while others require pre-approval for any compensated work outside your contract. The safest path is transparency. If in doubt, send a short note to your department chair or dean, outlining what you've been asked to do, the timeline, and the nature of compensation. Most will appreciate your professionalism and respond with quick guidance. It's far better to be proactive than to face an uncomfortable conversation later because someone learned about your side gig from a conference program or social media post.

If your consulting touches on sensitive or proprietary material, consider including a confidentiality clause in your contract. This protects both you and your client from unintended disclosure. For example, if you're advising on a yet-to-launch technology or a pending legal case, the client may already have their own nondisclosure agreement (NDA) ready. Read it carefully to understand your obligations, and don't hesitate to ask for clarification. Likewise, if you want to use insights from the project in future research or publications, bring that up early. Some clients are fine with it, especially if you anonymize the details, but otheAnother layer to consider is the emotional labor that can come with consulting, especially if you're working in spaces where your values are closely tied to your academic work. For example, a social scientist consulting with a government agency on community data may feel a personal stake in how that data is interpreted. It's important to set emotional boundaries as well as logistical ones. You are being hired for your expertise, not to fix systemic issues singlehandedly. That doesn't mean you shouldn't care—it means you need to build in recovery time, debrief with trusted peers, and remember that your role has limits. Burnout can sneak into consulting work just as easily as it does in teaching and research.

Your consulting work can also open up opportunities you didn't expect. Maybe a company invites you to do follow-up work. Maybe a conference organizer wants you to speak based on a project you completed. These are moments where you get to shape how your academic identity shows up in the real world. Do you want to be known for policy advising? For data storytelling? For technical writing that turns complex ideas into practical tools? You don't have to brand yourself like a marketing firm, but being aware of how your consulting engagements reflect your broader interests helps you steer your career instead of being pulled along by chance.

At some point, you may wonder how to grow your consulting work without overextending yourself. The answer usually lies in repeatable systems. Create templates for proposals, invoices, contracts, and emails so you're not reinventing the wheel every time. Block off "consulting hours" in your calendar so your academic work doesn't get cannibalized. Keep a spreadsheet—or use a simple CRM (Customer Relationship Management) tool—to track leads, engagements, and payments. You don't have to operate like a corporate machine, but treating your consulting like a real business gives you more time to focus on the actual work and less stress over logistics.

Another smart move is to build a "scope creep" clause into your agreements. Scope creep is when a project gradually expands beyond what was originally agreed upon. For example, the client may ask for one report, then a presentation, then another round of revisions—and suddenly you've done twice the work for the same fee. A clear contract can protect you by stating what's included and what triggers additional fees. You can phrase it in a friendly way, but the point is to draw a line between reasonable client expectations and free labor. It's the academic version of telling students, "Office hours are posted—please don't expect 3 a.m. email responses."

As your experience builds, you'll also start to see patterns in what types of projects are worth your time. Some pay well but are boring. Some are exciting but time-intensive. Some introduce you to people or fields that may matter later, even if the project itself is small. Trust your instincts, and if a gig feels off—even if the money looks good—pause. Ask questions. Sleep on it. Consulting should add to your life, not subtract from it. The most successful professors doing consulting work aren't chasing every opportunity; they're curating the right ones for their goals and values.

You'll also want to think about intellectual property when producing deliverables for a client. In academia, we're used to owning our ideas and publishing them freely. In consulting, the rules are different. If you write a report, build a dataset, or develop training materials for a client, they may own that work—even if it's based on your expertise. That's not necessarily a bad thing, but it's something to clarify upfront. If you want to retain the right to adapt or reuse the materials for other clients or in your teaching, negotiate that in advance. Copyright and ownership clauses should be clear, and ideally reviewed by someone with experience in academic consulting contracts.

Some professors also run into questions about whether their consulting counts as research, especially if it involves original data collection or policy recommendations. This can raise tricky issues about IRB (Institutional Review Board) review, authorship, and publishing. If you're conducting interviews or surveys as part of your consulting, ask your institution whether IRB oversight is required. If you want to publish findings from the work, discuss it with the client ahead of time. A good rule is to treat consulting like fieldwork: it may inform your scholarship, but it's not automatically part of your research portfolio unless certain boxes are checked.

When consulting work overlaps with your teaching, it can create interesting opportunities—and potential conflicts. Maybe you're consulting on a curriculum project while also designing a new course. Or maybe you're developing tools in a consulting role that you'd love to use in class. These synergies can be great, but check in with your institution to ensure you're not "double-dipping"—getting paid twice for the same work—or using proprietary materials without permission. A little planning goes a long way. Transparency protects you, and it helps everyone stay aligned about what's public, what's private, and what can be shared across roles.rs may need time to grant permission or request edits.

Another area professors often underestimate is how much time consulting takes—not just the work itself, but the communication, scheduling, follow-up, and administration. What starts as "just one meeting" can evolve into multiple email threads, progress calls, and revision requests. This is why it's important to account for all of your time, not just the hours you're producing a tangible product. If your client wants regular check-ins or detailed updates, that's part of the project too, and should be built into your timeline and fee. Think of it like writing a journal article: the research is only half of it—editing, submission, and responding to reviewer comments takes just as much time, if not more. Your consulting work deserves that same level of thoughtful planning.

Networking also plays a role in building a sustainable consulting practice. Many of the best opportunities come through word of mouth—colleagues who can vouch for your expertise, former clients who refer new ones, or people you meet at conferences and workshops. Keep track of who you work with, and don't be shy about following up after a successful engagement. A quick thank-you note, an offer to stay in touch, or a request for a testimonial can go a long way. These connections often lead to repeat business, collaborative projects, or unexpected doors opening down the road. Think of your consulting network as an extension of your scholarly community—it's just operating in different circles.

It's also okay to grow your consulting work slowly. You don't have to say yes to every offer or try to build an empire overnight. In fact, taking on too much too soon can dilute the quality of your work and leave you feeling scattered. Start with one or two projects a year. See how they fit into your teaching and research calendar. Learn what types of clients you enjoy and what projects drain you. Then, you can make informed decisions about when to scale up, pause, or pivot into new areas. Like academia itself, consulting is a long game—you're not trying to win the whole thing in one semester.

You might eventually find that consulting changes how you view your academic identity. When you're being paid for your expertise outside the classroom, it can be affirming in ways that university teaching and publishing aren't. It's not uncommon for professors to realize their value in new ways—especially if they've spent years underpaid, overworked, or stuck in bureaucratic systems. Consulting can give you leverage, not just financially, but emotionally. It reminds you that your skills have currency. That your insights matter. That your voice is valuable in more than just peer-reviewed journals. That kind of clarity can be powerful when you return to the classroom, to meetings, or even to the negotiation table.

Of course, not every consulting experience is positive. Sometimes, a client is slow to pay. Or the scope of work changes without warning. Or you discover midway through that your values don't align. These experiences can be frustrating, but they're also instructive. They teach you how to vet clients more carefully, how to set clearer boundaries, and how to protect your time and energy. Just like your first bad conference panel or committee meeting, a rough consulting gig doesn't mean you're not cut out for it. It just means you're learning. Keep notes. Reflect. And adjust your process for next time.

Some professors also find that consulting becomes a bridge to other career paths. What starts as a few side projects can evolve into a part-time business, a full-time career, or even a new identity beyond the academy. That's not the case for everyone, nor does it need to be. But it's worth acknowledging that the skills you hone through consulting—communication, negotiation, time management, marketing—are portable. They work just as well in nonprofits, startups, think tanks, or public service as they do in a classroom or lab. Consulting is not just a gig—it's training for a wider range of possibilities.

And finally, don't forget to celebrate your wins. When you land your first contract, invoice your first client, or get a glowing review, take a moment to appreciate what that means. You're translating years of study into real-world value. You're building something that didn't exist before. You're stepping into a space where academics don't always feel welcome—and making it your own. That's worth pausing for. Because while consulting is work, it's also affirmation. It's a reminder that knowledge has power—and that your time, your voice, and your experience are worthy of investment.

So whether you're thinking about taking on your first consulting gig or you've been at it for a while and want to refine your process, remember: you already have what it takes. The expertise, the integrity, the communication skills—it's all there. The rest is just structure. And once you build that foundation, consulting can become not just an extra paycheck, but a meaningful, empowering extension of your academic career. You don't need to reinvent yourself—you just need to recognize the value of what you already know, and learn how to offer it in a way that works for you.

Chapter 19: Expert Witness Work, Setting Rates, Retainers, and Managing Cross-Examination Risk

The first time a lawyer calls to ask whether you'd consider serving as an expert witness, you may feel equal parts intrigued and intimidated. Intrigued because expert work pays far better than typical academic side gigs and offers a front-row seat to real-world applications of your research. Intimidated because the courtroom is unfamiliar territory, packed with rules, deadlines, and high-stakes pressure you don't face in peer review. Accepting the invitation requires more than curiosity; it demands a solid grasp of how to price your time, structure your agreement, and protect your professional reputation under cross-examination. Done well, expert witnessing can become a rewarding, intellectually stimulating income stream—one that respects your academic commitments instead of derailing them.

Before you quote a fee, clarify your role. Attorneys usually need one of three services: a consulting expert who helps craft arguments behind the scenes, a testifying expert whose written report and courtroom testimony enter the public record, or occasionally both. Consulting assignments stay confidential and rarely make headlines, while testifying assignments expose your methods, credentials, and communication style to opposing counsel and, potentially, the media. Because testimony carries higher reputational and time risk, it commands higher pay. Think of it like teaching versus keynote speaking: both draw on your knowledge, but the public spotlight and scrutiny of a keynote warrant a premium rate.

Setting an hourly rate starts with a reality check on market norms. In many disciplines, novice academic experts charge $250–$350 per hour, mid-career professors run $400–$500, and high-profile, niche specialists can exceed $800. These rates may seem eye-popping compared to campus salaries, but remember: you're billing only for billable hours—time spent reviewing documents, drafting reports, or sitting for depositions—not for the years spent earning your expertise. One practical benchmark is to triple your effective university hourly rate (calculate your nine-month pay divided by total hours worked). This multiplier accounts for self-employment taxes, uncompensated prep time, and the elevated risk that comes with adversarial questioning.

A retainer is your first line of financial protection. Most experts ask the attorney to deposit an upfront amount—often 10–20 hours of work—into a trust account. You bill against that retainer monthly, replenishing it when the balance dips below a set threshold. Retainers signal that the client is serious, cover initial time commitments, and reduce collection headaches if the case settles abruptly. They also discourage last-minute cancellation, since unearned funds are refundable only under agreed terms. Spell out retainer size, replenishment triggers, and refund policies in writing; ambiguity invites conflict later.

Scope creep is common in litigation. What begins as a narrow opinion on, say, statistical sampling methods can balloon into multiple supplemental reports after new evidence surfaces. Protect yourself with a clear engagement letter that defines deliverables and specifies that any tasks beyond those deliverables require written authorization at your prevailing rate. Include minimum billing increments (e.g., 0.25 hours), differentials for expedited requests, and separate fees for travel days. The engagement letter is your syllabus for the legal semester—write it thoroughly so you can point back to it when deadlines tighten and expectations expand.

Cross-examination risk worries many academics, but preparation dissolves much of the fear. Opposing counsel's goal is to challenge your credibility, methodology, or impartiality. They may highlight minor errors in your CV, quote lines from old articles out of context, or push you to exceed the limits of your expertise. Your defense is rigorous pre-testimony prep: review every document you relied on, rehearse concise explanations of your methods, and clarify the boundaries of your opinion with the retaining attorney. Think of cross as an especially aggressive Q&A after a conference talk—one where anything inconsistent or overstated will be seized upon.

Universities differ on disclosure rules for expert work. Some require prior approval for any paid testimony; others treat it like ordinary consulting capped at one day per week. Conflicts of interest can arise if the litigation involves products you research, funding sources you rely on, or policies you publicly advocate. Before signing an engagement letter, scan your institution's policies and file any necessary paperwork. Transparency protects you if a reporter, trustee, or opposing lawyer digs into your outside activities. The best time to clear administrative hurdles is before subpoena season, not after.

Expert work can also sharpen your ability to translate research into accessible language. Attorneys and juries are not peer reviewers; they need your expertise explained in clear, confident, and jargon-free terms. That doesn't mean you have to oversimplify, but it does mean you need to avoid academic hedging like "on the one hand" or "arguably." In the courtroom, clarity wins. One good exercise is to practice summarizing your key findings to a friend outside your field or even a family member. If they understand it without blinking, you're on the right track. If they look confused or ask what certain terms mean, it's worth rewriting your talking points.

Report writing is central to most expert assignments, and it's a different animal than academic publishing. A strong expert report is factual, objective, and written for an audience that may never have taken a class in your subject. It outlines your qualifications, the materials you reviewed, the methodology you used, and the opinions you've reached. It should be carefully organized and free of speculative language. Attorneys may review and suggest edits to help with legal framing, but your credibility rests on maintaining your own voice and independent reasoning. Think of it as the professional version of a well-crafted syllabus: it represents you, and it will be read closely.

Deadlines in legal work are serious. Courts set firm timelines, and missing one can jeopardize the case or lead to your exclusion as a witness. Unlike academic publishing, there's little room for "I need another week." When you agree to a case, you're also agreeing to meet court-imposed deadlines, even if they land during midterms or spring break. Managing this requires honest scheduling from the start. Ask for a tentative case timeline, including when initial reports, depositions, and trial dates might fall. Don't assume "it'll be fine"—build buffer time into your own calendar to ensure you're not scrambling during crunch periods.

Depositions are where your expert mettle is really tested. Unlike a lecture or panel, you don't control the pacing, the questions, or even the room. You're seated, recorded, and under oath while opposing counsel probes your report, experience, and sometimes your tone. The key to surviving and thriving in a deposition is preparation. Practice answering questions with your attorney in advance, including ones that may seem redundant, hypothetical, or even hostile. Keep your answers focused and short. You're not there to teach a seminar—you're there to answer what was asked and nothing more. Silence is not your enemy; it gives the attorney time to ask another question, which might actually help your side.

One area that surprises many professors is how much of their academic life becomes fair game. Opposing counsel may comb through your CV, look at your faculty web page, and pull old interviews or social media posts. If you've made a strong public statement about a related issue, be ready to explain how it aligns—or doesn't—with your current testimony. This doesn't mean you need to delete or disown your past work, but it does mean being ready to own it clearly. Just like in a faculty review, inconsistencies or unexplained shifts in position can invite questions. Think through how your public and private personas align before you're asked under oath.

Payment structures can vary based on the attorney's preferences and your own systems. Some experts bill monthly, while others invoice after major milestones like the submission of a report or completion of a deposition.

Make sure your agreement includes when you get paid, what happens if a case settles or is dismissed, and who pays if you're asked to appear in court in another city. Travel expenses, parking, printing, and prep time should all be billable unless you've agreed otherwise. Keep records of everything, and don't be afraid to follow up if payment is delayed. Professionalism includes advocating for yourself, especially when your time is in demand.

At some point, you'll be asked to work on a case that gives you pause. Maybe it involves a politically charged issue, or you're not sure the data supports the client's position. One of the biggest mistakes a new expert can make is accepting a case they don't fully believe in. The money may be tempting, but if you're asked to stretch your findings or testify beyond your comfort zone, your reputation could suffer—and once that happens, it's hard to get it back. It's okay to walk away from a case that doesn't align with your ethics. Saying "no" professionally and early is far better than backing out midstream or getting grilled on the stand for opinions you don't fully stand behind.

Repeat clients are often a sign that you're doing something right. Attorneys prefer working with experts they trust—those who deliver on time, communicate clearly, and remain calm under pressure. If your first few engagements go well, you may find yourself added to a firm's go-to list for similar cases. This can be a huge advantage, not only financially, but also in terms of efficiency—each case will take less time to ramp up because you're familiar with the expectations. Still, even with repeat clients, don't skip the engagement letter or assume the terms are the same as last time. Each case is its own legal universe, and even a slight misunderstanding can create friction later on.

You might also want to consider setting an annual limit on how much expert work you take. Not because it's bad work—it's usually quite engaging—but because it can quickly eat into your bandwidth for research, teaching, and the other parts of academic life that drew you in to begin with. A helpful rule of thumb is to budget your consulting hours per semester just like you would teaching a course or serving on a committee. Some semesters may be lighter, and others heavier, but without a cap, it's easy for deadlines to pile up and stress to spike. By deciding in advance how many cases or hours you're willing to take on, you're more likely to protect your peace of mind and your academic goals.

Another angle to consider is how your expert witness work fits into your longer-term career narrative. For some professors, it becomes a side stream of income and nothing more. For others, it sparks an interest in public policy, legal reform, or even a future role in a government agency or nonprofit. There's no one right path here—but it helps to reflect on what you're building. Are you using expert work to test your market value outside of academia? Are you curious about how your research applies in legal or regulatory spaces? Are you looking to supplement retirement savings, pay down student loans, or create a cushion for your kids' education? Knowing your "why" can shape what cases you say yes to—and how much energy you want to devote to this path.

It's also wise to talk to a tax professional once you start making real money as an expert. That extra income is often classified as 1099 income, which means taxes aren't withheld, and you'll be responsible for setting aside a portion for federal, state, and self-employment taxes. A good CPA can help you estimate what to save, whether to pay quarterly, and even whether to form an LLC or S-corp for liability and tax benefits. These are not decisions you want to figure out in April with a big bill and no plan. If you're serious about this work—and especially if it becomes a regular source of income—it's worth getting professional help on the financial side.

As you gain experience, don't hesitate to adjust your rates. If you've successfully testified in court, written multiple reports, or received glowing feedback, you're not the same novice who took your first case. Many experts increase their rate by $25–$50 an hour each year or after every few major engagements. Some switch to flat-fee structures for certain deliverables, especially if they've learned how to estimate their time with precision. The point isn't to nickel-and-dime your clients, but to recognize the growing value of your expertise. Just as you wouldn't expect a full professor to be paid like a graduate student, your consulting rate should evolve alongside your credibility and experience.

In the end, expert witness work can be one of the most fascinating, challenging, and rewarding ways for professors to step outside the ivory tower and into the broader world. It forces you to clarify your ideas, defend your reasoning, and apply your knowledge where it matters most. It teaches you to protect your time, advocate for your value, and navigate complex systems with confidence. And it reminds you that the work you've done in quiet offices and classrooms can resonate far beyond campus walls. You don't need to become a courtroom regular to reap the benefits. But if you choose to step into this arena, do it with your eyes open, your boundaries firm, and your sense of purpose intact. That's how you turn expertise into opportunity—on your own terms.

Chapter 20: Speaking, Workshops, and MOOCs, Monetizing Your Voice Without Diluting Your Brand

The first time someone invites you to speak at a conference or lead a workshop, it can feel like a compliment more than an opportunity. You might think, "Sure, I'll share what I know," without considering whether you're being compensated fairly or whether the engagement fits into your long-term goals. But over time, these opportunities can add up—not just in exposure, but in income, relationships, and professional leverage. If you approach them with intention, speaking engagements, custom workshops, and even online courses like MOOCs can become a meaningful part of your career—not just something you squeeze in between faculty meetings. The key is to understand your value, package your knowledge strategically, and protect your personal brand along the way.

Most academics are used to talking for free. Conference panels, guest lectures, campus colloquia—these are often seen as part of the job, not sources of income. That mindset can carry over when someone outside the university invites you to speak, even if it's at a corporate retreat, government agency, or nonprofit training event. But here's the thing: if you're being asked to share your expertise in a setting that isn't part of your formal job duties, and especially if the audience isn't made up of fellow researchers, it's okay—and often expected—to be paid. Think of it like consulting with your voice. You're not charging for the hour you speak; you're charging for the years it took to know what to say.

Determining what to charge is part art, part research. For first-time engagements, you might start with $500 to $1,000 for a one-hour keynote or half-day workshop. As your reputation and demand grow, that can scale to several thousand dollars. Variables include audience size, travel, customization, and whether the talk is being recorded or reused. If you're unsure where to start, ask colleagues what they charge or search speaker bureau listings for benchmarks in your field. A simple way to test the waters is to ask the organizer, "Is there an honorarium or speaker budget associated with this?" Their answer will give you a sense of how to respond without overplaying or underselling your hand.

Workshops are where a lot of academics can shine. Unlike keynotes, which often require stage presence and storytelling polish, workshops lean into your natural strengths as a teacher. Whether it's a writing bootcamp, a stats refresher, or a diversity training session, you're helping people learn by doing—and that has real value. Many universities, foundations, and nonprofits are eager for interactive content but don't always know how to design it. You can step in with a clear format, outcomes, and time blocks, then charge for development and delivery. Just be careful not to recreate your own syllabus for free—customizing takes time, and that time deserves compensation.

MOOCs—Massive Open Online Courses—can be a tricky but powerful tool for monetization. At first, they were seen as free education for the masses, but now platforms like Coursera, edX, and Udemy have created hybrid models where instructors can be paid, either upfront or through revenue share. Creating a MOOC takes effort: filming, scripting, editing, and setting up quizzes or discussion boards. But once it's up, it becomes a digital asset—something people can buy or access while you sleep. Some professors use MOOCs to supplement classroom teaching or expand their impact beyond campus. Others turn them into lead generators for speaking, books, or consulting gigs. The trick is to build it once and make sure it aligns with your broader professional identity.

Brand dilution is a real concern. If you say yes to every speaking invite, accept every workshop, or post a dozen free webinars online, you can inadvertently cheapen the perception of your expertise. People may begin to expect you'll always show up for free, or that your time isn't in high demand. On the flip side, being too precious or unavailable can make you invisible. The goal is to be selective, strategic, and consistent. Choose opportunities that align with your values, audience, and messaging. And when you say yes, show up fully—because each appearance becomes part of your brand footprint, whether you intended it that way or not.

It's also worth developing a basic one-page "speaker sheet" or services outline. It doesn't have to be flashy—just a PDF that lists your speaking topics, audience takeaways, past clients (if any), and your contact information. This serves two purposes. First, it helps potential clients understand what you offer without you having to explain it from scratch each time. Second, it helps you define your lane. Are you a motivational speaker for early-career researchers? A methodologist who demystifies data? A voice for public scholarship? Having your offerings down on paper clarifies what you bring to the table—and reminds you to say no to gigs that don't fit.

Another key consideration is audience type. Who are you speaking to, and what do they hope to get from you? There's a big difference between a room full of high school teachers, a nonprofit board, a corporate HR team, or a group of first-generation college students. Each group brings a different level of knowledge, expectation, and need—and that should inform how you prepare and how you price. Don't assume that because an audience isn't academic, they won't understand or appreciate your depth. Often, non-academic audiences are the ones most grateful for accessible, engaging insights that feel both rigorous and real. And they're often the ones who return with future bookings or referrals.

As you grow in this space, your time becomes more valuable—not just in an hourly sense, but in terms of trade-offs. Every speaking event is time away from writing, mentoring, research, and personal life. That's why it's helpful to track the full cost of an engagement. That includes not just travel or prep hours, but the mental load of shifting gears and reentering your normal routines. If you're invited to speak during finals week, is it worth the stress? If the event pays $1,500 but takes three days out of your calendar, are you still ahead? These are questions only you can answer, but asking them early and often can save you from burnout masked as opportunity.

Intellectual property is another area worth understanding. If you design a slide deck or deliver a workshop, who owns the content? Are you giving the organization permission to record and share it freely? Do they expect to reuse your materials for future trainings without you? The answers vary depending on the agreement, so it's wise to clarify terms in writing. You don't need a lawyer for every gig, but you do need to ask questions like, "Will this be recorded?" or "Will participants receive copies of the slides?" Protecting your IP doesn't mean being stingy—it means making sure that the time and thought you invest isn't accidentally handed off for someone else's unlimited use.

Many faculty assume these types of activities are automatically covered by university policy, but the truth is more complicated. Some institutions require formal approval before outside speaking engagements, especially if you're using your title or talking about your research. Others have dollar thresholds for consulting or side income that trigger disclosure requirements. If you're unsure, check with your department chair or HR—not to ask permission, but to stay above board. The last thing you want is to be surprised by a conflict-of-interest issue when your only intention was to give back or earn a little extra. Staying transparent doesn't just protect your job—it shows that you take your professional responsibilities seriously.

Over time, many professors find a rhythm for what kinds of engagements light them up and what kinds just drain them. You might love interactive workshops but dread formal panels. You might feel energized by community college faculty but feel boxed in by corporate clients. Pay attention to those signals. One of the great freedoms of monetizing your voice is choosing where to show up. You don't have to be everywhere. You just have to be in the right rooms, saying the right things, to the right people. That's where the impact—and income—comes from.

As your reputation grows, inbound requests may increase. That's a good thing, but it also requires boundaries. Create a system that allows you to respond with clarity and confidence—whether that's a templated email, a personal assistant, or just a list of dates you're unavailable. Saying no gracefully is just as important as saying yes with enthusiasm. Something as simple as, "I appreciate the invitation, but I'm fully booked this semester," keeps the door open without overcommitting. The people who value your time will understand. The ones who don't probably weren't the right fit anyway.

Chapter 21: Royalties & Book Deals, Negotiating Advances, Subsidiary Rights, and Tax Treatment

Getting a book deal can feel like a dream come true, especially in academia where publishing is often tied to career advancement, tenure, and reputation. But once the excitement fades, you're left with a contract full of fine print and a lot of decisions that will affect your finances, time, and intellectual property. Whether you're publishing with a university press, a trade publisher, or even going the hybrid route, the truth is that book deals are both creative and commercial ventures. You're not just sharing your ideas with the world—you're also stepping into the business of publishing. And like any business deal, it's better to walk in with your eyes open and your calculator handy.

Let's start with advances, because that's often the first financial number that grabs your attention. An advance is essentially an upfront payment against your future royalties. In trade publishing—especially in nonfiction areas tied to expertise or public commentary—advances can range from a few thousand dollars to six figures, depending on the topic, platform, and perceived sales potential. University press books, by contrast, often don't come with advances at all, or if they do, they're modest—think $1,000 to $5,000. That said, don't confuse the size of the advance with the value of your work. Academic publishers may pay less up front, but your book could still bring long-term returns in visibility, consulting gigs, and career leverage.

One thing to clarify early is whether the advance is paid in a lump sum or in installments. Many publishers break it up—one third on signing, one third on manuscript delivery, and one third on publication. This matters because it affects your cash flow. That five-figure advance might feel less exciting once you realize it's spread out over two years and taxed as self-employment income. So when you're budgeting, don't treat the full amount as a windfall. Treat it like a contract job—because that's exactly what it is. You're being paid to deliver a product, and that product is your manuscript.

Then there are royalties, which kick in after the advance has been "earned out." That means once your book sells enough copies to repay the publisher the advance they gave you, you start earning a percentage on each sale. The royalty rate varies widely depending on format, publisher, and deal terms. Hardcovers might earn 10 to 15 percent of the list price; paperbacks might earn 7 to 10 percent. E-books tend to offer 25 percent of net revenue—meaning whatever the publisher gets after discounts, not the retail price. What's key here is that royalties aren't automatic. If your book doesn't earn out its advance, you keep the advance, but you won't see additional royalty checks. This is why a big advance isn't always the best deal—it raises the bar for your book's performance and may make the publisher less likely to invest in long-term marketing.

Subsidiary rights are another part of the deal that deserve your attention. These include the rights to turn your book into an audiobook, translate it into other languages, adapt it into a movie, or license it for a textbook or classroom use. Publishers often want to control these rights, but you can negotiate to retain some of them—especially if you have a platform or personal contacts in those markets. For example, you might agree to let the publisher handle foreign rights but keep the rights to create a podcast based on your book. If you retain a right and later sell it on your own, you keep the income. If the publisher sells it, you usually split the proceeds 50/50, minus their expenses. The key is to ask what rights are on the table and what happens if they're sold.

Copyright is another area where many authors assume they have more control than they do. In most traditional contracts, you retain the copyright, but you license exclusive publishing rights to the publisher. That means you can't take the manuscript and self-publish it later, or shop it to another publisher, without permission. But depending on the deal, you may be able to negotiate carve-outs for classroom use, personal website posting, or even turning a chapter into a journal article. Don't be afraid to ask for what you need—especially if the book grows out of your research or teaching and you want to use it in those spaces. A fair contract should protect both your creative control and the publisher's investment.

If you're working with a literary agent, they'll handle most of these negotiations. Agents typically earn 15 percent of all income from the book deal, including advances, royalties, and subsidiary rights. That might sound like a lot, but a good agent can often get you a bigger advance, better terms, and more opportunities down the line. If you're going without an agent—common in academic publishing—then you'll need to read the contract yourself or hire a publishing lawyer for a one-time review. That might cost a few hundred dollars, but it's worth it to understand what you're signing. Remember, you only get one chance to negotiate before the contract is locked in.

One thing that often surprises first-time authors is just how long everything takes. From contract to publication, it can easily be 18 to 24 months, especially with academic presses or traditional trade publishers. That timeline matters, especially if you're counting on the book to support a promotion case, raise your public profile, or generate income in a given tax year. If your advance is paid across milestones, remember that delays in editing, marketing, or printing can slow down your payments too. It's worth asking the publisher about their typical timeline and how quickly they process each payment. You're not being pushy—you're being financially aware, and that's something even editors respect.

Now let's talk taxes, because this is where many authors run into trouble. Advances and royalties are usually treated as self-employment income, meaning the publisher doesn't withhold taxes for you. That means you'll be responsible for paying quarterly estimated taxes, or you may owe a lump sum come April. It's easy to underestimate how much you'll owe, especially if this income is on top of your faculty salary. A good rule of thumb is to set aside 25 to 30 percent of any book income for taxes, especially if you don't have other deductions to offset it. You might also consider opening a separate savings account for this money so you don't accidentally spend what the IRS will eventually want.

If your book becomes part of a broader business—say you're building a speaking platform or offering courses based on the content—you may want to set up an LLC or sole proprietorship to manage the income. This can offer some liability protection and might simplify tax reporting, especially if you're claiming business expenses like travel, editing, or marketing support. Just be mindful of your university's policies around outside income and intellectual property. Some institutions require disclosure if you're earning significant revenue from work related to your faculty role. It's not about asking permission—it's about staying transparent and protecting yourself down the line.

Speaking of expenses, many authors spend more out of pocket than they expect. If you're self-promoting your book, you might pay for a website, social media ads, mailing lists, or a publicist. Academic authors often cover indexers, copyright permissions for figures, or even typesetting if the press doesn't provide it. Some of these expenses are reimbursed through grants or university support, but others come straight from your wallet. Keep receipts and track expenses carefully—they're tax deductible if they relate directly to the book. And if your book is part of a broader research project, see if grant funding can be used to offset production costs, especially for open access editions.

Another reality to keep in mind is that royalties often trickle in slowly, if at all. You may receive statements once or twice a year, and it's not unusual to wait six months to receive payment for sales made in the prior cycle. These checks are often small—$300 here, $500 there—and can feel anticlimactic after all the work that went into the book. That's why it helps to view the book not just as a revenue source, but as a credibility asset. A well-written, well-placed book can open doors to other income: consulting gigs, speaking engagements, media interviews, leadership roles. Don't measure its value by royalties alone.

Finally, it's worth understanding how book income fits into your overall financial picture. If this is your first time earning outside income, you might need to revisit your budget, retirement contributions, or savings plan. One strategy is to assign your book income a specific purpose—like funding a sabbatical, starting a college savings plan, or paying down debt. That way, the money has direction and impact, not just a temporary boost to your checking account. The same applies to future book deals. As your platform grows, think of your writing as part of a long-term financial and professional strategy—not a one-time side project.

It's also helpful to talk to other faculty who've published in your field or with your target press. Don't be afraid to ask them about what they negotiated, what they wish they'd done differently, or how they managed the financial side of the deal. Publishing is often shrouded in mystery, and those who've walked the path before you are often willing to share wisdom if you ask directly. Sometimes they'll point out clauses to avoid, or suggest literary agents who understand your niche. Other times, they'll simply reassure you that slow sales or odd royalty schedules are completely normal. There's value in peer mentorship here, especially when it comes to setting realistic expectations and spotting red flags early.

As your name becomes more recognized, you may receive offers from publishers you didn't approach—sometimes with flattering language and a tight deadline to sign. Be careful here. Some offers are legitimate; others are what the industry calls "vanity presses," which ask you to pay to publish under the guise of a partnership. Always read the contract and Google the press. Ask who will distribute the book, whether it will be in libraries or bookstores, and whether the publisher offers marketing support. If you're being asked to front thousands of dollars, slow down. Not all hybrid models are scams, but a rush to publish can lead to regret if you sign without understanding the business side.

Another wrinkle is how your university views the book in your tenure or promotion file. A university press publication may carry more academic weight, but a commercially successful trade book might raise your national profile, especially in applied fields. If your department values impact, media attention, or policy relevance, a trade book can be a strategic move. If they're more traditional, you may need to show how the book ties to your research or teaching. Either way, don't assume that the only path to legitimacy is through obscure presses or academic jargon. The best book for your career is the one that showcases your expertise, speaks to your audience, and reflects your voice.

From a long-term perspective, think of publishing as one pillar of your income portfolio—not the whole foundation. Some books are bestsellers. Most are not. But even modestly selling books can be stepping stones to other paid opportunities: invited talks, media commentary, policy consulting, or curriculum development. And when you've published more than one book, your backlist can continue earning royalties while you work on the next one. It's a slow build, but a steady one, if you're intentional. Treat your writing like an asset—something that can grow in value over time if nurtured and connected to a broader vision.

You might also consider self-publishing if you have a niche audience and clear marketing strategy. Self-publishing gives you full control over content, pricing, and rights—and it usually offers higher royalty rates per copy sold. But it also means you're the editor, marketer, distributor, and support staff unless you hire help. Many professors are well-positioned to self-publish supplemental textbooks, workbooks, or public-facing books based on years of classroom experience. If you go this route, learn the basics of ISBNs, formatting, and print-on-demand services. You don't need a massive platform—just a clear value proposition and a willingness to treat the book like a small business.

At the end of the day, book publishing is a blend of passion, strategy, and patience. It's one of the few income streams where your name stays on the product, your ideas continue working after you stop, and your influence can spread far beyond your zip code. Whether your book sells 300 copies or 30,000, the real win is that you've translated your knowledge into something lasting. So negotiate smart, plan for the financial side, and give yourself permission to be both scholar and entrepreneur. You're not just publishing—you're planting seeds. Some will take root now, some later, and some might surprise you years from now. But they all start with one thing: your voice, backed by clarity and confidence.

Chapter 22: Patents, Licensing, and Start-Ups, Turning Research into Equity and Cash Flow

Commercializing academic research can feel like venturing into a parallel universe—one with its own language, pace, and financial stakes. In the lab or archive, success means new knowledge; in the marketplace, success means problem-solving that people will actually pay for. The good news is that professors are often closer to marketable ideas than they realize. The challenge is translating those ideas into assets—patents, licenses, even start-up equity—without drowning in paperwork or compromising the integrity of your scholarship. Think of commercialization as an extension of the scientific method: observe a need, test a solution, collect data, and iterate. The difference is that your "data" here may include customer feedback, investor interest, and cash flow.

Let's start with patents, because they're the form of intellectual property most associated with research breakthroughs. A patent grants you—or, more likely, your university—exclusive rights to an invention for about twenty years. In exchange for public disclosure of how it works, you gain the legal power to stop others from making, using, or selling your invention without permission. But filing isn't cheap. Between attorney fees and government filing costs, a single U.S. patent can run $10,000 to $20,000 before international filings enter the picture. That's why universities have technology-transfer offices (TTOs): specialized teams who evaluate discoveries, decide whether they're worth patenting, and cover upfront costs in exchange for a share of future profits.

If your research yields something potentially patentable—say a new chemical compound, a software algorithm, or a medical device—the first step is a disclosure form to the TTO. Don't rush off and submit a journal article or conference abstract before filing; public disclosure can destroy patent rights in many countries. Think of it like sharing exam answers before the test is over. File first, publish later. Once the TTO vets your invention, they'll decide whether to pursue a provisional patent. This is a placeholder that secures a filing date but gives you a year to gather data, find partners, and refine claims before the full (and more expensive) patent application is due.

Licensing enters the story when someone else wants to use your patented technology. The university, as the legal owner, negotiates terms: an upfront fee, an annual maintenance fee, and royalties on product sales. Royalties might range from 1 to 10 percent, depending on the field and competitive landscape. The university then splits that income with you, typically 30 to 50 percent to the inventors after expenses. These numbers vary, so check your institution's policy. A modest but steady royalty stream can turn into a meaningful side income—enough to fund a lab tech, pay down student loans, or underwrite sabbatical travel—without extra hours on your part.

Sometimes, however, no company steps up to license your technology, or the offers that do come feel undervalued. That's when the start-up route becomes attractive. Spinning out a company allows you to control development, raise venture capital, and potentially capture a much larger share of the upside. Of course, it also piles on risk and workload. You'll need a business plan, a founding team, and investors willing to bet on unproven tech. Think of it like transitioning from writing a solo article to leading a multi-institution grant: the scope balloons, but so can the payoff. The TTO will still want its share—often in the form of equity plus a modest royalty—but you'll have more strategic control.

Equity compensation is where academics often feel out of their depth. Instead of a paycheck, you might receive common stock or options that vest over time. The basic idea is that you own a slice of the company in exchange for your intellectual contribution. If the company grows, so does the value of your equity. If it fizzles, the shares are worth little or nothing. To avoid nasty surprises, ask early how much equity you're getting, whether it's subject to dilution when new investors arrive, and what vesting schedule applies. A standard founder vesting timeline might be four years with a one-year cliff—meaning you earn 25percent of your shares after one year, with the rest vesting monthly thereafter.

Alongside equity, many faculty founders negotiate a consultancy or advisory agreement that pays a modest fee—say $1,000 a month for a few hours of guidance—to keep cash coming in until the company can afford real salaries. If you take on an official executive role, like Chief Scientific Officer, be ready for heavier time commitments, fiduciary duties, and potential conflicts with your university job. Some schools allow part-time leave or shared-equity arrangements; others require you to choose. Mapping out these commitments in advance ensures you don't promise venture investors 40 hours a week you simply don't have.

Venture investors care about three things: technology, team, and total addressable market. As the academic inventor, you are core to the first two. Yet investors also worry that professors have limited availability and little business experience. One way to reassure them is to recruit a seasoned co-founder or CEO early—someone comfortable with fundraising, hiring, and go-to-market strategy. That lets you remain the scientific North Star while delegating day-to-day operations. Think of it like collaborating with a statistician on a complex study: you steer the research question, they steer the methodology, and together you deliver something stronger than either could alone.

Conflict-of-interest (COI) rules loom large once equity enters the picture. Universities don't want faculty grading their own homework—publishing favorable papers about a drug they also own stock in, for example. Most institutions require an annual COI disclosure listing your outside roles, equity stakes, and consulting income. The goal isn't to block your start-up; it's to set guardrails. You might need to recuse yourself from certain purchasing decisions, limit student involvement in company-funded projects, or appoint an independent data monitor for clinical studies. Completing the paperwork feels tedious, but failing to do so can jeopardize both your job and the company's credibility.

Timing your departure—partial or total—from the university is another pivotal decision. Some founders take a one-year leave of absence to get the company through prototype or SeriesA funding, then return to academia with a board seat and equity. Others negotiate a "reduced FTE" arrangement, teaching one course per year while actively growing the venture. A few make a clean break, betting that the start-up's upside outweighs tenure security. There's no universal answer, but ask yourself where your presence adds the most value. If the science is stable and what the company needs is market traction, maybe you can stay on campus while a commercial CEO drives the next phase.

Licensing negotiations hinge on future cash-flow projections—numbers that are inherently speculative. Companies prefer low royalties tied to sales; universities push for upfront fees or milestone payments to hedge risk. A middle-ground approach is to propose staged royalties that rise as revenue benchmarks are hit, or convertible equity that allows the university to swap future royalties for additional shares later. Remember, both sides benefit from a deal that lets the technology flourish. If the royalty is so high it scares away investors, everybody loses. Treat the conversation like a collaborative grant budget meeting: transparent assumptions, shared risk, and mutual incentive to deliver outcomes.

International patents widen the moat around your invention but multiply costs. The Patent Cooperation Treaty (PCT) offers a unified filing that preserves rights in numerous countries for up to thirty months, buying time to gauge global interest. Ask the TTO which regions matter for your field—maybe Europe and Japan for pharmaceuticals, or China and India for agricultural tech. Filing everywhere "just in case" can drain resources better spent on prototype development or clinical trials. Patents are tools, not trophies; file strategically, not nostalgically. A focused portfolio often beats a sprawling, underfunded one.

Once a product reaches the market, reporting and audit clauses kick in. Licensees must send periodic sales statements and royalty checks, but tracking can get messy if multiple SKUs or bundled products include your technology. Don't assume the accounting will police itself. Universities typically reserve audit rights, but audits happen rarely unless red flags appear. Keep communication lines open with the licensee and ask for clear SKU-level reporting early. A simple Excel sheet in year one can prevent six-figure discrepancies in year five. Think of it as maintaining lab notebooks—documentation today guards against disputes tomorrow.

Finally, plan an exit—even if it's years away. What happens if the company is acquired, goes public, or winds down? Acquisition can trigger accelerated vesting or bonus payouts; bankruptcy can wipe your equity entirely. Understanding liquidation preferences, dilution scenarios, and IPO lock-ups equips you to make informed decisions along the journey. You don't need to master every legal nuance, but you should know enough to ask pointed questions and hire counsel when stakes escalate. Remember, commercialization is a marathon sprinkled with sprints. Pace yourself, stay curious, and surround yourself with partners who respect both your scholarship and your entrepreneurial spark.

Chapter 23: Board Service & Advisory Roles: Compensation Types, Fiduciary Duties, and Time Commitments

Board service can look glamorous from the outside—think polished conference rooms and catered lunches—but at its core it is a roll-up-your-sleeves commitment to guide an organization with wisdom and integrity while protecting other people's money and dreams. Imagine being the co-pilot of a flight carrying employees, customers, and shareholders; you are not at the controls every second, yet your judgment can keep the plane on course or send it into turbulence. That combination of influence and accountability is why invitations to join a board feel flattering and weighty all at once. Before sending back a thrilled yes, it helps to understand exactly what you are agreeing to in dollars, duties, and day-to-day rhythm. In the next few pages we will walk through the practical realities—compensation, fiduciary obligations, and time commitments—so you can decide whether this opportunity aligns with your goals, bandwidth, and risk tolerance. My aim is to speak plainly, share real stories, and leave you with a toolbox of questions to ask before signing on the dotted line.

Compensation is usually the first topic to surface at cocktail parties, and it comes in more flavors than a summer snow-cone stand. Some boards pay a straight annual retainer, wired into your bank account quarterly like clockwork, which feels a lot like a predictable paycheck for advice. Others sweeten the pot with equity—restricted stock or options—that might be worth little today but could create substantial upside if the company thrives, a bit like accepting chips in a poker game rather than immediate cash. There are hybrid models that combine both, plus meeting fees that function as a taxi meter: the more sessions you attend, the more you earn. Committee chairs and lead directors often receive an extra stipend to reflect heavier workloads; think of it as a captain's armband acknowledging additional responsibility on the field. Finally, early-stage startups sometimes offer nothing but coffee and a handshake, betting that mission alignment or future equity value will compensate for the present-day sacrifice. The key takeaway is to map compensation against risk, effort, and your own liquidity needs rather than assuming every board seat is a golden ticket.

Cash retainers appeal to professionals who value steady income and prefer not to juggle tax complexities tied to equity. For example, Malcolm, a semi-retired banker, serves on the board of a regional credit union and receives twenty thousand dollars a year—enough to justify his time yet small enough that no one questions his motives when tough decisions arise. His tax situation stays simple because the retainer flows as ordinary income, reported on a straightforward 1099. Compare that with Priya, who joined a biotech startup at the Series B stage and accepted options priced at a few pennies per share; five years later, a public listing turned those options into a seven-figure windfall, though she also wrestled with alternative minimum tax and lock-up periods. Both arrangements can be smart, but clarity about vesting schedules, clawback provisions, and blackout windows helps you avoid surprises. Remember that board pay is seldom "set and forget"—it intertwines with your broader financial plan, so looping in your tax professional early is prudent.

Equity compensation deserves a closer look because it links your pocketbook to the company's performance, thereby aligning incentives but amplifying volatility. Picture planting a fruit tree: you water it with meeting prep, fertilize it with strategic guidance, and hope it bears sweet returns in a few seasons. The upside can feel exhilarating—especially if the share price jumps tenfold—but the tree can also wither if the business falters or regulators swoop in. Vesting schedules matter because unvested shares usually evaporate if you resign early, so ask how long you must serve before ownership becomes permanent. Moreover, find out whether shares settle automatically or require you to exercise options—meaning you pay out of pocket and potentially owe taxes before realizing cash proceeds. A rule of thumb I share with wealth-management clients is to treat unvested equity as possibility, not reality, until it clears your brokerage statement.

Beyond money, board work is fundamentally a fiduciary assignment, which is a fancy legal way of saying you must act in someone else's best interest with loyalty and care. Think of the role like being a trustee of a friend's life savings: you read every document twice, question vague language, and never treat the funds as your personal piggy bank. Corporate directors owe a duty of care, which requires reasonable diligence—reading materials in advance, attending meetings, and challenging assumptions with respectful skepticism. They also owe a duty of loyalty, meaning you avoid conflicts, disclose any potential self-dealing, and prioritize the organization's welfare over your own. In nonprofit settings, an additional duty of obedience enters the picture, compelling you to honor the mission and comply with applicable laws. Breaching these duties can invite lawsuits, reputational damage, and sleepless nights, so understanding them upfront is non-negotiable.

Let's ground fiduciary duty in a real scenario. Suppose you sit on the board of a community hospital exploring the purchase of a new electronic medical record system, and your cousin owns one of the bidding vendors. Even if his product is stellar, you must disclose the relationship and, in many cases, recuse yourself from the vote to preserve impartiality. Failing to do so could spark accusations of self-dealing, undermine board cohesion, and jeopardize patient trust. On the flip side, demonstrating transparency can enhance your credibility; I have seen directors earn colleagues' respect by over-disclosing ties, thereby modeling ethical behavior for the entire organization. The actionable takeaway is simple: keep a running list of personal interests—investments, relatives, consulting gigs—that could intersect with board matters, and share it with the corporate secretary annually or whenever circumstances change. Trust flourishes in the sunlight of disclosure.

Duty of care often trips up well-meaning directors who underestimate the time required to stay informed. Board packets can stretch to 300 pages, laden with financial statements, regulatory updates, and competitive analyses. If you skim or skip because "I'll just ask questions in the meeting," you risk missing red flags like declining cash flow or whistle-blower complaints buried in a footnote. Courts apply the business-judgment rule, generally deferring to your decisions if you acted in good faith and with adequate information, but ignorance is a weak defense when disaster strikes. Set aside uninterrupted time before each meeting—perhaps a Saturday morning with coffee—to digest materials, jot questions, and highlight sections needing clarification. That discipline not only shields you legally but also elevates the strategic conversation, earning gratitude from management and fellow directors.

Time commitment is the sleeper issue that turns enthusiastic volunteers into frazzled travelers. A typical public company board meets four to six times a year for a full day, plus committee meetings that can double the workload for audit, compensation, or governance chairs. Add travel, pre-reads, and emergency calls, and you might spend twenty-five to forty days annually—comparable to taking on a meaningful side hustle. Early-stage startups and nonprofits can be deceptively demanding, too, because lean staff means directors roll up sleeves on everything from fundraising to drafting policies. One director I coached expected quarterly Zoom calls but soon found herself fielding nightly Slack messages during a crisis product recall. Before joining, ask for a candid calendar estimate broken down by routine and peak periods, then check it against your own commitments to ensure you can show up fully rather than merely phone in.

Seasonality also affects workloads; retailers need heightened board attention during holiday inventory ramps, while banks focus heavily on first-quarter regulatory filings. A board in merger talks may convene weekly until the deal closes, turning your schedule upside-down. Experienced directors often maintain a "white-space buffer" of five to ten unscheduled days per quarter to absorb surprises without canceling family vacations or client obligations. If your main job already runs at capacity, consider whether the additional board seat pushes you beyond sustainable bandwidth. Burnout erodes sound judgment and can embarrass you if you nod through presentations without grasping the core issues. Healthy boundaries, including the right to decline last-minute travel if it clashes with prior commitments, preserve both your sanity and your effectiveness.

When evaluating compensation in light of time and risk, calculate an implied hourly rate to see whether it meets your personal threshold. For instance, a fifty-thousand-dollar retainer diluted over forty days equates to twelve-hundred-fifty dollars per day, or roughly one-hundred-fifty dollars per hour if you work an eight-hour stretch. That may feel fair if you enjoy the mission and network benefits, but less so if those hours displace higher-earning consulting work. Equity complicates the math because future value is uncertain; I encourage clients to create three scenarios—downside, base, and upside—then weigh the average against their opportunity cost. Remember to include ancillary time like onboarding training, mandatory site visits, and continuing-education sessions required for regulated industries. Transparent math sets realistic expectations and prevents resentment later.

Speaking of training, savvy boards invest in director education, covering topics such as cybersecurity, ESG, or industry-specific regulations. These sessions can add another two to three days per year but pay dividends in sharper oversight and reduced liability. Susan, a former marketing executive, credits a one-day cybersecurity boot camp with alerting her to gaps in her company's data-breach response, leading to an early fix that saved millions. In heavily regulated sectors—think banking or utilities—continuing education may be mandatory, with logged hours subject to auditor review. If the organization covers travel and tuition, view it as professional development; if not, factor those costs into your compensation calculus. Staying current not only protects the enterprise but also enhances your resume for future board opportunities.

Liability insurance, known as D&O (directors and officers) coverage, is another pillar of risk management. Without it, a lawsuit could put your personal assets on the line, even if you acted responsibly. The policy limits should match industry norms—hundreds of millions for Fortune 500 firms, lower for private or nonprofit entities—and be paired with robust indemnification provisions in the bylaws. Always request a summary of coverage, including exclusions like fraud, and have your own attorney skim the fine print. A real-estate developer I know accepted a board seat at a charitable foundation only to discover later that their D&O policy lapsed due to budget cuts, leaving him exposed during a donor lawsuit; it took six stressful months to resolve. Ensuring adequate coverage up front is like wearing a seatbelt—you hope never to test it, but you'll be glad it's there in a collision.

Cultural fit matters as much as technical skill, because boards function like small teams where trust and respectful debate drive better outcomes. Pay attention to how directors interact during your interview: do they probe constructively or play gotcha games? Is dissent welcomed or brushed aside by dominant personalities? A well-composed board balances backgrounds—finance, operations, technology, human resources—so conversations are multifaceted rather than echo chambers. If you feel pressure to rubber-stamp management rather than challenge assumptions, consider that a warning sign. Joining a dysfunctional board can be like moving into a beautiful house with termites—the problems stay hidden until costly repairs become unavoidable.

Many professionals seek board seats for networking, résumé enhancement, or to give back, yet overlook the reputational downside if the organization stumbles. When a company restates earnings or a nonprofit mishandles funds, headlines rarely differentiate between negligent and diligent directors; everyone's name appears together. Before accepting, review recent financial statements, audits, and press coverage to spot red flags like high executive turnover or regulatory investigations. Reach out to former board members for candid insight—why they left can be more telling than why current directors stay. Your professional brand, built over decades, is worth protecting by doing this diligence even if it feels awkward. As one seasoned director told me, "I never invest in a stock without research, so why would I invest my reputation blindly?"

Balancing multiple board roles introduces potential conflicts and fatigue, so establish a personal cap—perhaps three public company boards or five total mandates, depending on complexity. Each additional seat compounds your meeting calendar and reading list, increasing the odds of missed detail. Institutional investors scrutinize "over-boarded" directors, sometimes voting against re-election when they believe attention is spread too thin. If you already sit on several boards, disclose that upfront so the nominating committee can judge whether you have room to contribute fully. Conversely, serving on both a corporate board and a nonprofit can create enriching cross-pollination, as long as you compartmentalize proprietary information and allocate time fairly. Self-awareness about your limits signals professionalism and protects all parties.

Let's turn to advisory roles, which differ from formal board service yet often carry similar expectations minus the fiduciary weight. Advisory board members—sometimes called mentors or ambassadors—typically provide strategic counsel without voting rights, making the position attractive to entrepreneurs who crave guidance but want to keep governance nimble. Compensation ranges from a small equity grant to per-meeting stipends or simply brand visibility. Because legal duties are lighter, liability is lower, though reputational stakes remain if the venture behaves unethically. Time commitments can be flexible—monthly calls, ad hoc brainstorming, or a quarterly dinner—so clarify cadence and deliverables before diving in. If you thrive on strategy but prefer fewer legal entanglements, an advisory seat can scratch the itch.

Real-life example: Jordan, a digital-marketing expert, joined the advisory council of a craft-beer startup, receiving one-quarter of one percent in equity that vested over two years. He spent roughly eight hours a month reviewing campaigns and making introductions, generating mutual wins; the company's taproom traffic doubled, and Jordan's expertise gained visible proof points for his consulting firm. Advisory roles can also act as stepping-stones to full board service, allowing both parties to test chemistry. Keep in mind that state laws differ on potential liability even for non-fiduciary advisors, so ask whether the company extends D&O

coverage or at least includes you in indemnification clauses. Transparency about expectations, compensation, and risk keeps relationships smooth and productive.

For both board and advisory positions, negotiations should feel collaborative rather than adversarial. Approach the conversation like designing a win-win project scope: outline tasks, timelines, resources, and success metrics. If the organization pushes back on what seems like basic protections—insurance, clear role description, timely information flow—consider how they'll respond when stakes are higher. Seasoned negotiators focus on alignment: when compensation and commitment feel balanced, enthusiasm stays high and turnover stays low. Remember that walking away can be the most strategic move if terms don't match your needs; an empty calendar slot can later be filled with a better-fit opportunity. As my mentor once said, "Every 'no' makes room for the right 'yes.'"

Succession planning is the hallmark of a mature board. Ask whether term limits or mandatory retirement ages exist, how new directors are groomed, and whether an emergency plan covers sudden vacancies. Robust succession keeps fresh perspectives flowing and prevents stagnation—think of it as crop rotation for governance. If you join an aging board without clear replenishment strategy, you may inherit heavier duties as peers retire without replacements in sight. Conversely, boards that regularly onboard new talent foster vibrant debate and professional development. Evaluating succession before you jump in reflects foresight and signals that you value long-term institutional health.

Once onboard, cultivate effective working habits: arrive prepared, speak concisely, listen actively, and follow through on commitments. Early in my career, I watched a director earn widespread respect simply by summarizing complex issues in plain language right before crucial votes, enabling less technical members to grasp nuances. Emulate that clarity by asking management to translate acronyms or provide one-page dashboards if materials become opaque. Building relationships outside formal meetings—coffee with the CFO, site tours with plant managers—adds context that improves decision-making. Still, maintain independence; you're a guardrail, not a cheerleader. Your superpower is constructive skepticism wrapped in collegial tone.

Finally, align your board journey with personal purpose. Some people chase prestige or pay only to discover the subject matter bores them, leading to disengagement that serves no one. Reflect on the mission, industry, and leadership style that energize you, whether it's environmental stewardship, advancing medical innovation, or shepherding a family business through generational transition. When your values sync with the organization's goals, meetings feel like energizing brainstorming sessions rather than chores. That alignment enriches both sides: the company gains a passionate advocate, and you gain meaningful stories, networks, and yes—sometimes rewarding compensation. Board service done right is less about accumulating titles and more about stewarding impact that outlasts any single director's tenure, and that legacy is compensation of a different, profound kind.

Ask ChatGPT

Chapter 24: Summer Salary Strategies: Grant Funding, Teaching Loads, and Vacation Trade-Offs

Summer rolls around on campus like a quiet Sunday morning—hallways echo, coffee shops shorten their hours, and the frantic pace of the spring semester gives way to birdsong and lawn-mower hum—but for many faculty members the question of how to keep paychecks flowing never goes dormant. Alice, a mid-career biologist, remembers her first July on the tenure track when she stared at a half-sized paycheck and realized her nine-month contract did exactly what it said on the tin. It felt a little like discovering the hotel minibar prices after you've already opened a juice—you can't put it back and you have to swallow the cost. She learned that mapping out summer salary in January is kinder to the nerves than scrambling in May. Think of it as packing sunscreen before the beach rather than hunting for an overpriced bottle at the resort gift shop. Planning early converts the summer gap from a surprise invoice into a manageable line item.

Grant funding is the marquee strategy most research-active faculty chase, and with good reason: external sponsors frequently allow investigators to pay themselves up to two or three months of additional salary. Picture a garden hose connected to a municipal water line; as long as the grant is active, money flows directly into your summer paycheck stream. The catch is that you must water the right plants—meaning the research aims in your proposal—and document every drop with time-and-effort reports. Some agencies cap summer compensation at a percentage of your base, while others let you bill against the actual daily rate, so reading the fine print is not optional. I know a chemist who assumed her NSF award covered her full August month, only to discover the 2/9 rule limited her draw to twenty-two percent of annual pay; she ended up eating ramen and raiding the travel budget to close the gap. The lesson is to build grant budgets with explicit summer lines and to clarify agency caps before the proposal leaves your inbox.

Timing proposals is part art, part logistics, because the award cycle often runs a season or two behind academic needs. If you submit in November and receive notice in June, the earliest funds can hit your account might be late July, which helps in August but leaves June hanging. Veteran grant-writers hedge with a portfolio approach—one award in year two, another in year three—so at least one hose stays open each summer. Universities sometimes offer bridge funding to tide you over while a renewal is pending, and this safety net can feel like a temporary credit card advance from a benevolent relative. But bridge money often converts to a loan if the grant fails, so treat it like borrowing tools from a neighbor: return them quickly and in good condition. A pragmatic move is to bank a month of salary from the previous year's discretionary funds when possible, creating your own micro-bridge without institutional IOUs.

Not every scholar will win the grant lottery every season, which is where summer teaching enters the picture as a solid, though sometimes underappreciated, pillar. Teaching a condensed course can feel like hosting a dinner party every night for three weeks—intense, satisfying, but also exhausting. Universities pay anywhere from one-eighth to one-sixth of base salary for a three-credit class, and that paycheck shows up reliably without paperwork marathons. My economist friend Miguel teaches intro micro in June, pockets two extra mortgage payments, and still takes July to visit his family in Argentina. The key is to weigh opportunity cost: if prepping a new course crowds out writing a grant resubmission, you might lose future summers' funding for a short-term gain. In fields where research deadlines dictate promotion prospects, that trade-off deserves sober reflection.

Teaching load negotiations offer more flexibility than many faculty realize, especially at institutions hungry for online summer enrollment. One colleague convinced her dean to let her prerecord half the lectures in March, freeing up travel time later while still satisfying contact-hour requirements. Think of it like cooking freezer meals in advance so you can spend evenings at the park instead of the stove. Another lever is course bundling—teach two back-to-back sessions in June for double pay and a completely free July and August—but remember stamina: marathon grading sessions can bleed into the rest of summer if you're not disciplined. Successful "bundle teachers" schedule daily grading blocks like gym appointments, preventing the paper stack from morphing into a weekend-eating monster. And if you're a lab instructor, ask whether the course can run with a teaching assistant handling bench prep; sometimes that assistantship cost is lower than the grant time you'd otherwise sacrifice.

Consulting and service contracts provide a third income stream that pairs nicely with academic calendars because industry projects often spike when businesses accelerate initiatives between fiscal years. A civil-engineering professor I mentor supplements her salary by modeling storm-water runoff for local municipalities each summer; the city gets expert analysis at a competitive rate, and she gains fresh data for journal articles plus a generous consulting fee. Universities typically let you devote one day per week to outside work during the academic year and more during breaks, but you must disclose the activity and ensure no conflict with grant-funded tasks. Think of consulting rules as the speed limits of fiscal traffic: stay within lanes and everyone arrives safely. One cautionary tale involves a historian who accepted paid curatorial work that overlapped an NEH grant; auditors flagged duplicate effort and clawed back funds, teaching the entire department a painful lesson about double-dipping. Transparency with both sponsor and institution is the cheapest insurance policy you can buy.

Balancing money-making strategies with genuine downtime is the emotional heart of summer planning. Vacation isn't just a luxury; it's the academic version of changing the oil in your mental engine. Skipping rest to chase every dollar can leave you stalled on the highway come September, staring at a blinking check-engine light of burnout. A psychology professor once told me she schedules her vacation into her grant proposals by allocating a zero-charged twelfth week labeled "project shutdown and travel"; reviewers seldom object, and her dean appreciates that she returns refreshed rather than resentful. If external funds can't cover that gap, she simply budgets the unpaid week into her household finances, viewing it as a preventive healthcare expense. Remember, vacation trade-offs are measured not only in lost income but also in preserved creativity and family goodwill, currencies that yield long-term dividends.

Family dynamics often dictate whether you choose the grant, teaching, or travel path. Faculty with school-age children may prioritize July freedom for camps and grandparents, making June teaching the optimal compromise. Dual-academic couples juggle overlapping grant deadlines like synchronized swimmers; if both chase full summer salary every year, someone might miss the metaphorical oxygen of rest. One math professor I know alternates with his partner: she pursues grant salary in even-numbered summers while he teaches, then they switch, ensuring at least one adult is flexible for childcare and research each year. It's like splitting driving duties on a cross-country road trip—everyone gets a turn behind the wheel and a chance to nap in the passenger seat. Treating summer strategy as a household puzzle rather than a solo quest lightens the load and fosters mutual support.

Financially, it helps to view your nine-month base as a foundation and any summer earnings as variable "roof money" that can be stored for lean years when grants fall through. Setting up a dedicated high-yield savings account for surplus summer pay insulates the rest of your budget from feast-or-famine swings. One humanities professor squirrels away half of every teaching check into such an account, labeling it the "sabbatical snowball," which later funds conference travel and manuscript workshops without chasing last-minute funding. Think of it as building a storm shelter in sunny weather; you hope not to use it, but when a tornado in the form of grant rejection hits, you're glad it's stocked. Automating transfers on payday removes temptation to overspend and turns financial discipline into a background habit.

University payroll calendars impose another twist: some institutions spread your 12-month pay evenly even if you work only nine months, while others halt checks in May unless you secure supplemental funding. Knowing which system you're in prevents panic at the mailbox. If your campus offers twelve-month distribution by request, consider the psychological benefits of steady income versus the slightly higher pretax advantage of lump-sum summer pay. It's akin to choosing between a steady drip coffee maker and a French press—both deliver caffeine, but the experience differs. Whichever you select, coordinate with your accountant to handle quarterly tax estimates because extra summer income can bump you into a new bracket or trigger self-employment liabilities if classified as consulting. The IRS cares less about academic calendars and more about accurate withholding.

Bridge funding, whether institutional or departmental, can rescue you from timing gaps but should be approached with realistic exit strategies. My colleague in computer science once accepted two months of departmental bridge on the assumption her DARPA grant would renew; when budget cuts killed the renewal, she negotiated to convert the advance into fall course overloads rather than repay in cash. This creative solution preserved her family's summer road-trip plans but demanded heavy September workloads, proving that every lifeline comes with strings. Before taking bridge money, map the worst-case scenario and discuss repayment alternatives with your chair—perhaps spreading the load across service assignments or mentoring programs. It's easier to negotiate flexible terms while everyone still believes the grant will materialize than after disappointment sets in.

Diversifying funding sources decreases reliance on a single grant. Collaborative awards let co-principal investigators each charge partial summer salary, reducing each person's burden while strengthening the proposal with interdisciplinary flair. Picture four friends sharing a picnic basket; everyone brings a dish, and no one carries the whole meal. Interinstitutional collaborations can also unlock larger federal mechanisms like Centers or Networks grants, where the pot is big enough to finance multiple summers for several years. Of course, shared awards require clear communication about authorship, budget use, and timeline so that the picnic doesn't devolve into food fights. A written memorandum of understanding among collaborators can prevent awkward exchanges when invoice approvals start routing across campuses.

Sabbatical planning intersects with summer salary in intricate ways because many institutions permit paid leave only if you forgo outside earnings or cap them at a fraction of base. Aligning a sabbatical with an existing grant that pays equipment and grad student costs—but not salary—can free you to travel for archival research or industry externships without triggering clawbacks. Alternatively, some faculty bank sabbatical months by deferring grant draws until the leave year, effectively smoothing pay across longer spans. Think of sabbatical as the academic equivalent of a pit stop in a race; what matters is fueling effectively without violating pit-lane speed limits set by policy. Knowing the rules two years in advance equips you to position grant renewals or teaching hiatuses for maximum synergy.

Taxes often sneak up like ants at a picnic if you forget they love sugar as much as you do. Summer salary spikes can alter your withholding calibration, especially if grant funds land in a lump rather than as steady pay. One physicist friend underestimated his quarterly payments after a lucrative Department of Energy contract and faced a five-figure penalty the following April. His accountant later set up an automated 20-percent transfer from each grant paycheck into a separate tax account—a financial equivalent of brushing crumbs off the picnic blanket before ants arrive. If consulting income flows through a sole proprietorship or LLC, you may also owe self-employment tax and should investigate retirement vehicles like a SEP-IRA to lower liability while building long-term wealth.

Building a summer budget, much like drafting a syllabus, clarifies expectations and sets the pace for the season. Start by listing non-negotiable expenses—mortgage, insurance, student-loan payments—then layer variable costs like vacation travel, daycare, or conference fees. Match these against the net income scenarios from grants, teaching, or consulting and play what-if games: what if only one of three proposals funds? What if enrollment in your course falls short and pay prorates downward? Keeping a conservative baseline forces you to live within "C-minus" funding and treat any upside as bonus. One colleague's mantra is "plan for ramen, spend on risotto only when the check clears," a delicious metaphor for prudent optimism. Adjust your budget each May when actual award notices firm up, the way you update a syllabus once enrollment settles.

Mentally, many faculty find relief in assigning each summer a theme—Grant Summer, Book Summer, Family Summer—so salary strategies align with the primary objective rather than competing with it. During Book Summer, a historian might decline teaching and accept partial pay loss to finish a manuscript, trusting the resulting publication will boost future grant competitiveness. In Grant Summer, the same professor may front-load proposal writing and accept heavier teaching the following year to rebalance income. Themes act like the season label on a Netflix show; they set audience expectations—your family, your department, your own inner critic—so everyone knows the plot arc and measures success accordingly. This narrative framing transforms what could feel like random hustle into a coherent chapter of your career story.

When considering vacation trade-offs, remember that travel itself can sometimes be folded into scholarly life. Field research in Provence might double as a family getaway if you schedule data collection in the mornings and leave afternoons free for markets and museums. University per-diem rules can complicate reimbursing spouses or kids, but careful separation of expenses and transparent accounting avoids ethical gray zones. One linguistic anthropologist I know rents an Airbnb with an extra bedroom during fieldwork, paying personally for the larger space while the grant covers her single-room equivalent rate; everyone wins. Vacation doesn't always mean beaches either—digital detox at a cabin three hours away can cost less than airfare and still deliver the mental recharge you need to hit September fresh. Weigh destination glamor against financial strain with the same analytical eye you apply to research design.

Some faculty hesitate to pursue summer salary aggressively because they fear appearing money-oriented, especially in humanities circles where grant culture is newer. But securing funds to pay yourself is not greed; it is stewardship of your expertise and a buffer against burnout that ultimately benefits students and scholarship. Framing salary as "support for research continuity" rather than "extra pay" can shift departmental attitudes. A literature scholar successfully advocated for internal grant expansion by showing how steady summer compensation sped up book production and increased the department's visibility in national rankings. Her dean now treats the program as an investment, proving that clear articulation of benefits can transform cultural skepticism into institutional support.

Finally, remember that summer strategies evolve across a career. Early-stage faculty may hustle every grant and course to build a dossier; mid-career professors often pivot toward balance, integrating family travel and health priorities; senior scholars sometimes scale back to mentoring grants and guest-lecturing gigs that keep them engaged without full-time demands. Think of summer salary planning like adjusting sail trim over a voyage: the wind shifts, the boat ages, the destination map changes. Regularly revisit your goals, health, and household needs to tune the balance of grant work, teaching, consulting, and rest. By treating summer as a strategic asset rather than a seasonal scramble, you turn the hottest months into fertile ground for both financial stability and the intellectual growth that drew you into academia in the first place.

Chapter 25: Creating an LLC or S-Corp, When, Why, and How for Professorial Side Income

Creating an LLC or electing S-Corp status may sound like paperwork reserved for Silicon Valley tech founders, yet for professors who moonlight as consultants, authors, or speakers, these structures can be the difference between operating a lemonade stand on your driveway and running a professionally branded café on Main Street, complete with health inspections, liability shields, and an accountant who knows your coffee beans from your payroll beans. When you take your first honorarium check in exchange for a workshop or expert witness testimony, you have already crossed the line from hobby to business in the eyes of the IRS, and that means your personal Social Security number and your university paycheck are now in the same bucket as the laptop you buy for side projects and the travel you expense to conferences. An LLC—short for limited liability company—creates a legal fence around that bucket so a lawsuit over a consulting misstep does not spill into your mortgage or retirement fund, while an S-Corp—which is really a tax election layered onto an LLC or corporation—adds a tax-saving sprinkler system that can keep more cash irrigating your garden of research or family vacations. The catch is that fences and sprinklers both cost money to install and maintain, so you need to weigh the price of state filings, payroll compliance, and bookkeeping against the savings from self-employment tax reduction and the peace of mind that comes with a clean separation of church and state between your professorial salary and your entrepreneurial hustle. Think of the LLC as a sturdy backpack that keeps your lunch from getting squished against your textbooks, and think of the S-Corp as the insulated lunchbox inside that backpack, controlling the temperature so your yogurt stays fresh and the ice pack does not leak into your lecture notes. Many professors start with a sole proprietorship by default, because they file a Schedule C with their 1040 and call it a day, but as side income creeps past ten or twenty thousand dollars a year they notice the self-employment tax bite swelling like a mosquito sting, and that irritation is usually the moment they book a chat with a CPA who suggests entity formation as a soothing salve.

Deciding when to pull the trigger on an LLC starts with an honest look at risk, revenue, and runway, a trio I encourage my faculty clients to write on a sticky note and attach to their monitor before they open the Secretary of State website. Risk means the chance that a client, conference attendee, or book reader could claim your advice caused them financial harm and come after your assets, even if the lawsuit barely holds water; revenue measures the dollars you expect to run through your side gig over the next twelve to twenty-four months, not pie-in-the-sky royalties a decade out; runway refers to how long you plan to operate this venture and whether you envision scaling it beyond an occasional Saturday Zoom session. If your consulting involves high-stakes topics—say, medical device regulation or multi-million-dollar patent litigation—the liability component alone can justify forming an LLC even if you earn only a few thousand in year one, because a single lawsuit could exceed your university's professional liability coverage, which often does not extend to private moonlighting. Conversely, if you run a small peer-review-editing service that earns five hundred dollars a summer, your risk is minimal and it may make sense to stay a sole prop until revenue grows or you partner with colleagues, at which point joint ownership nudges you toward an entity anyway. Runway matters because state fees and annual reports can cost several hundred dollars a year; forming an LLC in January only to let it dissolve by December wastes cash better spent on research assistants. My rule of thumb: once gross side-gig income passes the $10,000 mark or your work involves advice that could influence someone else's financial or legal position, schedule a consultation with a tax advisor to explore whether an LLC—and eventually S-Corp treatment—would serve you well.

Understanding why an S-Corp can save money requires a quick tour through the self-employment tax maze, but I promise to keep jargon in the back seat and let plain language drive. When you run a sole proprietorship or an LLC taxed as a sole prop, every dollar of net profit faces the 15.3-percent self-employment tax, which combines the Social Security and Medicare payroll taxes that your university normally handles on your W-2 income; you basically pay both the employer and employee halves on your side hustle. Electing S-Corp status lets you split your earnings into two buckets: reasonable salary and profit distribution, where only the salary portion bears payroll taxes while the profit escapes that 15.3-percent bite, though it still pays regular income tax. Picture your revenue as water pouring into a two-chamber pitcher: the first chamber—the salary—fills to a level the IRS deems reasonable for someone with your skills and workload, and the overflow drips into the second chamber—profit—which you can pour into personal savings without soaking it in self-employment tax. If you clear forty thousand dollars in profit and decide that twenty-eight thousand is a fair salary, you save roughly two-thousand dollars in payroll taxes, a sum that compounds nicely in a retirement account or pays for next year's sabbatical airfare. The IRS watches this pitcher closely, so lowballing salary to a token amount invites penalties; to stay safe, benchmark against industry surveys, keep records of hours worked, and document how you arrived at the salary figure, like explaining your grading rubric to an inquisitive student.

Setting up an LLC is simpler than writing a syllabus, though both benefit from clear objectives and deadline reminders. First, you choose a state—often where you live and work—to file articles of organization, paying a fee that ranges from fifty dollars in Kentucky to eight-hundred in California; some professors pick Delaware or Wyoming for favorable laws, but if you consult primarily in your home state, registering locally avoids foreign-entity paperwork. Next, you draft an operating agreement, even if you are the sole owner, because banks and potential collaborators may request it, and because spelling out management rules now avoids future headaches if you bring on grad-student co-owners or sell the business. Then you obtain an Employer Identification Number from the IRS website, a process faster than ordering coffee on a mobile app, and you open a dedicated business checking account to quarantine income and expenses. Finally, if you plan to hire research assistants or pay yourself a salary under S-Corp status, you register for state payroll tax accounts, which sounds daunting but typically involves a few online forms. These steps transform your side gig into a toddler with its own Social Security card and piggy bank, distinct from your household finances, which simplifies bookkeeping come April and strengthens your liability shield.

Electing S-Corp status is like adding a turbocharger to your LLC engine—it boosts efficiency but requires regular maintenance lest the engine seize. You file IRS Form 2553 within two months and fifteen days of the LLC's formation date or any future tax year; miss that window and you can request late election relief, but better to mark your calendar and avoid groveling. Once elected, you must run payroll for yourself, issuing W-2s, withholding taxes, and remitting them quarterly, either through a service like Gusto or with your university's payroll office if they allow faculty moonlighting entities; skipping payroll is the number-one reason S-Corps get audited and penalties mushroom. Year-end brings Form 1120-S, the corporate return that flows into your personal return via a K-1, a document many professors first encounter with the same trepidation students feel opening their first bluebook exam. To keep administrative load reasonable, I recommend S-Corp election only when net profit consistently exceeds thirty-five to forty thousand dollars, because below that the tax savings rarely offset payroll service fees and accountant billable hours. Like upgrading from public transit to car ownership, the convenience shines at scale but not if you drive only once a month.

A real-life example grounds these numbers: Dr. Chen, a computer-science associate professor, earns one-hundred-and-twenty thousand at her university and an additional fifty thousand advising two startups. For the first two years she reported the side income as sole-prop profit, paying roughly seven-and-a-half thousand in self-employment tax on top of federal and state income tax. Her CPA suggested forming Chen Consulting LLC and electing S-Corp status; they set her salary at thirty-five thousand, leaving fifteen thousand as profit distribution, which saved about two-and-a-quarter thousand dollars annually in payroll tax while costing one thousand in payroll and filing fees, netting a twelve-hundred-dollar gain plus stronger liability protection. Over five years that saving built a down payment on an investment property she and her spouse purchased as a retirement nest egg. Dr. Chen says the best part is psychological: the LLC's separate bank card keeps her from buying office gadgets on personal amnesia, forcing mindful spending that clarified her profit margins.

Liability protection, while not absolute, is the LLC's signature feature and plays out like wearing a lab coat and goggles in a chemistry demonstration—accidents can still happen, but protective gear reduces burns. If a corporate client sues over advice that caused a product delay, the plaintiff must pierce the LLC veil to reach your personal assets, a hurdle they cannot clear unless you co-mingled funds or committed fraud. Keeping meticulous records—separate bank accounts, signed contracts under the entity's name, and documented meetings—strengthens the veil the way double-stitched gloves protect better than single-layer ones. University indemnification typically covers activities within your appointment, but outside work often falls in a gray zone; an LLC fills that gap the way travel insurance covers your luggage on conference trips. Remember that professional liability insurance, or errors-and-omissions coverage, can layer atop the LLC like adding a face shield over goggles, further reducing legal splashback; premiums for academics range from five-hundred to fifteen-hundred dollars annually depending on specialty and revenue.

Choosing between an LLC taxed as a sole prop and one electing S-Corp status resembles selecting between a reliable sedan and a hybrid version of the same model: both get you to campus but the hybrid uses fuel more efficiently, provided you drive enough miles to justify the higher purchase price. In lower-revenue years, you may skip the S-Corp and file Schedule C; when revenue spikes thanks to a bestseller textbook or a flurry of corporate workshops, you can elect S-Corp beginning the next tax year. There's no penalty for toggling once, but flipping back and forth annually raises eyebrows at the IRS; aim for stability unless circumstances dramatically shift. Some professors form two entities—one LLC for royalty income that requires little labor and another S-Corp for consulting—though maintaining dual books doubles costs and complexity, so weigh simplicity against optimization. A quick litmus test: if you cannot explain your entity structure to a grad student in under three minutes, it is probably too complex for your lifestyle.

State tax rules can tilt the equation: Tennessee imposes a franchise and excise tax on LLCs regardless of profit, while Texas levies a gross-receipts-based margin tax above certain thresholds. Professors in high-fee states might delay formalization or register in a different state if most clients are remote, but beware nexus laws that treat income as sourced where services are performed, not where the LLC resides. Multi-state complexity resembles juggling office hours across time zones—doable, but only with a robust calendar and clear boundaries. Local licenses add another layer; some cities require a professional-service permit even for home-based businesses, and fines for noncompliance can wipe out your first speaking fee. A quick call to your municipal clerk, akin to asking the librarian before removing a rare book, saves headaches later.

Bookkeeping under an LLC or S-Corp need not devour evenings if you adopt cloud accounting software and weekly routines as casually as grading homework over coffee. Connect your business bank and credit card feeds to categorize expenses—software subscriptions, conference airfare, home-office percentage of internet—so your Profit & Loss statement stays updated and ready for quarterly estimated tax payments. Reconciling monthly ensures you catch duplicates or personal expenses that slipped through, maintaining the liability veil and smoothing audit defenses. Paying yourself through owner draws (LLC) or payroll (S-Corp) on a regular schedule mimics university paycycles and helps household budgeting, preventing the feast-or-famine swings that can stress family finances. Finally, store digital receipts in cloud folders named by year and vendor, an organizational habit that beats the shoebox method and delights accountants come tax season.

Speaking of taxes, estimated payments under an S-Corp shift from personal quarterly vouchers to monthly or semi-weekly payroll deposits for withheld taxes plus quarterly corporate estimates on profits, a rhythm change similar to switching from semester to quarter teaching calendars. Your payroll service calculates federal and state deposits and issues W-2s in January, sparing you the spreadsheet acrobatics of manual calculations. Corporate profits flow to you via a K-1, prompting quarterly estimated tax vouchers on your personal side, so set calendar alerts to avoid surprises. Some professors automate savings into a tax account, treating it like a lab fee: money earmarked for equipment may not fund pizza, and tax funds should never buy conference swag. When cash flow surges, bump estimates mid-year to dodge underpayment penalties, a strategy akin to offering extra office hours before exams to avoid student panic.

University policies on external entities vary and must be honored like IRB protocols. Many schools cap outside work at one-day-per-week averaged across the academic year, requiring disclosure forms and sometimes conflict-of-interest committee review if clients overlap with your grant funding. An LLC does not exempt you from these rules; rather, it clarifies boundaries and provides documentation to show that consulting income is separate from sponsored research. Some professors negotiate course releases in exchange for bringing large contracts through the university's research foundation, but that shifts revenue to the institution and may reduce personal earnings while adding administrative overhead. Evaluate whether routing work through your entity or the university best aligns with your goals, recognizing that legacy-building and student support might trump sheer net pay in certain projects, just as co-authoring with students sometimes outweighs solo publications in tenure dossiers.

Retirement planning is an unsung hero of entity formation because an S-Corp enables higher tax-advantaged contributions through a Solo 401(k) or SEP-IRA compared to a sole prop. The Solo 401(k) allows both employee deferrals and employer profit-sharing contributions, letting a high-earning professor sock away over sixty thousand dollars pre-tax if profit supports it. That contribution not only trims current taxable income but compounds for future sabbaticals or retirement adventures. Your university retirement plan's limits are separate, but combined contributions can trigger the overall employee cap, so coordinate with your benefits office and CPA to avoid excess contributions that require messy corrections. Think of retirement buckets like nested Matryoshka dolls: each fits snugly inside the next, but forcing one too big into the wrong slot cracks the wood.

Health-care deductions intersect subtly with entity choice: an S-Corp owner who pays personal health insurance can deduct premiums above the line, but only if the S-Corp reimburses or pays them and the cost does not exceed S-Corp wages, yet another reason not to set salary artificially low. If your spouse's employer covers your family, the deduction moot point, but note that health reimbursement arrangements or QSEHRAs can let the S-Corp reimburse individual marketplace premiums, transforming a personal expense into a business deduction under certain rules. Consult a benefits-savvy accountant before implementing, because nondiscrimination clauses apply like library silence rules: break them and everyone suffers. Disability insurance and professional liability premiums similarly become business deductions, stretching each consulting dollar further toward net profit.

Exit strategy may seem premature when your side gig is a fledgling, but entities shine brightest when you plan beyond today's lecture. Should you decide to sell your curriculum materials to a publisher or merge your analytics consulting with a larger firm, having an established LLC with clean books speeds due diligence and boosts valuation, the way well-organized lecture notes make sabbatical handovers painless. Even winding down is smoother: dissolving an LLC involves formal filings that close tax accounts and protect you from future claims, whereas a sole prop's end often leaves lingering tax IDs and clients unclear about liability. Estate planning benefits too; ownership shares in an LLC can pass to heirs via a living trust, maintaining continuity if your teenage daughter wants to inherit the family data-science brand you built from your basement. View entity creation as planting an oak tree: you relish shade today but its true strength appears decades later.

Throughout my years advising faculty entrepreneurs, the happiest ones treat their LLC or S-Corp like a teaching assistant—supportive, organized, and responsible—rather than a capricious overlord demanding late-night attention. They schedule quarterly finance retreats, sometimes at a campus café, to review profit, adjust salary, and forecast upcoming projects, much the way curriculum committees evaluate program outcomes. They keep a running document of frequently asked questions—Why did I choose this salary? Which states require nexus filings? Who signs the engagement letter?—so future them can solve puzzles without digging through old emails. They enlist professionals—CPA, attorney, payroll service—the way they assemble a dissertation committee, selecting advisors who challenge assumptions and keep the work on track. And they remember the core goal: to translate academic expertise into societal value while generating fair compensation and shielding personal finances, a mission as noble as any research agenda.

At the end of the day, forming an LLC or electing S-Corp status is neither a magic wand nor a bureaucratic nightmare; it is a strategic tool, like statistical software or a well-constructed lit-review matrix, whose utility depends on thoughtful application. Run the numbers, weigh the risks, consult experts, and revisit your decision annually as revenue, regulations, and life circumstances evolve. When done right, your entity becomes an ally that handles tax efficiency and liability containment in the background, freeing you to focus on what drew you to academia: curiosity, mentorship, and the joy of sharing ideas beyond campus walls. Whether you dream of retiring early to write novels, funding a student scholarship from consulting proceeds, or simply paying for family adventures without draining your 403(b), the correct business structure can turn those aspirations into a sustainable, well-protected reality. And that, perhaps, is the most gratifying lesson: by embracing entrepreneurship wisely, professors need not choose between ivory-tower ideals and real-world reward—they can savor the best of both, cup of coffee in hand, confident that their intellectual labor and their personal finances are now aligned and empowered for the journeys ahead.

Chapter 26: Travel Reimbursements & Per Diem, Keeping Receipts, Avoiding Audits, Maximizing Deductions

Travel reimbursement rules may look like dense legalese, but at their core they are simply the ground rules for telling a credible money story: you took a trip for work, you spent real dollars, and you want to shift those costs from your personal wallet to the organization or the tax return. Think of it like recounting a weekend camping adventure to a friend—you describe where you went, why you went, and what supplies you used, and your friend trusts you because the story hangs together. Auditors function like that skeptical friend who raises an eyebrow if your fuel receipt predates the trip or your tent rental appears twice, so building a clear, chronological narrative is half the battle. Start each journey by writing down the business purpose in plain English—"presented paper on marine plastics at OceanCon 2025"—because purpose frames every dollar of expense. Keep that sentence at the top of your folder, digital or paper, so anyone reviewing the packet can grasp context before diving into receipts. A purposeful story converts random numbers into justified investments and earns reimbursements with far less friction.

Per diem, the government's daily meal and incidentals allowance, operates like an all-inclusive resort wristband: once you have it, you may dine within the resort's limits without signing a check for every sandwich. Instead of itemizing each muffin and latte, you receive a fixed dollar amount based on city and date, and as long as you remain below that cap, no receipts for meals are required. The upside is simplicity—no more fishing wadded coffee slips from your pocket—and protection against lost documentation that could otherwise disqualify a deduction. The downside surfaces if you are a thrifty eater in a high-rate city like NewYork, because the flat allowance can feel like fireworks money burning a hole in your pocket. Wise travelers compare the per diem to expected actual costs before choosing, just as savvy shoppers compare an unlimited data plan to pay-as-you-go. Remember that auditors do not begrudge you the full per diem as long as you were eligible; what triggers concern is switching methods mid-trip or mixing per diem with receipt-based meals without clear segregation.

Reimbursements based on actual expenses are closer to a pay-as-you-go taxi meter, ticking upward with every fare and requiring proof of each segment. This model suits researchers who snack lightly but spend heavily on specialized lab shipping or field permits, enabling precise matching of reimbursement to cost. Under actuals, the IRS demands contemporaneous documentation—generally a dated receipt showing amount, vendor, and what was purchased—so tossing your Uber email into a dedicated folder as soon as it lands in your inbox keeps you compliant. Most universities set a floor—often $75—below which receipts for meals or incidentals are optional, but auditors can still ask why a lunch was unusually expensive, so jotting a note that you covered a collaborator's entrée can pre-empt awkward questions. Decide early whether your trip will run on per diem or actuals, because hybrid accounting complicates both storytelling and spreadsheets. When in doubt, ask your grants officer; they care less about penny chasing and more about consistency that stands up to federal scrutiny.

Receipts are the breadcrumbs that lead auditors back to the truth, and losing them is like letting pigeons eat the trail before anyone verifies your route. Old-school travelers tape paper slips to a yellowing ledger, but a smartphone camera or a dedicated scanning app such as Adobe Scan creates a PDF within seconds, reducing the chances of coffee stains wiping out your defense. Make scanning a muscle memory: board the plane, snap the boarding pass; pay hotel bill, snap the folio; order taxi, screenshot the fare summary. Store images in cloud folders named by trip and date so you can retrieve them even if your phone meets a watery fate. Digital receipts not only survive coffee spills but also feed directly into expense software, saving hours of manual data entry. Think of the phone camera as an umbrella: you may not predict when the compliance rain will fall, but having it handy keeps you dry.

Mileage logs for personal vehicles seem tedious until you realize they convert your odometer into a cash-back license plate. The IRS sets a cents-per-mile rate each year—58.5¢ for 2025—covering fuel, maintenance, and depreciation, and to claim it you need a contemporaneous log showing date, destination, business purpose, and miles driven. Apps such as MileIQ run quietly in the background, auto-tracking trips the way a FitBit counts steps, and asking you to swipe right for business, left for personal. If you prefer pen and paper, a small notebook in the glove compartment coupled with the discipline of logging before you exit the car can work just as well. Remember that commuting miles from home to your regular office are not deductible; only incremental distances created by a business errand count. Treat the log like a lab notebook: accurate, timely, and immune to creative fiction.

The business-purpose narrative extends beyond the headline to every line item—why did you take that taxi, who was at dinner, and what agenda did you cover? Brief notes such as "Taxi from hotel to client site for 9a.m. meeting" or "Dinner with graduate student co-investigator to plan field protocol" meet IRS standards and jog your memory months later. Without purpose statements, receipts morph into numbers divorced from justification, tempting auditors to disallow them. Think of purpose as metadata on a digital photo; without it, the image loses context and searchable value. Habitual note-taking feels awkward at first, but voice-memos converted to text can streamline the process, and some expense apps prompt you automatically so you never leave a blank. Consistency turns explanations from an afterthought into the natural companion of every transaction.

Foreign travel introduces exchange rates, VAT, and multilingual receipts, but the same storytelling principles apply: document, convert, and justify. Credit-card statements showing both local and U.S. dollar amounts satisfy conversion rules, although attaching a daily treasury rate printout shields you if the card statement arrives after reimbursement closes. VAT refunds, common in Europe, belong to the granting agency or employer if they reimbursed the expense, so track any refunds like overdue library books you must return. When local vendors email invoices in French or Japanese, annotate the PDF with a brief English translation—"laboratory glassware"—to aid reviewers who last studied that language in high school. Traveling researchers often tape a small envelope inside their field notebook and slide cash receipts into it at day's end, ensuring nothing vanishes into damp backpacks or rental-car consoles. Treat currency conversion like lab unit conversion: methodical, documented, and defensible.

Advances, those small loans issued ahead of travel, feel like a parental allowance: helpful, but requiring an end-of-summer reckoning. Many finance offices give you ten to thirty days post-trip to reconcile, and missing the deadline can trigger payroll deductions or taxable income classification. Keep the advance in a separate checking sub-account or even a labeled envelope so it never blends with personal funds, and draw from it only for trip costs; this segregation simplifies the final accounting. If you spend less than the advance, return the surplus promptly and attach a copy of the deposit receipt to your expense report to prove closure. Failure to settle timely is a red flag akin to unreturned library books—one incident may pass, but multiple infractions invite heavier oversight. Advances work best when treated like borrowed lab equipment: record it, use it carefully, and return it in good order.

Combining personal days with business travel can slash airfare yet complicate deductions, a bit like adding a family detour to a conference road trip. The IRS allows transportation costs to remain fully deductible if the trip is primarily for business, defined by the majority of days being business activity, but hotel and meals on purely personal days are not. Keep a calendar showing which days were conference sessions, client visits, or fieldwork versus museum tours or beach lounging; this visual proves the predominance of business purpose. Split receipts where necessary—hotel bill lines for weekend nights may become nondeductible, while weekday nights stay eligible—and annotate accordingly. For airfares that are the same price regardless of extra days, the full ticket might remain deductible, but document fare comparisons at booking to back up the claim. Think of personal extensions as side quests in a video game: enjoyable, but kept separate from the main mission to preserve score integrity.

Spousal or companion travel deductions are restricted unless the person is an employee whose presence serves a bona fide business purpose, not merely moral support. A spouse who co-presents research data or manages equipment setup can qualify; one who tours wineries while you lecture cannot. To claim, add your spouse to the trip budget as you would a research assistant: include role description, deliverables, and any compensation. Airfare and fifty percent of meals become deductible if documented, but auditors scrutinize such claims, so gather conference programs listing your spouse's session or letters from clients affirming their role. When only your room cost remains equal with or without the spouse—think one king bed versus two queens—no allocation is necessary, but meals must still be split. Treat the deduction like a group-project grade: credit only valid contributors.

Grant-funded per diem rates sometimes differ from federal GSA tables, especially for international aid agencies that impose austerity caps. Always defer to the lowest allowable rate unless the grant explicitly authorizes a higher standard; overbilling a grant is tantamount to mischarging taxpayers. If university policy is stricter than the grant, you must follow campus rules; if the grant is stricter, the grant prevails, making policy a floor, not a ceiling. Discrepancies can be managed by blending per diem and actuals—perhaps actual lodging within a capped hotel rate and per diem meals—but obtain pre-approval in writing. Grant officers view deviations the same way IRB boards view protocol changes: fine when justified and documented, perilous if hidden. Safeguard your reputation by flagging anomalies early rather than hoping finance ignores them.

Meals and incidentals (M&I) within per diem often puzzle travelers who wonder whether their morning latte counts as "incidental" or "meal." The IRS lumps small expenses like tips, dry-cleaning, and phone calls into incidentals, but generous GSA tables roll incidentals into the same dollar figure as meals, meaning you simply spend the pot as you see fit. Some universities break the M&I rate into breakfast, lunch, and dinner percentages—25, 30, 45, respectively—and require deduction of the relevant segment if a meal is provided by the conference. Attaching the conference agenda showing hosted lunches satisfies this offset requirement, proving you did not double-dip. Imagine you receive a fixed box of puzzle pieces; if the conference supplies one piece, you must remove it before assembling your reimbursement puzzle. The math may feel nitpicky, yet these rules maintain public trust that funds support actual nutritional needs, not gourmet indulgence.

Hotel taxes, resort fees, and tourism levies can stack like hidden layers in a mille-feuille pastry, inflating nightly costs beyond the advertised rate. Most grants allow reimbursement of mandatory taxes but not optional add-ons such as spa access or minibar raids, so ask the desk to separate charges at checkout. Snapping a photo of the folio before departing prevents lost documentation and captures the final itemization, which sometimes differs from the reservation email. If a hotel insists on a resort fee covering gym access you never use, the fee remains reimbursable because it is compulsory, yet note "mandatory fee" on the receipt to silence queries. When foreign VAT is recoverable, some universities use third-party services to reclaim it, so flag VAT amounts separately to maximize institutional refunds. Treat these taxes like substitute teaching duties: unavoidable but trackable, and sometimes they come back as credit if processed correctly.

Airfare selection balances cost containment with human wellbeing; red-eyes in cramped economy may tick the lowest-fare box but sabotage next-day presentations. Many policies allow premium economy or business class when flying internationally or when preparing to present within hours of landing, provided justification accompanies the expense. Save screenshots of fare comparisons at booking time, because airlines' dynamic pricing mutates daily, and auditors respect contemporaneous evidence over hindsight estimates. If you upgrade using personal miles, you may still claim the coach fare as reimbursement, but disclose the upgrade to avoid perceived double benefits. Conversely, accepting a free seat from a corporate partner could be a taxable gift, so coordinate with HR before finalizing. Navigating airfare rules resembles selecting research equipment: cheapest is not always best if it jeopardizes results.

Ground transportation options—ride-sharing, public transit, rental cars—offer flexibility, but rate caps and preferred-vendor agreements constrain choices. Universities often favor ride-sharing for trips under thirty miles and rentals for longer hauls, basing the decision on total cost including parking. Document comparison screenshots or map mileage routes to prove your choice minimized expenses consistent with policy. Fuel receipts for rental cars must match the rental period, and skipping the refill forces the agency's premium pricing, which auditors may disallow, so schedule a gas stop on the way to return the vehicle. Keep toll receipts too; many state highways no longer issue paper tickets, so the rental's toll summary or a Transponder statement serves as proof. Treat your transportation decision like selecting statistical software: choose the tool that fits the task, price it responsibly, and document the rationale.

Conference registration fees paid months in advance sometimes blur into travel costs, but classifying them separately clarifies budget categories and prevents double counting if the sponsoring society offers a refund for presenters. When a fee bundle includes meals, list the included meals on your expense report so you remember to deduct them from per diem. If the fee provides digital proceedings, note that as a non-travel research expense, charging it to the appropriate grant line. Early-bird discounts save money but risk non-refundable losses if travel is later canceled; trip insurance or refundable tickets mitigate this risk and may be reimbursable if allowed by policy. Think of registration like booking lab reagents—you balance early discounts against the possibility of protocol changes.

Audit triggers resemble allergy symptoms—subtle at first then suddenly debilitating if ignored. Patterns such as round-number receipts, identical taxi fares on different days, or meal costs exceeding 75percent of per diem raise software flags. Splitting a hotel room among five researchers without clear cost allocation or submitting expenses months late also invites scrutiny. Good faith back-up—conference schedules, shared-room letters, and timely submission—functions like antihistamine, calming the system. The ultimate defense is transparency: when a cost seems odd, attach an explanatory note rather than hoping the reviewer won't notice. Auditors are humans trained to spot anomalies, and proactive context converts potential charges into verified, allowable costs.

Tax deductions for unreimbursed travel disappeared for employees under the 2017 Tax Cuts and Jobs Act, but self-employed faculty using LLCs or S-Corps still deduct travel tied to their side gigs. Keep dual documentation streams—one for employer-paid trips, one for business-entity trips—to avoid mixing apples and oranges. If your university partially reimburses you and your consulting entity covers the rest, allocate expenses proportionally and keep copies of both reports to substantiate the split. Remember that meals remain fifty-percent deductible, though Congress briefly allowed one-hundred-percent deduction for restaurant meals in 2021–2022; always check the current year's rules. Treat these deductions like selective herbicide: apply only where weeds actually grow, or risk killing the lawn.

Creating a repeatable system turns travel accounting from a chaotic scavenger hunt into a smooth assembly line. Block fifteen minutes at day's end on every trip to scan receipts, name files, and jot purpose notes before fatigue erases memory. Use auto-forward rules in your email to route booking confirmations to an "Expenses-Pending" folder, so nothing falls through inbox cracks. Sync your calendar with expense software so meeting titles populate business-purpose fields automatically, slashing manual typing. Quarterly, reconcile credit-card statements against your expense ledger, spotting duplicates or omissions while memories remain fresh. These rituals resemble weekly lab maintenance: unglamorous but essential to prevent contamination that could ruin months of data.

In the grand scheme of academic life, travel receipts may seem mundane compared to grants won or papers published, yet mastering them safeguards the funding that powers those achievements and defends your integrity.

Every boarding pass scanned, every per diem rate double-checked, and every note about who shared dinner with you fortifies a transparent chain of evidence that can withstand scrutiny. That peace of mind frees cognitive bandwidth for science, teaching, and mentoring rather than midnight hunts for a two-month-old taxi slip. When you view travel accounting as storytelling—not bureaucratic drudgery but a narrative of responsible stewardship—compliance becomes a natural extension of scholarly rigor. And the next time an auditor knocks, you can greet them with the calm confidence of a researcher who knows every data point is cataloged, every method documented, and every conclusion defensible, both in the lab and in the ledger.

Chapter 27: IRS Red Flags for Faculty, Common Audit Triggers and How to Stay Compliant

Faculty life offers a buffet of income streams—salaries, summer stipends, consulting fees, book royalties, honoraria—and the IRS knows it, which is why professors sometimes land on the agency's watch-list even when they think everything is tidy. The first red flag is underreported side income: every 1099 your publisher, conference, or corporate client files must match your return exactly, so resist the urge to delay reporting a late-arriving form. Picture the IRS database as a giant matching game of index cards; if your deck is missing one, the computer immediately sets it aside for human review. To stay compliant, keep a spreadsheet that logs every contract or speaking gig the day you sign it, then reconcile the sheet against the pile of tax documents that trickles in each January. That five-minute habit saves you the headache of an automated notice months later and preserves your coffee budget for something tastier than audit stress.

A close cousin to unreported income is the "hobby loss" trigger, which pings when a professor shows consulting revenue year after year but never a profit. The IRS expects a bona fide business to break even three out of five years, so chronic losses look less like entrepreneurship and more like an expensive pastime. Imagine a student who keeps dropping a course yet claims to be mastering the material—eventually the advisor asks tough questions. To avoid hobby classification, document a clear profit motive:

keep a business plan, record marketing efforts, and save emails where clients negotiate fees. When profit proves elusive, scale back expenses or raise rates rather than letting red ink pile up like ungraded exams.

Exaggerated home-office deductions also attract attention because the line between personal and professional space blurs when your study doubles as a guestroom. The IRS rule is strict: the area must be used regularly and exclusively for business, not just occasionally for grading papers. Think of it as reserving a lab bench—you can't stash your groceries there on weekends and still call it research space. Measure the square footage precisely, calculate the percentage of your home it represents, and keep dated photos in case an auditor asks for proof. If the room doubles as a nursery during sabbatical, don't claim it that year; flexibility now beats penalties later.

Travel expenses raise eyebrows when per-diem rates seem lavish or destinations align suspiciously with vacation hot spots. The IRS compares your deductions to GSA tables and peer norms, so a five-star beachfront hotel during a regional conference sparks questions. Picture an auditor scrolling conference agendas while looking at your resort receipt—if the dots don't connect, you'll be invited to explain. Maintain a detailed itinerary with session schedules, meeting notes, and evidence that the hotel was the conference venue or the lowest practical cost. When tacking personal days onto business travel, prorate lodging and meals to reflect only the work portion.

Large charitable contributions relative to income are another audit magnet because generosity sometimes masks inflated deductions. The moment your donations exceed about 20percent of adjusted gross income, the IRS computer kicks out a query for substantiation. Treat every gift receipt like a research citation: include date, amount, and a statement that no goods or services were received in exchange. Non-cash donations such as lab equipment or books valued over five thousand dollars need a formal appraisal, not a best guess scribbled on the receipt. By documenting rigorously, you turn potential suspicion into a non-event.

Foreign bank accounts and research stipends paid overseas trigger

Form8938 and FBAR filing requirements; ignoring them is like leaving a section blank on a grant application—reviewers notice. If you spend a semester on exchange in Germany and open a local bank account for daily expenses, the highest annual balance may well cross the reporting threshold. File the forms even if the account earns no interest; penalties for omission dwarf the hassle of disclosure. Keep copies of account statements in your tax file and note currency conversions, ensuring every euro converts consistently with official rates. Transparency transforms an audit risk into routine paperwork.

Misreporting graduate-student wages can also raise flags, particularly when stipends are wrongly labeled as independent-contractor payments. Universities treat students as employees for payroll tax and FICA exemptions; paying them through your LLC to skirt withholdings looks like misclassification. Comparable to labeling a seminar as lab credit when it's clearly a lecture, the mismatch stands out. To stay safe, run all graduate worker payments through official payroll channels, even if that means higher bureaucracy. Your future self will thank you when the IRS passes by your return without a second glance.

Overly aggressive retirement contributions beyond IRS limits ripple onto Form5329 and often pop audit alarms. Professors juggling 403(b) deferrals, 457(b) plans, and side-gig Solo401(k)s sometimes exceed the combined employee cap, unaware that different buckets share one ceiling. Imagine stuffing too many books into a locker: the door won't shut, and someone will notice. Use a year-end checklist to total all deferrals and adjust December paychecks if needed. Excess contributions can be withdrawn by April15 to dodge penalties, but only if you spot the overage in time.

Rental property losses can offset only limited amounts of ordinary income unless you qualify as a real-estate professional, a status few faculty truly meet. Taking full losses while logging minimal landlord hours is like claiming lab credit without attending sessions—auditors are skeptical. Maintain a time log of property management activities and be prepared to show tenancy ads, maintenance invoices, and mileage logs. Alternatively, consider electing to aggregate rental and personal real-estate services if you genuinely clock the hours. Honesty in classification steers you clear of harsh recapture taxes later.

High medical-expense deductions relative to income can appear suspicious, especially when claimed without proper documentation. Save every invoice, prescription, and proof of payment because auditors request them more frequently at elevated deduction levels. Think of it as keeping raw data for a published study—you never know which detail a peer reviewer will question. Remember that only expenses exceeding 7.5percent of AGI are deductible, so double-check math before filing. Electronic health portals can export statements, providing an easy audit shield.

Underpayment of estimated taxes creates a trail of interest notices that sometimes snowball into audits, much like late assignment submissions attract a professor's scrutiny. Side-gig earnings, stock sales, and royalty spikes require quarterly estimates using Form1040-ES or an automatic payroll increase. Set calendar reminders for April, June, September, and January so you never miss a due date, and adjust mid-year when income surges. Meeting the safe-harbor thresholds—100percent of prior-year tax or 90percent of current-year—locks the IRS out of underpayment penalties. Consistent, timely payments paint you as a compliant taxpayer rather than a target.

Math errors and mismatched Social Security numbers sound trivial, but they are leading causes of correspondence audits because computers flag them instantly. Review returns line-by-line like proofreading a manuscript, or better yet, use reputable software to catch arithmetic slips. If you hand off records to a preparer, ask for a draft copy well before filing so you can confirm names, numbers, and faculty ID spelling quirks. A return without typos is like a grant proposal without formatting errors—basic, but still impressive. Neatness counts more with the IRS than most realize.

Claiming the American Opportunity or Lifetime Learning Credits for multiple years beyond eligibility draws scrutiny, particularly when children age out of college. Keep a simple grid of each dependent, credit years used, and 1098-T forms received, preventing accidental double dipping. Think of it as tracking grading curves: once a student finishes the course, you can't keep awarding points. Providing the IRS with clear tuition statements and proof of payment extinguishes most objections quickly. Stay vigilant when kids transfer, take gap years, or pursue graduate programs because eligibility rules shift.

Inaccurate basis calculations on stock sales—from university retirement plan conversions or employee-stock-purchase programs—can overstate losses or understate gains, tempting audits. Broker 1099-B forms sometimes leave basis blank for older holdings, putting the burden on you. Keep trade confirmations and annual statements the way you archive syllabi—organized and accessible. Matching sale proceeds with correct basis neutralizes suspicion and reduces capital-gain tax surprises. When unsure, consult your broker before filing, not after an IRS letter arrives.

Using round numbers throughout ScheduleC or ScheduleA screams estimation and triggers human review, because real life rarely ends in zeros. Record expenses down to the cent, or at least the dollar, just as you would list lab measurements with precision. Round figures suggest you back-filled numbers rather than logging actual costs. If you honestly paid exactly $7,000 in rent, note the lease agreement in your file; otherwise expect questions. Precision shows respect for the process and defuses red flags before they wave.

Large refundable credits, especially earned income credits, seldom apply to tenured faculty but may surface when family income dips due to sabbatical. The IRS monitors EIC claims closely for fraud, so ensure your earned income and investment income meet thresholds. If a sabbatical grant pushes you above limits, skip the credit to avoid clawbacks. Keeping explanatory sabbatical letters and grant documentation handy helps resolve any queries. Honesty about income composition is the safest route.

Failing to file or misreporting FormT for tuition and fees when you distribute scholarship funds or tuition reductions to graduate assistants attracts scrutiny, because the IRS cross-checks FormT with students' education credits. Work with your bursar to ensure accurate reporting of qualified expenses and adjustments. Retain scholarship award letters and distribution logs to substantiate the figures. It's akin to double-checking bibliographies in co-authored papers so references line up. Clean coordination keeps both you and your students free from unpleasant surprises.

Improper classification of personal expenses—such as family cell phones, grocery bills, or personal Amazon purchases—through your LLC or S-Corp is a bright flashing light. The IRS expects a clear boundary between business and household costs, much like IRB panels expect consent forms separate from data collection sheets. Use dedicated business accounts and cards, reimburse the company for any accidental personal charges, and annotate unusual transactions immediately. An annual review meeting with your accountant serves as quality control, catching leaks before they flood an audit. Accountability beats scrambling to justify charges retroactively.

Failure to file required informational returns—1099-NEC for freelance editors or W-9 collection from guest speakers—draws penalties and signals sloppy bookkeeping. When you pay more than six hundred dollars to an independent contractor, file the form by the January deadline or face steep fines. Keep a contractor checklist like a lab-safety protocol: collect W-9s, note services rendered, and verify taxpayer IDs. Electronic filing tools make the process nearly painless, so no excuses. Proper paperwork demonstrates professionalism to both contractors and the IRS.

Finally, ignoring state-tax nexus rules when consulting across borders leaves a trail of inconsistent filings that state auditors trade like juicy gossip with the IRS. If you earn income in multiple states—say, virtual workshops for California districts while living in Illinois—research whether you must file non-resident returns. Use calendar flags to note days physically worked in each state and keep invoices tagged by client location. Think of state taxes as co-authors on your financial manuscript: they need their share of credit, and omitting them invites disputes. Complying with varying thresholds may feel tedious, but keeping ahead of state notices prevents multilayered headaches down the road.

Staying compliant boils down to one principle familiar to any scholar: meticulous record-keeping paired with honest intent. When every deduction has a story, every income stream a matching form, and every claim documentation to back it up, audits shrink from ominous thunderclouds to routine drizzle. Practicing these habits may feel dull compared with research breakthroughs, yet they protect the resources that fund those discoveries. By treating taxes with the same intellectual rigor you apply to your discipline, you transform potential IRS red flags into green lights for a worry-free academic career. After all, the goal is to spend your office hours mentoring students and advancing knowledge, not fending off auditors—though if they do call, you'll be ready with folders labeled, receipts scanned, and a clear narrative that lets them walk away satisfied and silent.

Part IV · Growing & Protecting Wealth Through the Career Arc

Part IV explores the financial evolution faculty members experience as their careers mature, responsibilities grow, and income often reaches its peak. This section provides a roadmap for turning mid- to late-career earnings into lasting wealth, while simultaneously guarding against the financial risks that can derail decades of progress. It covers topics such as advanced retirement planning, estate strategies, real estate decisions, insurance essentials, and integrating side income or consulting ventures into a long-term plan. Readers will also learn how to navigate big-picture questions—like when to scale back, how to exit university life gracefully, and how to balance legacy goals with current lifestyle. Through relatable examples and practical guidance, this part empowers faculty to shift from accumulation to preservation with clarity, confidence, and purpose.

Chapter 28: Investment Basics for Scholars, Asset Allocation, Index Funds, and Rebalancing

Investing can feel like stepping into a noisy trading pit full of cryptic jargon, yet the fundamentals remain surprisingly straightforward once you translate them into everyday language. Imagine that every dollar you earn is a diligent graduate assistant: you can let it idle in the break room earning nothing but stale coffee, or you can assign it research projects that grow its knowledge—and your wealth—over time. Scholars already understand compound intellectual growth; financial compounding works the same way, with gains building on prior gains if given enough semesters to run. Your paycheck covers today's needs, but investments power sabbaticals, late-career flexibility, and a dignified retirement. The sooner those graduate-assistant dollars start their research in the financial markets, the more prolific their publication record becomes on your balance sheet.

Most professors rely heavily on a single income source—the university—and that concentration risk mirrors a lab dependent on one funding agency: great when things flow, nerve-wracking when budgets tighten. Diversifying income streams through investing spreads risk the way interdisciplinary grants hedge against any single rejection. Cash in a savings account earns safety but barely any return, like a paper stuck in a desk drawer never submitted for peer review. By moving a portion into productive assets—stocks, bonds, and real estate funds—you invite the broader economy to co-author your financial future. Accepting measured risk is the admission ticket to higher expected returns, and understanding how different assets behave is the syllabus for that course.

Risk and reward operate like the tension between publishing speed and journal prestige: high-impact venues demand patience and resilience, while lower-tier outlets provide quicker but smaller citations. Stocks historically deliver higher average returns than bonds but carry stomach-churning volatility, meaning their value might drop significantly in any given year. Bonds act more like methodical literature reviews—steady, lower-variability, but unlikely to make headlines. Cash is the lab thermostat: crucial for short-term stability yet offering no intellectual thrill or financial lift. The art of investing lies in mixing these elements so they complement rather than sabotage each other.

Asset allocation is simply the recipe for that mix, expressed as percentages of stocks, bonds, and cash tailored to your goals and nerves. A younger scholar might choose 80percent stocks and 20percent bonds, betting on decades of market participation, whereas a near-retiree could flip that ratio to preserve capital. Think of it as course load selection: an early-stage PhD candidate tackles advanced theory classes, while a finishing student emphasizes dissertation writing and job-market prep. Your allocation should evolve as deadlines—also known as life milestones—approach. The key is choosing a starting mix intentionally instead of drifting into whatever funds the university's default plan assigns.

Stocks represent tiny ownership slices of companies, granting you a claim on their profits and growth. When you buy a share of a broad stock index you effectively supervise a global research team of thousands of firms working day and night. The price of that share bounces with news cycles—earnings reports, political shifts, technological breakthroughs—much like citation counts rise and fall with academic trends. Over long horizons, however, corporate earnings have trended upward because human ingenuity and productivity keep pushing boundaries. By owning stocks you align your wealth with that upward arc of innovation.

Bonds, on the other hand, are IOUs issued by governments and corporations that pay periodic interest and return principal at maturity, functioning like a fixed-term grant that awards predictable disbursements. Because bond issuers promise to repay on set dates, bond prices typically fluctuate less than stocks, offering a stabilizing counterweight during market storms. If stock holdings are the high-risk, high-reward experiments in your financial lab, bonds are the proven protocols that keep funding steady even when flashy projects stall. Yet they are not risk-free: interest-rate changes and issuer defaults can still bite, so diversification within bonds—mixing government, corporate, and international issues—remains wise.

Cash equivalents such as money-market funds and short-term CDs resemble departmental petty cash: handy for near-term expenses, but costly to hoard because inflation quietly erodes purchasing power. Holding three to six months of living costs in an emergency fund shields you from unexpected job gaps or roof leaks, just as a departmental reserve covers equipment repairs. Beyond that buffer, excess idle cash slows overall portfolio growth. By consciously parking only what you genuinely need, you let the remainder hustle in more productive arenas.

Determining personal risk tolerance is both art and self-reflection, akin to choosing between qualitative interviews and quantitative surveys for a research project. One gauge is how you slept during the last market downturn: if headlines cost you hours of shut-eye, you may need a lower stock allocation. Another is time horizon: faculty in their thirties have decades to recover from market dips, whereas those eyeing retirement within five years require more ballast. Risk capacity and risk tolerance must meet in the middle; a long horizon means little if anxiety pushes you to sell at the bottom. Write down an allocation you believe you can stomach, then imagine it dropping 25percent overnight; if that mental exercise triggers panic, tweak until discomfort turns into determined patience.

Once you select an allocation, implementing it with low-cost index funds is like sourcing peer-reviewed datasets instead of reinventing the wheel. Index funds track broad market benchmarks—such as the S&P500 for U.S. large caps or the Bloomberg U.S. Aggregate for bonds—by holding every constituent in proportion, eliminating the guesswork of stock picking.

They charge razor-thin fees, often under 0.05percent, leaving more of your returns in your pocket. Scholars appreciate efficiency, and index funds embody it by capturing market performance without the overhead of star managers who rarely outperform after expenses. They also simplify tracking progress, because fund performance closely mirrors published index data you can verify independently.

Exchange-traded funds, or ETFs, deliver index investing through a security traded like a stock, offering intraday pricing and sometimes lower expense ratios than comparable mutual funds. For buy-and-hold investors the operational differences are minor; what matters is sticking with low-cost, diversified vehicles. Avoid the lure of niche thematic ETFs that promise exposure to trendy sectors—these behave like narrow research topics that fizzle after a brief citation burst. A core holding in a total-market or all-world index fund covers thousands of companies, reducing the impact of any single failure. Simple, broad exposure outperforms fancy packaging over full market cycles.

Many scholars wonder whether they should attempt active management to "beat the market," akin to writing a groundbreaking monograph versus contributing to an established anthology. Evidence shows that consistently outperforming after fees is exceedingly rare, and choosing the managers who will do so in advance is almost impossible. Indexing embraces humility, acknowledging that collective market wisdom sets prices efficiently. By avoiding costly trading and management fees, you secure what the market gives rather than chasing mirages. Your time is better spent refining research than predicting next quarter's winners.

Behavioral pitfalls can derail even sound strategies, as investors are human before they are rational. Confirmation bias, loss aversion, and recency bias tempt you to buy high after euphoria and sell low after crashes, just as scholars sometimes chase fashionable topics at the expense of rigorous inquiry. The antidote is a written investment policy statement outlining your allocation, rebalancing schedule, and performance benchmarks. When fear or greed strike, the document functions like a pre-registered research plan, guiding you back to methodical discipline. Share the statement with a trusted colleague or financial advisor to add accountability.

Setting up the right accounts maximizes tax efficiency and aligns investments with specific goals. Most universities offer 403(b) or 457(b) plans that shelter contributions from immediate taxation, allowing tax-deferred growth similar to grant money in a protected budget line. Traditional IRAs provide another pre-tax option, while Roth IRAs flip the script: you pay taxes upfront but withdraw contributions and growth tax-free in retirement, akin to funding an open-access publication now for perpetual future access. Taxable brokerage accounts, though lacking upfront breaks, offer flexibility and favorable long-term capital-gain rates. The general hierarchy is to max employer match opportunities first, then diversify across account types to hedge future tax-rate uncertainty.

Tax efficiency continues inside the portfolio through asset location—the art of placing tax-heavy bonds in tax-advantaged accounts and tax-optimized stock index funds in taxable ones. Dividends and interest resemble grant overhead: unavoidable but manageable if you park them where they cause the least drag. International index funds with automatic foreign-tax credits can live happily in taxable accounts, while high-yield bond funds may belong inside a 403(b). By aligning asset placement with tax characteristics, you squeeze extra compound growth without increasing risk, like choosing the optimal statistical test for your data structure.

Rebalancing is the periodic act of restoring your chosen allocation after market movements shift the weights. When stocks surge, they overweight your portfolio, raising risk; when they plunge, they underweight it, reducing growth potential. Rebalancing forces you to sell high and buy low, a counterintuitive yet profitable discipline analogous to peer-review edits that trim verbose sections and bolster weak arguments. Whether you rebalance annually on your birthday or whenever a holding drifts more than five percentage points from target, consistency matters more than precision. Automation through target-date or balanced index funds can handle the task if you prefer a set-and-forget approach.

Calendar-based rebalancing suits scholars who crave simplicity: pick a date—say New Year's Day—review current weights, and execute trades.

Threshold-based rebalancing responds to market volatility, trimming or topping up when drift exceeds predefined bands, similar to adjusting course readings when student feedback indicates confusion. Both methods work; choose the one you'll stick to. Remember transaction costs and taxable gains when selling in brokerage accounts; use new contributions or dividends to nudge allocations whenever possible, minimizing taxable events.

Dollar-cost averaging helps manage emotional timing by investing fixed amounts at regular intervals regardless of market level, echoing how universities deduct retirement contributions each paycheck. Buying more shares when prices dip and fewer when prices rise smooths purchase cost over time. While lump-sum investing historically outperforms when markets trend up, the psychological comfort of gradual entry can safeguard you from bailing out after a sudden drop. If a windfall like a book advance arrives, depositing half immediately and spreading the rest over six months balances math and mindset.

Your allocation should evolve as you progress from assistant professor to emeritus, mirroring the shift from building a CV to mentoring the next generation. Gradually tilting toward bonds reduces volatility when portfolio withdrawals begin funding retirement. Yet retaining some equities combats inflation, which erodes fixed income the way outdated citations weaken a literature review. A common glide path moves from 80/20 stock-bond in early career to 50/50 by retirement, though personal circumstances—pension presence, health, legacy goals—may justify deviations. Revisit your plan every three to five years or upon significant life changes such as marriage, sabbatical abroad, or inheritance.

In the end, investment success for scholars hinges less on predicting markets and more on cultivating habits that parallel good research: gather data, design a sensible framework, execute consistently, and review outcomes against objectives. Asset allocation provides the blueprint, index funds supply the building materials, and rebalancing keeps the structure sound as environmental forces shift. With these basics mastered, you can delegate the day-to-day to automated contributions and focus energy on teaching, discovery, and mentoring. Let your money publish its own steady stream of returns while you advance knowledge, confident that both endeavors benefit from patience, discipline, and a respect for evidence.

Chapter 29: Tax-Efficient Investing, Backdoor Roths, HSAs, and 457(b) Deferred Comp Plans

Tax efficiency in investing is a bit like soundproofing a music studio: you still have to play the notes well, but the right insulation keeps outside noise—in this case, unnecessary taxes—from muddying your performance. The core idea is that every dollar you save in tax today can keep compounding right alongside the rest of your portfolio, producing returns on money that would otherwise have gone to the government long before you needed it. Instead of treating taxes as an after-the-fact surprise each April, savvy investors design their savings plan so that Uncle Sam quietly waits his turn—or sometimes never gets invited to the party at all. By layering different account types—pre-tax, tax-free, and taxable—you spread your future withdrawals across multiple buckets, giving yourself flexibility no matter how Congress tinkers with rates down the road. This chapter explores three powerful tools in that toolbox: the "backdoor" Roth IRA strategy for high earners, the under-appreciated health savings account, and the 457(b) deferred compensation plan often available to academics and nonprofit employees.

The Roth IRA itself is straightforward: you contribute after-tax dollars now, the account grows tax-free, and qualified withdrawals come out without a cent owed to the IRS. That's a sweet deal for young faculty or anyone who expects to be in a higher bracket later, yet it comes with an income phase-out that blocks many mid-career professors from direct contributions. The workaround is what practitioners call the backdoor Roth: first you place money into a non-deductible traditional IRA, then convert it almost immediately to a Roth, paying tax only on any growth during that brief holding period. Think of it as walking through two adjoining rooms—one technically open to everyone and one that would otherwise turn you away at the door—just long enough to change your coat. Because conversions have no income limit, the strategy stays perfectly legal, provided you mind one crucial trapdoor called the pro-rata rule, which can surprise those with pre-tax money lingering in any traditional IRAs.

The pro-rata rule treats all traditional IRA balances as one pot when calculating taxes on a conversion, so if you own, say, fifty thousand dollars of old deductible contributions, your small non-deductible deposit becomes diluted in the eyes of the IRS. Suddenly that "almost untaxed" move turns partly taxable because the government views each conversion dollar as a blend of pre- and after-tax money. Avoiding this requires clearing or sheltering prior IRA balances before attempting the backdoor process: rolling them into an employer 403(b) or 401(k) plan walls them off so the IRS pro-rata calculation shows only after-tax funds. It's like separating white laundry from reds so nothing bleeds color onto your freshly converted account. Though the paperwork can feel daunting, most custodians handle rollovers seamlessly, and the one-time effort can save thousands in unnecessary taxes over decades of compounded gains.

Timing matters, too. Some advisers recommend depositing the non-deductible IRA contribution and waiting a month to convert, fearing the IRS might frown on a same-day flip, while others see no written requirement for such a delay. The IRS has yet to challenge prompt conversions, but to sleep well at night you might choose a short cooling-off period, akin to letting fresh paint set before you touch the wall. Either way, file Form8606 with your tax return to document the basis, because losing track now risks paying tax on that money twice later. Keeping immaculate records is your defense if an audit ever asks you to prove which dollars have already been taxed. Like detailed lab notes, thorough documentation turns potential headaches into routine clarifications.

Once the money sits in the Roth, your future self reaps three key benefits: tax-free growth, tax-free withdrawals, and no required minimum distributions (RMDs) in retirement. Not having to take forced withdrawals means you control your tax bracket in your seventies rather than the IRS doing it for you. Further, heirs receive Roth dollars income-tax free, making the account a potent estate-planning vehicle even if Congress requires faster beneficiary drawdowns nowadays. For professors who may move in and out of teaching roles or take lucrative consulting assignments later, locking in today's comparatively low tax rates via a Roth hedge can smooth future surprises. Think of it as publishing a pivotal paper now that keeps boosting your tenure file long after you've stopped updating it actively.

Next comes the health savings account, or HSA, which many experts dub the "triple-tax-advantaged unicorn" of personal finance. Contributions reduce your taxable income like a traditional 403(b), growth compounds tax-free like in a Roth, and qualified medical withdrawals escape tax entirely—three distinct benefits stacked in one wrapper. To qualify, you must pair it with a high-deductible health plan, a phrase that scares off some academics accustomed to low-cost copays, yet many institutions have tempered those deductibles with employer contributions to the HSA, softening the blow. Even if your annual healthcare spending is minimal, treating the HSA as a stealth retirement account for future medical costs can pay huge dividends, given healthcare inflation's relentless pace. By paying current out-of-pocket expenses with after-tax dollars and saving the receipts, you preserve the right to reimburse yourself decades later, effectively turning the HSA into an auxiliary Roth if you wish.

Picture an HSA like a lab fridge: you can store experimental reagents for years, pulling them out when the protocol demands. Each medical bill you pay now becomes a future claim ticket; scanning those receipts and filing them in a cloud folder creates an evidence trail should the IRS question a large reimbursement down the line. Meanwhile the invested balance enjoys decades of growth, often in the same low-cost index funds you hold elsewhere. Unlike flexible-spending accounts, HSAs carry no "use-it-or-lose-it" deadline, giving you latitude to choose the optimal withdrawal moment. After age sixty-five, non-medical withdrawals become penalty-free though still taxable, essentially converting the account into a traditional IRA fallback, but most retirees welcome the ability to fund Medicare premiums tax-free from the HSA instead.

Managing HSA investments requires a mindset shift, because many custodians default contributions into cash or a money-market sweep paying negligible interest. To harness the real power, you must log in and elect investment options once your balance crosses any required cash threshold. Set an annual reminder—perhaps during open enrollment season—to rebalance and increase equity exposure while you are years from needing the funds. The expense ratios inside some employer-selected HSA platforms can be surprisingly high, so investigate whether you can transfer balances periodically to a lower-cost provider while leaving payroll contributions at the original custodian. Treat it the way you'd treat long-term field data: organized, regularly reviewed, and optimized for clarity and efficiency.

We turn now to the 457(b) deferred compensation plan offered by many public universities and charitable hospitals, a cousin to the more familiar 403(b) but with unique superpowers. Contributions reduce taxable income today and grow tax-deferred like any pre-tax account, yet withdrawals after separation from service—no age fifty-nine-and-a-half requirement—face only ordinary income tax, not penalties. That flexibility can bridge early-retirement years before Social Security or while Roth conversions are most attractive. Imagine the 457(b) as a reserve reading room: accessible once you leave campus, even if the main stacks remain closed. Funding one may appear redundant if you already max a 403(b), but since the IRS regards them as separate buckets, high-earning scholars can double their tax-deferred space, socking away more than forty-thousand dollars combined each year.

A common worry revolves around the security of 457(b) assets, technically part of the employer's general funds and therefore subject to creditor claims if the institution fails. While public entities like state universities pose minimal default risk, private-hospital 457(b)s warrant scrutiny—you wouldn't park research samples in a freezer notorious for power outages.

Assess the employer's financial health and diversification; if concerns linger, prioritize your 403(b) first, then allocate to the 457(b) only if comfortable. For most tenured professors, the advantage of penalty-free early access outweighs the low probability of institutional collapse. Nevertheless, diversification across account types and institutions remains wise, ensuring no single failure jeopardizes retirement security.

Coordinating these accounts within your overall savings hierarchy involves balancing current tax relief, future tax diversification, and liquidity needs. A practical sequence for many faculty is: capture any 403(b) match, fully fund the HSA, execute the backdoor Roth, then divide additional dollars between 457(b) and taxable brokerage accounts depending on retirement timeline and appetite for flexibility. This arrangement feels like planning a balanced teaching load: required core courses first, then electives that align with personal research goals. Because each account has different withdrawal rules, spreading contributions smooths cash-flow options later, letting you dial income up or down to manage tax brackets or healthcare subsidies.

Keep in mind that tax policy is a moving target—Congress can alter contribution limits, conversion rules, or deduction thresholds with shifting political winds. The best hedge is maintaining multiple account structures so that whichever direction rates go, you have a bucket poised to deliver funds efficiently. In statistical terms, think of it as building a robust model rather than relying on a single predictor variable. Annual reviews during tax-prep season or after salary changes will ensure your plan keeps up with new legislation and institutional offerings. Staying nimble does not mean tinkering constantly but does call for intentional adjustments when variables materially shift.

Execution details matter. Use automatic payroll deductions where possible to sidestep decision fatigue; the money never hits your checking account, so the temptation to spend drifts away like an unread email marked spam. For the backdoor Roth, calendar two to-dos each January: contribute to your traditional IRA, then schedule the conversion whether you prefer immediately or after a short buffer. For the HSA, elect the maximum family or single contribution during open enrollment and adjust mid-year if eligible raises occur. For the 457(b), set a fixed percentage rather than a flat dollar amount if you anticipate annual merit increases, preserving your savings rate automatically. These micro-systems accumulate in the background, freeing cognitive bandwidth for teaching and research.

Tax forms often intimidate even data-savvy academics, yet treating them as lab protocols rather than bureaucratic monsters reframes the task. Form8606 logs your Roth conversion basis; IRSForm8889 chronicles HSA contributions and withdrawals; the W-2 Box12 code G or H reveals your 457(b) totals. When forms arrive each January, file them into labeled digital folders—"2025 Retirement Docs"—and cross-check with paystubs before forwarding to your CPA or preparing returns. A fifteen-minute reconciliation now prevents messy amended returns later, akin to catching a citation error before journal submission. When in doubt, lean on payroll or benefits offices—they handle these questions daily and usually welcome proactive inquiries.

Real-life examples illuminate the theory. Consider Dr. Alvarez, age forty-five, earning $140,000 with a spouse who teaches high-school science. They max Dr. Alvarez's 403(b) at $23,000, contribute $8,300 to the family HSA, perform a $7,000 backdoor Roth each, and fund the university 457(b) with an additional $23,000. Combined, they defer or shelter over $68,000 annually, cutting current taxable income to roughly $72,000, which lowers their effective rate and qualifies them for a modest child-tax-credit phase-in. Meanwhile the HSA balance grows in a total-market index fund, and the 457(b) gives them a path to semi-retirement at fifty-five without penalties. Their taxable brokerage remains modest, yet they have enough liquidity in the HSA—via those saved receipts—and the 457(b) to cover gap years until Social Security.

Contrast that with Professor Chen, single and already tenured, earning $200,000 with substantial consulting revenue. She rolls an old SEP-IRA into her current 403(b) to clear the pro-rata hurdle, then makes annual backdoor Roth contributions and chooses an aggressive equity allocation in that account. Because she expects consulting income variability, she only contributes half the maximum to her 457(b), directing the remainder to a taxable index-fund portfolio for flexibility. She uses her HSA primarily for current medical expenses but invests any surplus above $5,000, rebalancing annually. Her diversified buckets prepare her for either an early exit or a continued full-professor track, depending on how the consulting business evolves.

Common pitfalls still ensnare the unprepared. Forgetting to file Form8606 results in double taxation on converted funds, while leaving pre-tax IRA dollars untouched before a backdoor move triggers the pro-rata complication. Similarly, using HSA funds at a drugstore without tracking the receipt erodes the opportunity for future tax-free reimbursements. And failing to update 457(b) beneficiaries can misalign estate plans, especially after life events like divorce or remarriage. Treat each misstep as a preventable lab accident: protocols, checklists, and periodic audits of your own system keep errors rare and recoverable.

Technology helps. Expense-tracking apps scan medical receipts and tag them for HSA reimbursement; retirement dashboards aggregate 403(b), Roth, and 457(b) balances to reveal allocation drift. Setting text alerts for payroll contribution changes acts like a field monitor that pings when data collection pauses unexpectedly. Even a simple spreadsheet listing account, annual limit, year-to-date contribution, and beneficiary names serves as a living lab notebook guiding future adjustments. The incremental friction of maintaining that file pales in comparison to the costly friction of tax mistakes.

Eventually withdrawals come into play, whether for an early-career sabbatical, midlife career change, or full retirement. Strategically drawing from the 457(b) first can create space in lower tax brackets for partial Roth conversions, lowering lifetime taxes. HSA reimbursements of decades-old medical receipts can fund cruises or roof repairs tax-free, acting as a buffer in years when market downturns discourage tapping equities. Required minimum distributions from pre-tax 403(b)s can then land after seventy-three, by which time your Roth account keeps growing quietly without mandated withdrawals. This choreography turns tax codes into a waltz rather than a mosh pit, smoothing lifetime cash-flow.

Each of these accounts reflects a simple principle: the less you pay to taxes and fees, the more capital compounds on your behalf. Backdoor Roths lock in tax-free growth, HSAs offer triple advantages with healthcare flexibility, and 457(b)s extend tax-deferral space while granting early access unmatched by other plans. Harnessing them together is like assembling an interdisciplinary research team: each member shines in a different scenario, but the collective outperforms any single expert. Your job is to set up the structures, automate contributions, and revisit allocations with the same diligence you bring to grant-proposal revisions.

Along the way, keep perspective. No tax strategy substitutes for a solid savings rate, just as no statistical tool rescues flawed study design. Start with the basics—spend less than you earn, invest in diversified low-cost funds—then layer on these advanced accounts to amplify the outcome. If confusion strikes, consult a fee-only planner the way you might seek a methods specialist's input on a tricky dataset. The incremental cost of expert advice often pales beside decades of compounding benefits from a well-executed plan.

In the end, tax-efficient investing is less about gaming the system and more about understanding its rules so thoroughly that you let them work for you. By weaving backdoor Roths, HSAs, and 457(b) plans into your financial fabric, you create a resilient wardrobe that adapts to academic salary freezes, consulting windfalls, healthcare surprises, and evolving retirement visions. Once these accounts are humming, you can re-focus on teaching, research, and family, confident that each paycheck contains not only today's fulfillment but tomorrow's security. And that, perhaps, is the best definition of tenure—knowing your intellectual and financial futures are both safeguarded by design, leaving you free to chase the questions that truly inspire you.

Chapter 30: Real Estate Beyond the Primary Home, Rental Properties, REITs, and College-Town Risks

For many academics, buying a home is the first big step into real estate, but curiosity often grows about what lies beyond the primary residence. Rental properties, real estate investment trusts (REITs), and other forms of real estate exposure can provide income, long-term appreciation, and portfolio diversification. Still, like any other investment, real estate comes with risks, headaches, and trade-offs that are important to understand before jumping in. You may have a colleague who raves about their second house generating passive income or someone who swears by REIT dividends in their retirement portfolio. This chapter is here to help you separate hype from substance, laying out what's possible, what's probable, and what to watch out for, especially in college towns where faculty often first dip their toes into landlording.

Rental property ownership can look like a dream on paper—steady rent checks, appreciation over time, and the ability to deduct expenses such as mortgage interest and maintenance. In reality, it's more like a hybrid job between investment and part-time property manager, especially if you're not using a professional company. Even in the best neighborhoods, tenants call when pipes burst, leases need renewing, or something mysterious happens to the garbage disposal. If you buy a place intending to rent to students, those problems often multiply, as the turnover tends to be higher, and maintenance issues may escalate faster due to wear and tear. One faculty member I know bought a duplex near campus and made decent returns, but she jokes that she also earned a Ph.D. in drywall repair and crisis texting with parents about their kids' parties.

Getting financing for an investment property is slightly more complicated than buying your primary home. Lenders usually want a larger down payment—often 20 to 25 percent—and interest rates can be higher, particularly if the property won't be owner-occupied. That's because lenders see more risk in rentals; if money gets tight, most people will protect their own home first and let the rental fall behind. You'll also need to show that you have sufficient cash reserves to cover the mortgage if the unit sits vacant or major repairs come up. Think of the underwriting process like writing a grant proposal—you're trying to convince the lender your plan is solid, your budget realistic, and your execution dependable under pressure.

Cash flow is one of the most important things to understand when investing in rental property. Positive cash flow means that after your mortgage, taxes, insurance, and other expenses, there's still money left over each month. Negative cash flow means you're paying out of pocket to keep the place running, which may be fine if appreciation is strong and your long-term plan is to sell. But consistent losses can bleed your finances dry and turn a promising investment into an expensive stressor. It's a little like teaching a new course—you may lose time early figuring it out, but if the department never funds a TA or buys the right materials, that class will keep draining your energy semester after semester.

Maintenance is a sneaky variable in rental real estate. Roofs leak, dishwashers die, tenants lock themselves out, and your phone may ring at the least convenient times. You can outsource to a property management company, but they usually charge 8 to 12 percent of the rent and sometimes add markups on repairs. The trade-off is between time and money—do you want to personally drive over with a plunger, or would you rather pay someone to do it and accept slightly lower returns? Some faculty enjoy the hands-on element; others find it pulls them away from their research and writing. The key is to be honest with yourself about how much time and patience you're really willing to devote.

Location is another huge factor, especially for faculty buying in college towns. These markets often feel stable because of constant student demand, but that same turnover creates wear on the property, unpredictable vacancies, and issues with noise, parties, or late rent. Local laws may limit student occupancy per unit, and towns with a high proportion of rentals sometimes crack down on short-term leases or enforce strict inspection codes. One professor bought a triplex near campus, only to learn he needed a rental permit requiring expensive safety upgrades like a new fire escape. Before buying in a college town, research zoning laws, tenant ordinances, and school calendars just like you'd research archival access before a sabbatical trip.

Some faculty think about buying real estate in their child's future college town, imagining that they can offset tuition costs by owning a home or condo and renting rooms to roommates. This plan can work well, but it introduces complexity, especially if you'll be an out-of-state landlord. You'll need to set up reliable management, understand local tenant laws, and ensure your child is comfortable living in a shared space while you act as both landlord and parent. There are also tax implications—if you let your child live rent-free, you may not be able to deduct all expenses. One family I know did this successfully for four years, but they treated it like a small business, not a shortcut to savings.

If the idea of managing properties feels too hands-on, REITs—real estate investment trusts—offer another way to gain exposure to real estate without owning physical property. REITs are companies that own or finance real estate across sectors like commercial buildings, apartments, data centers, and even healthcare facilities. You can buy shares of publicly traded REITs in your retirement or brokerage account, and they tend to pay regular dividends, which can be attractive for long-term income. It's like buying stock in an entire apartment complex without ever needing to mow the lawn or answer tenant emails. While REITs can fluctuate with the stock market, they add diversification and can serve as a valuable complement to traditional stocks and bonds.

REITs do have tax considerations that investors should understand.

Because they're required to pay out at least 90 percent of taxable income as dividends, they often generate more taxable income than regular stocks. This makes them better suited for tax-advantaged accounts like IRAs or 403(b)s, where you don't pay taxes on dividends each year. Putting REITs in a taxable brokerage account can lead to surprise tax bills if you're not careful, especially if you reinvest the dividends. The takeaway here is simple: location matters not just for buildings but for where you park your investments. Treat tax planning for REITs the same way you would for deciding whether to hold bonds in a Roth or traditional IRA.

There's also the option of investing in real estate syndications or crowdfunding platforms, which pool money from multiple investors to buy larger properties. These platforms typically require higher minimums and are less liquid, meaning your money may be tied up for five to ten years. Still, for faculty who want exposure to commercial or multi-unit properties without owning them directly, these can be a middle ground between DIY rentals and REITs. Just be sure to read the fine print—fees can be high, and not all platforms are equally transparent. Think of them like collaborative research grants: they can be fruitful, but you'd better trust your partners and understand your deliverables.

Before diving into any real estate investment, it's smart to assess your overall financial picture. How much emergency cash do you have on hand? What's your current debt load? How diversified are your existing investments? Rental property, for instance, ties up a large chunk of capital and may require extra funds at inconvenient times. One of the most common mistakes is underestimating how illiquid real estate can be—you can't sell a toilet or one-third of a roof to raise money in a hurry. A diversified portfolio lets you absorb real estate bumps without jeopardizing your financial goals.

Taxes are another major consideration when investing in property. Rental income is taxed as ordinary income, but you can deduct expenses such as mortgage interest, property taxes, insurance, repairs, and depreciation. Depreciation is a big one—it lets you reduce your taxable income even if the property is appreciating in value. However, when you sell, the IRS recaptures some of that depreciation, meaning a potentially higher tax bill down the road. To navigate this, many investors use strategies like 1031 exchanges to defer taxes, but those are best done with help from a seasoned accountant. Think of tax planning for real estate like designing a syllabus—it's not just about what you teach now, but how the course fits together by the end.

Real estate also comes with liability risk, especially if someone is injured on your property or sues over a dispute. Landlord insurance helps, but you may also want to consider forming an LLC to hold your rental properties. An LLC can provide legal separation between your personal assets and the property, limiting your risk if something goes wrong. It's not foolproof, and it comes with costs and paperwork, but for faculty with growing portfolios, it's worth discussing with a legal or tax advisor. Think of it as building a firewall between your academic life and your investment life—you hope you never need it, but you'll be glad it's there if sparks fly.

Real estate investing can affect your financial aid eligibility or income-based repayment plans if you have student loans. Rental income is counted when calculating adjusted gross income, which may reduce your eligibility for certain loan programs or tax credits. The same goes for parents helping children with college—owning property that generates income could impact need-based financial aid calculations. If you're applying for FAFSA or managing a Public Service Loan Forgiveness plan, be sure to understand how real estate income plays into your broader financial picture. Even a modest side property could have unintended consequences if it tips your income over a threshold.

Time is the hidden cost in real estate investing. Faculty already juggle teaching, research, grading, committees, and sometimes side consulting. Adding property management to that list may be energizing for some but overwhelming for others. If you're short on time but still interested in the asset class, REITs or passive syndications may better fit your lifestyle. The most successful investors choose the model that fits their personality, bandwidth, and risk tolerance. There's no prize for being the busiest landlord—only for building a strategy that supports your bigger life goals.

One final word of caution: real estate markets, like academic trends, go through cycles. What seems like a gold mine today may cool off tomorrow. Rents can decline, property values can fall, and local laws can change in ways that upend your plan. During COVID-19, for example, eviction moratoriums and sudden shifts in student housing demand hit many college-town landlords hard. Resilience in real estate, like resilience in research, comes from adaptability, good preparation, and humility about what you can't control. If you assume every plan will hit at least one unexpected bump, you'll be less rattled when it happens.

At its best, real estate beyond your primary home can be a solid wealth-building tool and a smart way to diversify your investments. It can produce income, hedge against inflation, and add real-world value to your portfolio. But it's not passive, not foolproof, and not something to enter without clear eyes and a long-term mindset. Just like getting tenure or publishing a book, success comes from planning, effort, and patience—not just enthusiasm and good intentions. Whether you're ready to buy a duplex, invest in REITs, or simply learn the landscape, understanding the nuances of real estate will serve you well as you grow your financial future.

Chapter 31: Caring for Aging Parents, Financial Support, Power of Attorney, and Long-Term-Care Insurance

Saving for a child's education is a bit like planning a cross-country research sabbatical—you need a map, flexible funding sources, and contingency plans if weather or budgets shift unexpectedly. The moment a baby arrives, relatives start dreaming about future diplomas, but tuition costs can climb faster than any merit raise, so putting a strategy in place early gives compounding more semesters to work. The cornerstone tool for most families is the 529 plan, a state-sponsored investment account that grows tax-deferred and offers tax-free withdrawals for qualified education expenses. Each state sponsors at least one, and you're not locked into your own state's plan, though home-state residents sometimes get an income-tax deduction on contributions. Choosing a 529 feels similar to selecting a graduate program: look at fees, investment choices, performance history, and any perk that boosts the value proposition without tying your hands later.

Inside a 529, you can pick age-based portfolios that gradually shift from stocks to bonds as the future student nears enrollment, a set-it-and-forget-it option that reassures busy parents and grandparents. Alternatively, you can build a custom mix of index funds or socially responsible tracks if you're comfortable rebalancing every few years. The real magic lies in the tax break; earnings withdrawn for tuition, mandatory fees, books, and even certain room-and-board costs sail past federal taxes entirely. Some plans now extend to K–12 tuition and apprenticeship programs, though using funds early shrinks college-year balances, so weigh the trade-offs carefully. Think of the 529 as a specialized lab grant—it comes with broad latitude inside your research goals but must be spent on the approved project to retain its tax-free status.

Contribution limits to 529s are generous—effectively tied to lifetime gift-tax exclusion amounts—so large lump sums from grandparents are permissible, and a special five-year gift-splitting rule lets a donor front-load up to five times the annual gift exclusion without filing extra paperwork. This can jump-start growth, especially if tuition inflation keeps outrunning conservative investment returns. The flip side is market risk; a big deposit before a downturn may sting, so staggered contributions can hedge timing. Automated monthly transfers smooth volatility, turning savings into another utility bill for the household budget. The earlier you start, the lighter the monthly lift, because compounding does more of the heavy lifting just like early data collection eases the final sprint on a dissertation.

Changing beneficiaries is one of the 529's underrated features. If the older child earns a full scholarship or decides to enlist instead of enroll, you can pivot leftover funds to a younger sibling, first cousin, or even yourself for that long-deferred sabbatical coursework. The IRS views education as a family affair, so moving funds among relatives avoids taxes or penalties, provided the new student remains in the same generational cohort. Should all educational avenues close, you may withdraw the money, paying ordinary income tax plus a ten-percent penalty on the earnings portion, but only taxes on your original contributions if you claimed a state deduction. Scholarship offsets create another escape hatch: funds equal to the amount of tax-free scholarship received can be withdrawn penalty-free, though still subject to income tax on gains. Consider it a tuition refund on compounding—less ideal than staying the course but far better than a total loss.

While 529s shine for college goals, custodial accounts—UTMAs and UGMAs—offer broader spending flexibility at the cost of less favorable financial-aid treatment and taxable earnings. Set up under the Uniform

Transfers to Minors Act or Uniform Gifts to Minors Act, these accounts hold assets "in trust" until the child reaches the age of majority, typically eighteen to twenty-one depending on state. Unlike 529s, funds can be used for anything benefiting the minor, from summer programs to a first apartment's security deposit. That freedom tempts some parents who want multi-purpose savings vehicles, but remember that ownership switches to the child at adulthood, legally empowering them to cash out for a sports car if they choose. It's analogous to handing over a completed research grant with no further oversight—the hope is they stay on mission, but the decision is ultimately theirs.

Taxes on custodial accounts follow the so-called "kiddie-tax" rules. A small slice of unearned income may be tax-free, the next chunk is taxed at the child's lower rate, and anything beyond falls under parents' top marginal bracket. If grandparents funnel large dividend-paying stocks into a UTMA, December 31 can bring surprise liability that reduces net returns. Families who value tax efficiency often hold growth-oriented index funds with minimal payouts until the child is older and in a lower bracket. The calculus resembles choosing between publishing in open-access journals that charge upfront fees or traditional titles with longer payoffs—you optimize based on timing, cost, and future flexibility.

Financial-aid formulas treat 529s owned by parents as parental assets, assessed at up to about 5.6percent when determining Expected Family Contribution, whereas custodial accounts count as the student's assets, assessed at a steeper 20percent. That difference can shrink aid eligibility, so families eyeing need-based assistance often prioritize 529s over UTMAs to keep the asset hit small. Conversely, grandparents owning a 529 can sidestep the asset count entirely, but distributions used to pay tuition once showed up as student income on the FAFSA and hurt aid. Rule changes starting with the simplified FAFSA for the 2024–25 year treat those distributions more leniently, reducing this pitfall, yet timing still matters—using grandparent 529s in junior and senior years limits any potential baseline-year income effect. Financial planning here feels like scheduling conference travel around teaching obligations—sequencing matters to avoid unintended conflicts.

Balancing multiple funding sources demands a clear hierarchy. Generally, aim to maximize tax-advantaged 529 contributions first, then consider custodial accounts for gifts beyond college needs or for children likely to receive scholarships where flexible uses could prevail. An HSA earmarked for future medical costs or a Roth IRA in your own name may outrank a UTMA if preserving parental control and tax efficiency matter more than giving the child early spending autonomy. Each family's map differs, but writing a short investment policy statement—just like drafting a course syllabus—clarifies priorities and reduces debate when relatives propose well-meaning but misaligned gifts. Sharing that document with grandparents keeps everyone rowing in the same fiscal direction.

Scholarships, grants, and fellowships can alter your funding landscape quickly. If your student wins a full-ride athletic package or a merit tuition waiver, your 529 may look overfunded overnight. Don't panic; as mentioned, you can shift beneficiaries, hold funds for graduate school, or withdraw scholarship-equal amounts penalty-free. Some parents deliberately aim for a 529 surplus, figuring any leftover can fund advanced degrees or even future grandkids after a generation-skip transfer. Others throttle contributions around sophomore year of high school once merit prospects crystallize. Adapting your plan is a bit like revising a research proposal after preliminary findings—you pivot but keep the overarching objective in sight.

Investment choices inside education accounts deserve attention but not obsession. Age-based 529 portfolios track glide paths that grow more conservative as matriculation nears, protecting against market crashes that could slash tuition savings at the eleventh hour. DIY investors who prefer index funds should still schedule annual reviews to ensure stock-heavy allocations dial back risk accordingly. The worst scenario is a 50-percent drawdown senior year followed by a forced sale to pay the bursar, an outcome akin to losing a hard drive two weeks before manuscript submission. Risk management here is about smoothing tuition bills regardless of market weather.

Some families explore prepaid tuition plans, locking in today's prices at in-state public universities. These function differently from investment-based 529s, more like purchasing "education insurance." They can be ideal if you're certain a child will attend a state school but less flexible if they choose a private or out-of-state institution, where credits may transfer at average tuition rates, not full cost. With university funding ebbing and flows uncertain, some plans have faced solvency questions, so read actuarial reports before committing. Think of prepaid tuition as buying an annuity in the form of future course credits—security trades off against choice.

Creative funding sources such as employer scholarships, state grants, and service-based programs like AmeriCorps can dovetail with your savings strategy. These sometimes reduce the qualified expenses you can pay with 529 money, so coordinate usage to avoid penalties. For instance, a tuition-exclusive scholarship may free you to use 529 dollars on housing and meal plans, still qualified under the rules. Careful matching of expense categories to funding sources prevents waste, similar to aligning specific grant funds to allowable research costs in a multi-sponsor project.

Grandparents looking to make a significant legacy impact often weigh direct tuition payments versus 529 contributions. The IRS excludes tuition paid directly to a college from gift-tax calculations, allowing large transfers without dipping into the lifetime exemption. However, those payments bypass the power of tax-free compounding and can inadvertently lower need-based aid in the year they're made. Contributing to a parent-owned 529 may offer greater long-term leverage and flexibility. Deciding between the two mirrors the trade-off between upfront seed funding for a lab versus endowing a fellowship—both help students, but timelines and tax contexts differ.

If you have multiple children or grandchildren, equity issues arise. Market returns can vary widely between a firstborn's and a younger sibling's enrollment years, leading to uneven account balances even with equal contributions. Some families counteract this by pooling 529 funds in one master account and switching beneficiaries as needed, evening out market luck. Others set rigid contribution schedules but pledge to top up if the market short-changes a later child. Transparency and documented intentions help avert feelings of unfairness, much like published grading rubrics stave off student resentment.

When kids reach high school, involving them in the funding conversation pays dividends beyond dollars. Showing them account statements and explaining how contributions, market gains, and scholarships intersect demystifies costs and fosters ownership. A teen who understands the value of scholarships may study harder, knowing the payoff reduces the family's draw on savings. That awareness also curbs entitlement attitudes around spending choices: a child who sees what dorm upgrades mean in foregone 529 growth may opt for a standard roommate instead of a single suite. Financial literacy, in this sense, is another compounding asset.

Special-needs considerations can modify the education-funding toolkit. For beneficiaries with disabilities, 529 ABLE accounts allow tax-advantaged saving for qualified expenses—including education—without jeopardizing means-tested benefits. Contributions are capped lower than traditional 529s but integrate seamlessly if college is still part of the plan. Coordinating ABLE and 529 strategies demands careful titling and beneficiary designations, akin to balancing multiple co-authors on a complex paper while preserving voice and compliance. Consulting a special-needs planner ensures tax, legal, and benefit angles align.

Loans enter the picture when savings, scholarships, and cash flow fall short. Federal student loans offer income-driven repayment and forgiveness paths valuable for those entering public service, including academia. Families sometimes deliberately use loans early, preserving 529 money for graduate tuition where borrowing options are pricier. Yet over-reliance on loans can burden future budgets and derail retirement saving. The trick is assessing loan terms much like measuring a lab chemical—exact dosages can propel the experiment, but excess spoils the solution.

Annual gift-tax exclusions currently permit any individual to give $18,000 per recipient each year without filing returns, a handy benchmark for grandparents eager to chip in. Coordinating among multiple donors and beneficiaries avoids accidental over-gifting, which burns lifetime exemption unnecessarily. A simple shared spreadsheet labeled "2026 Education Gifts" keeps track of who gave what, mirroring shared lab inventory lists that prevent double-ordering reagents. Clear communication reduces administrative drag and fosters familial goodwill.

Estate planning and education funding often intersect. Naming a successor owner for a 529 ensures continuity if the primary owner passes away; without this, accounts can get tangled in probate, freezing funds just when tuition bills loom. Trusts can also own 529 plans, though the paperwork grows. Meanwhile, custodial accounts automatically become the child's asset at majority, impacting inheritance dynamics. Grandpa may intend a grandchild's UTMA as college money, but once control transfers, that money factors into the grandchild's own estate. Reviewing titling regularly is like updating co-author affiliations—easy to overlook until it causes confusion at publication time.

Finally, all these moving parts work best inside a bigger family financial plan. If parents are under-funded for retirement, prioritizing an education kitty at the expense of their own future could mean leaning on the very child they sought to help. The adage "you can borrow for college but not for retirement" carries weight, though nuance exists. A balanced approach channels surplus cash first toward emergency reserves and retirement matches, then into education vehicles according to time horizon and tax advantage. Regular check-ins—perhaps at semester breaks—keep the strategy aligned with changing income, tuition forecasts, and scholarship prospects.

With thoughtful planning, 529 plans, UTMA/UGMA accounts, and scholarship offsets become complementary instruments in an orchestra tuned to the family's values, risk tolerance, and goals. Each option has strengths and blind spots, and their synergy shifts as kids progress from kindergarten excitement to cap-and-gown reality. Rather than chasing the perfect single solution, successful families craft a flexible ensemble that can modulate volume, tempo, and timbre as the score demands. After all, the purpose of funding education is not merely to foot a bill but to empower young minds to explore, create, and contribute without the weight of financial chains, ensuring the next generation of scholars starts life already moving forward instead of digging out of debt.

Chapter 32: Family & Friends Asking for Money, Scripts, Boundaries, and Formal Loan Agreements

When someone you care about asks you for money, especially a close friend or family member, it doesn't just tap your wallet—it touches your heart, your values, your history, and sometimes your guilt. Whether it's a sibling in a tough spot, a cousin with a new business idea, or a lifelong friend who needs help covering rent, these moments can feel like a pressure cooker of love, loyalty, and financial risk. Many people wrestle with whether saying "no" is selfish or smart, or whether saying "yes" might compromise their own financial goals or complicate a personal relationship. It's not just about numbers—it's about boundaries, communication, and being able to live with the outcome, whichever way you go. That's why this chapter is about more than just money; it's about making intentional choices that reflect your values while protecting your peace.

Let's start with the reality: once people know you're "doing okay"—whether that means you got a new job, inherited money, or simply make steady income—they may see you as someone with extra. In some families or friend groups, there's an unspoken assumption that one person will be the financial safety net, especially if they've historically stepped up before. Sometimes you're asked directly, and sometimes it's more subtle—like a story about unpaid bills or a "joke" about how they need your help. You may feel flattered, burdened, obligated, or even resentful. That mix of emotions is normal, but what matters is how you respond—ideally with clarity, compassion, and a plan that puts both parties on solid ground.

It helps to think ahead and develop what I call a "giving policy." Just like a university has a syllabus or a company has HR policies, having a personal guideline around lending or giving money keeps you from scrambling in the moment. You might decide, for example, that you're open to giving small gifts under $200 with no strings, but anything above that requires a conversation and some documentation. Or maybe you've committed to saying no to loans but yes to helping in other ways, like co-signing on a lease, helping with a resume, or giving a one-time non-repayable gift. The more you've thought about your stance ahead of time, the easier it is to avoid emotional whiplash when someone puts you on the spot. Your policy doesn't have to be public, but it should be something you believe in—and something you stick to, even when the requestor is someone you love.

Let's talk scripts, because saying no or setting conditions can be awkward, especially if you grew up in a family where money was shared without discussion or questions. One script could be, "I care about you, and I really want to see you succeed, but I've committed to not lending money to friends or family because I've seen how it can strain relationships." Another version might be, "I can't lend money right now, but I can help you brainstorm options or connect you with resources." If you do want to give or lend but on your terms, you might say, "I'm willing to help with $1,000 as a gift, but I'm not in a position to cover the full amount you asked for." Scripts work best when they're honest, clear, and delivered without apology. You're allowed to protect your finances just like you'd lock your front door—not because you don't trust your family, but because boundaries are healthy and necessary.

Sometimes you do want to help, but you don't want to be taken advantage of—or worse, resented when it's time to repay. That's where a formal loan agreement comes in. It doesn't have to be fancy, but it should include the amount, repayment terms, timeline, and what happens if the borrower can't pay it back. You can even write something like, "This is a loan, not a gift, and we're agreeing to $100 per month starting September 1 until it's paid off." You both sign and date it. It may feel strange or even cold, but think of it like a syllabus: it sets expectations clearly from the start and protects the relationship from misunderstandings. If someone refuses to sign a simple agreement, that's a red flag—and possibly your answer right there.

Of course, many people never repay loans, even when they have the best of intentions. Life happens—jobs fall through, emergencies pop up, or they just stop returning your texts. If that happens, it's important to remember that your response isn't just about the money; it's about your peace of mind. Some people choose to forgive the loan entirely, reframing it as a gift in hindsight. Others cut off future financial help but preserve the relationship. Still others let the relationship drift, which can be painful but necessary. There's no right answer, but if you do lend, you should be emotionally prepared for the possibility that you won't get it back. Only lend what you can afford to lose—not just financially, but emotionally too.

There's also a cultural element to all this. In many communities, especially where economic disparity has existed for generations, the idea of "we all rise together" is sacred. If one person breaks through financially, it can feel like an unspoken contract that they'll help lift others too. That's noble—but it has to be sustainable. You can't pour from an empty cup. Helping family doesn't always mean giving money. Sometimes it means creating opportunities, providing education, or leading by example. Saying no to one-time requests doesn't make you selfish; it may make you strategic, especially if your long-term goal is to fund your own child's education, build wealth, or retire with dignity.

One technique that helps is the "budget bucket" method. Set aside a portion of your monthly or annual budget as your "helping" fund—just like you'd budget for travel or holiday gifts. Then, when someone asks, you can check your bucket. If it's empty, you say, "I've already committed my giving funds this month, but I can check back with you next quarter." If it's full, you help within that limit. This method gives you structure while keeping generosity in your life. It also lets you say "I'm not saying no—I'm saying not yet, or not all, or not right now."

If you're feeling pressured or emotionally manipulated, that's a sign to pause. Just like you'd raise an eyebrow if a student demands an A without earning it, you can question a request that comes with guilt trips, ultimatums, or past favors used as leverage. You're not obligated to rescue everyone, especially if it puts your own stability at risk. You might say, "I know this is hard, but I need to make financial choices that are sustainable for me. I hope you can respect that." And if they don't respect it? That tells you something important. Financial boundaries are often the clearest mirrors of relationship health.

It's also wise to distinguish between "can't" and "won't." Some people truly can't afford to help, and that's the end of the story. But others—especially those with some wiggle room—feel conflicted about whether they *should* help. If that's you, then your job is to clarify what feels right to you. Will helping this person align with your values and give you peace, or will it make you anxious, resentful, or financially vulnerable? Imagine looking back in five years—will you be proud of this decision, or regret it? That kind of reflection beats any spreadsheet.

And then there's the issue of fairness. What if one sibling is always asking, and the others never do? What if you help one cousin and suddenly the family grapevine lights up with requests from people you haven't spoken to in years? Be prepared: money moves through networks. Helping one person can open the door for others. You can anticipate this by setting clear expectations. "This is a one-time gift." Or, "I'm happy to help this time, but please don't assume I can say yes in the future." Setting the precedent on your terms protects you from becoming the unofficial ATM of the family.

Some requests come from people with great intentions—starting a business, going back to school, launching a nonprofit. These goals are admirable, but they still need a plan. Before giving money, ask questions: "What's your timeline? What's your backup plan if this doesn't work? How will this loan be used specifically?" If they get defensive or vague, you've learned something. But if they're organized, open, and coachable, then maybe your support—whether financial or advisory—could really make a difference. Just make sure you believe in the plan as much as the person.

Documentation isn't just for loans. If you give a gift, make it clear that it's a gift. Say it in writing. This avoids confusion later if someone says, "I thought that $5,000 was a loan and I planned to repay you." Clarity up front prevents resentment down the line. If you want the money back, say so—and put it in writing. If you don't, say that too. You don't need to make it awkward. Just say, "This is a gift to support you during this time. There's no need to pay me back." Done.

Emotionally, it can help to process the situation with someone neutral—a therapist, financial advisor, or trusted friend. Talking it out gives you space to weigh your options without pressure. Don't make big financial decisions when you're emotionally flooded—whether it's guilt, excitement, or fear. Step back. Sleep on it. Look at your budget. Run the numbers. Say, "Let me think about it and get back to you." That sentence alone has saved more friendships than any loan ever could.

Sometimes the most loving answer is not a financial one. Maybe you say no to cash but yes to childcare support, driving them to interviews, or connecting them with someone who can help. Money is just one way to show up. You don't owe people your savings to prove your love. Relationships are built on consistency, not currency. Let your actions speak louder than your checkbook.

Finally, remember that your job is to steward your resources wisely, not to play hero or martyr. You're allowed to prioritize your peace, your goals, and your boundaries. You can be generous and discerning. You can love people and still say no. The key is being intentional. Know your limits. Communicate them clearly. And always, always keep the relationships that matter more than the money at the center of your decisions. That's how you honor both your values and your future.

Chapter 33: Charitable Giving & Donor-Advised Funds, Aligning Philanthropy with Academic Values

Charitable giving is often portrayed as a spontaneous act—an envelope passed at a campus event, a texted donation after a disaster—but scholars know that deep impact usually stems from deliberate inquiry and long-term planning. When you view philanthropy the way you approach research, suddenly questions emerge about evidence of effectiveness, alignment with personal values, and sustainability of outcomes. In academic life, we push students to back claims with data; why not bring the same rigor to donating? By applying the tools of our trade—critical thinking, documentation, peer review—we can turn generosity into a disciplined practice that amplifies good rather than scattering dollars like confetti. The result is not colder giving but clearer giving, infused with the same curiosity and intentionality that drive scholarship.

The first step is to articulate your philanthropic thesis statement. Just as a research project starts with a question or hypothesis, purposeful giving begins with defining what problem you hope to address. Maybe you care about first-generation college access because you once navigated that maze alone, or perhaps your fieldwork highlighted health inequities that still keep you up at night. Write these motivations down, because clarity on paper becomes guardrails when a flood of appeals arrives in your inbox. Having a written statement does not lock you into one focus forever, but it anchors decisions so you are steering the ship rather than drifting wherever waves of guilt or hype push you.

Next, translate that thesis into measurable objectives. In the classroom, you define learning outcomes; similarly, in philanthropy, you can list desired outputs and long-term impacts. If you aim to support STEM education for underrepresented communities, your short-term output might be funding twenty scholarships this year, while your long-term impact could be increasing graduation rates in five years. Setting metrics may feel clinical, yet it prevents feel-good donations that look impressive but do little to move the needle. Think of metrics as the syllabus schedule—students still experience serendipity, but the timeline ensures you cover critical content before finals.

Now the money mechanics: donor-advised funds, or DAFs, are like flexible research endowments you create for yourself. You deposit cash, appreciated stock, or even royalty income into an account hosted by a public charity or community foundation, receive an immediate tax deduction, and then recommend grants over time to organizations that meet your criteria. A DAF removes December 31 pressure—just as a teaching release grants time to refine syllabi, a DAF grants time to vet nonprofits without sacrificing tax benefits in the year you contribute. The assets can be invested for growth, meaning your philanthropic "endowment" potentially yields more giving capacity down the road.

Setting up a DAF is easier than filing IRB paperwork. Most large financial custodians offer platforms with minimum initial gifts ranging from $5,000 to $25,000, and the online forms usually take less than an hour. You name the fund—perhaps the "Smith Family Academic Equity Fund"—select an investment pool that matches your risk tolerance, and designate successor advisors so your philanthropic vision outlives you. Fees typically run 0.6 to 1.0percent annually plus the underlying fund expenses, so weigh the costs against the convenience and tax perks. The key benefit is administrative: the DAF issues your donation receipt, handles confirmations to recipient charities, and aggregates records come tax season.

A common tax strategy is "bunching" deductions by making large DAF contributions in high-income years, surpassing the standard deduction threshold, then granting smaller disbursements annually while taking the standard deduction in off years. This approach mirrors front-loading lab supplies with one big grant then drawing them down incrementally as experiments progress. Another tactic is donating appreciated securities, which erases capital-gain tax and turbocharges the gift value compared with selling the shares first and donating cash. If you acquired tech stocks during a sabbatical stint in industry, funneling them into the DAF might save thousands in taxes while boosting the amount available for future grants.

Selecting grantees becomes a research exercise. You can consult platforms like Charity Navigator for quantitative data—financial health, transparency scores—but qualitative due diligence matters too. Request annual reports, interview program directors, or visit project sites virtually, much like reviewing manuscripts or evaluating doctoral defenses. An academic lens can spot red flags that glossy brochures miss, such as lack of robust evaluation methods or mission creep away from stated aims. Your grants can even include stipends for independent program assessment, turning your dollars into both service delivery and knowledge generation.

Aligning philanthropy with academic values also means considering open access and public scholarship. If you donate to educational nonprofits, ask whether their curricula will be freely available or locked behind paywalls. Funding a research nonprofit? Condition the grant on publishing findings under Creative Commons licenses. In effect, you are extending the open-science movement into the nonprofit arena, ensuring that the public—not just a board of directors—benefits from the knowledge produced. This stipulation echoes university commitments to knowledge dissemination and magnifies impact without extra dollars.

DAFs are not perfect. Critics argue they can become parking lots where money sits indefinitely while communities face urgent needs. To keep yourself honest, create a payout rule, such as granting at least five percent of the fund annually, mirroring private-foundation requirements. Place it in writing as a self-imposed accountability measure, and schedule an annual "grantmaking retreat," perhaps every spring break, to review impact reports and approve new disbursements. Consider inviting trusted colleagues or family members to serve as an informal advisory committee, providing the peer-review feedback loop academics value.

Sometimes donors worry that using a DAF obscures transparency because grants can be anonymous. Anonymity has legitimate uses—protecting privacy or avoiding fundraising spam—but if you believe public disclosure motivates others to give, choose to reveal your name on selected grants. Transparency fosters a culture of generosity much like publishing data cultivates replication. You control the dial; anonymity does not have to be all or nothing.

If a DAF feels too institutional, direct giving remains powerful. Automatic monthly donations to a local literacy center or a first-generation student fund provide steady cash flow that nonprofits can count on. The recurring model parallels your salary distribution—predictable, budget-friendly, and easy to increase when raises arrive. Set donations on autopay just like retirement contributions, ensuring generosity is a line item, not a leftover. Then use the DAF for episodic, larger gifts driven by strategic reviews.

Don't overlook the potential of in-kind expertise. As an academic, your knowledge—grant writing, data analysis, curriculum design—holds market value. Offering pro-bono consulting alongside a financial grant often multiplies the effect. One biology professor I know donated $3,000 to a community science museum and helped design an exhibit on local biodiversity, doubling attendance numbers and future donations. The lesson: pair your checkbook with your CV to create impact beyond what either could do solo.

Family engagement can deepen both legacy and learning. Allow children or grandchildren to recommend a percentage of annual grants, teaching them due diligence and budgeting. Provide guidance but not a veto, fostering agency and values transmission. Many DAF platforms enable multi-generational advisors, so the fund becomes a classroom where philanthropy methods are handed down like research traditions. The conversation shifts from "What do we own?" to "What problems do we solve together?"

When life circumstances shift—sabbatical abroad, salary change, health issues—review your giving plan just as you would update a course syllabus mid-semester if enrollment unexpectedly doubled. Flexibility ensures your philanthropy remains proportionate and aligned with current priorities. A formula approach, like donating a fixed percentage of side-consulting income, scales automatically and avoids decision fatigue. That way, a lucrative keynote becomes a win for both your personal goals and the causes you champion.

Some scholars worry that giving restricts personal financial freedom, especially amid rising housing and healthcare costs. But philanthropy and personal security are not mutually exclusive; they coexist in a balanced financial plan. Allocate resources to emergency funds, retirement, and debt reduction first, then direct surplus to charitable vehicles. This mirrors responsible lab management: keep contingency funds for broken equipment while still funding student research travel. Disciplined stewardship makes generosity sustainable rather than stressful.

Strategic giving can also dovetail with career objectives. Funding graduate fellowships or departmental initiatives can enhance your program's reputation and attract talent, provided conflicts of interest are managed transparently. A political scientist I advise channels royalties from her popular textbook into an endowed lecture series on civic engagement, aligning her scholarship with philanthropy while boosting departmental visibility. Clear guidelines—managed by the university foundation, not her directly—prevent undue influence on curriculum or hiring.

In an era of social justice reckoning, many academics evaluate whether their philanthropy addresses systemic inequities or merely alleviates symptoms. Conduct a portfolio review: categorize each grant by issue area, geographic reach, and theory of change. Aim for a blend that meets immediate needs and funds advocacy or policy work tackling root causes. This mirrors a balanced research agenda that bridges descriptive studies with intervention trials. If your giving skews heavily toward your alma mater's athletic fund, consider reallocating some share to community colleges or scholarship programs serving marginalized students.

Legacy planning converts philanthropy from an annual act to an enduring narrative. Designating your DAF or a percentage of your estate to continue supporting chosen causes ensures your values live on after your final lecture. Drafting an ethical will—an informal letter explaining why you supported certain organizations—offers heirs a roadmap for future grant decisions. Think of it as the introduction section to your life's final research paper, contextualizing your hypotheses and anticipated impacts for future collaborators.

Finally, remember that philanthropy, like teaching, is iterative. You test hypotheses, collect feedback, and refine methods over time. Celebrate wins—a program graduation rate spike, a newly tenured faculty member you funded—but also scrutinize shortfalls candidly. If an organization under-delivers or shifts away from your mission, pivot grants elsewhere without guilt. Intellectual humility—the admission that data should guide decisions—applies to giving as much as to scholarship.

Charitable giving aligned with academic values transforms generosity from sporadic impulse to sustained, evidence-based practice. Whether you channel resources through donor-advised funds, direct gifts, or a hybrid model, the key is treating philanthropy with the same rigor, curiosity, and integrity that animate your professional life. When you do, every dollar becomes a footnote in a larger story of impact, transparency, and shared knowledge—qualities that scholars have championed for centuries and that the world needs now more than ever.

Chapter 34: Estate Planning for Academics, Wills, Trusts, and Digital Legacy of Research

Estate planning may sound like something reserved for aristocrats with mansions and oil portraits, yet for academics it is simply the disciplined habit of deciding who will inherit the fruits of your teaching, research, and retirement accounts before a court decides for you. Scholars spend decades curating syllabi, mentoring students, filing grants, and publishing work that outlives classroom lectures, but many postpone writing even a basic will because they feel too young, too busy, or too intimidated by legal jargon. The irony is that the clearer your intellectual property and financial wishes are on paper, the freer you can feel to focus on scholarship while you are alive. A will functions like a syllabus for your estate: it explains what happens, who is responsible, and where resources should go, sparing loved ones from confusion at a moment already clouded by grief. Without one, state intestacy laws impose a one-size-fits-all distribution that rarely aligns with an academic's nuanced family dynamics or professional commitments.

A solid will begins with inventory, just like a literature review starts with a comprehensive search of existing scholarship. List all tangible assets—home, car, personal library, lab equipment you personally own—and all intangible ones such as retirement accounts, royalties, and digital subscriptions. Knowing what exists clarifies what needs direction and prevents accidentally omitting that niche journal royalty stream that steadily arrives each quarter. Most professors ignore smaller sources of income, but even modest sums can fuel scholarships or research stipends if documented properly. Once the inventory is complete, decide beneficiaries thoughtfully, keeping in mind personal relationships and philanthropic passions. Designate an executor who blends financial acumen with emotional steadiness, ideally someone comfortable dealing with publishers, HR departments, and family in equal measure.

Trusts often enter the conversation when an academic wants finer control or privacy than a will alone can offer. A revocable living trust acts like a binder where you transfer ownership of assets while alive, yet retain full control; upon death, the successor trustee follows instructions without the delays or public exposure of probate court. This structure appeals to scholars who own property in multiple states—reducing multi-state probate costs—or who envision royalties flowing for decades after their passing. Irrevocable trusts, while more rigid, help shield assets from estate taxes or creditors and can guarantee that endowed funds remain restricted to specified academic programs. Trusts do involve more initial paperwork and sometimes ongoing administration fees, but the smoother transition often justifies the effort for anyone with complex intellectual property.

Speaking of intellectual property, researchers accumulate copyrights, data sets, and sometimes patents that continue generating revenue and reputation post-mortem. Academia's collaborative nature means ownership can be split among universities, co-authors, and funding agencies, so clarifying your personal stake is vital. Work-for-hire clauses, university IP policies, and grant contracts all influence how your estate can control or profit from future licensing. An estate plan should specify whether you wish royalties to support heirs, a departmental fund, or an open-access archive benefiting the broader scholarly community. Including a literary executor—someone savvy about academic publishing—to manage negotiations with presses or journals can preserve your intellectual legacy while maximizing financial returns.

Digital legacy extends beyond Google Scholar profiles and institutional repositories; it includes email archives, course-management platforms, cloud-stored lecture recordings, and even social media accounts where your academic persona lives. Appoint a digital executor empowered to access, preserve, or delete these assets according to your wishes, providing passwords through a secure vault or attorney escrow. Decide whether you want lab notebooks uploaded to an open server, unfinished manuscripts completed by a former postdoc, or personal reflections withheld from public view. Universities increasingly offer guidance on data stewardship, but ultimate authority may still rest with your estate, so do not assume institutional servers guarantee perpetual availability. Digital clutter can overwhelm loved ones; clear instructions transform potential chaos into an organized archive scholars can mine for generations.

Beneficiary designations on retirement accounts and life-insurance policies bypass wills entirely, transferring directly to named individuals or entities, so updating them after marriage, divorce, or the birth of children is non-negotiable. A mismatch—such as an ex-partner still listed on a 403(b) even though the will leaves everything to a new spouse—will result in the account going to the ex. Calendar a biennial beneficiary review, perhaps every time you file your promotion materials or submit an annual report. If your goal is philanthropic, consider naming a university foundation or donor-advised fund as contingent beneficiary to endow scholarships. Remember, beneficiary paperwork is often fill-in-the-blanks, requiring no attorney once your broader plan is set, yet it wields outsized legal power.

Letters of instruction complement formal documents by offering context, guidance, and personal messages that legal instruments cannot capture. In one letter you might explain the significance of bequeathing your annotated copy of Kant's *Critique of Pure Reason* to a particular doctoral student or why royalty income should fund travel grants for first-generation scholars. These letters carry no legal authority but influence executors and trustees in day-to-day decisions, bridging emotional gaps left by legal language. Keep them concise, update as needed, and store with your will or trust documents. Think of them as the teaching notes that accompany a dense slide deck: they translate abstract points into human terms.

Power of attorney and health-care proxies round out the planning picture by covering incapacity rather than death. A durable financial power of attorney allows a trusted agent to handle royalty checks, grant renewals, or even lab-animal care if you are hospitalized. Meanwhile, an advance directive paired with a medical proxy clarifies treatment preferences and authorizes someone to make health decisions aligned with your values. Academics often assume rationality will prevail in hospitals, yet families under stress can disagree about aggressive interventions versus palliative care. Filling out these documents is no harder than submitting an IRB amendment, and it spares loved ones from wrenching guesswork.

International scholars face cross-border challenges: dual citizenship, property overseas, and multiple pension systems can expose estates to conflicting laws. If you own an apartment in Paris and a condo in Pennsylvania, each jurisdiction might claim probate authority, complicating timelines and taxes. An attorney versed in international estate law can coordinate treaties and tax credits, perhaps recommending separate "situs" wills for each country. Failure to plan may freeze assets while courts determine rightful heirs, disrupting mortgage payments and research access for whoever inherits. For globetrotting academics, estate planning is as critical as keeping passports current.

Insurance plays a supporting role, funding bequests or covering estate taxes so cherished assets need not be sold quickly. Term life insurance is often sufficient, providing a tax-free lump sum at low cost during peak earning years and while dependents are young. Permanent insurance can fund trusts or equalize inheritances when illiquid assets—like a family farm or valuable art—go to one heir. Disability insurance, likewise, protects income if illness strikes before retirement, preserving the estate plan's assumptions. Rather than viewing insurance as a product, treat it as a grant that activates only under adverse scenarios.

Guardianship decisions for minor children or dependents stand among the most emotional choices. Selecting a guardian involves balancing love, logistical capability, and alignment with your educational values. Perhaps you want kids to remain near a particular school district or be raised by someone who shares your commitment to the arts. Specify a guardian in your will and name backups in case first choices cannot serve. Without this clarity, courts will appoint guardians based on statutory priorities, which may ignore nuances like sibling proximity or cultural heritage vital to you.

Taxes can erode estates through federal and state levies, though most academics' net worth will fall below the current federal exemption, which exceeds $13million per individual. Nonetheless, state inheritance taxes may apply, and future legislation could lower thresholds. Charitable bequests—either outright or via charitable remainder trusts—can reduce taxable estates while supporting scholarship funds or community programs. If you anticipate significant royalties from a forthcoming textbook series or patented technology, planning early to channel income streams into tax-advantaged structures shields both heirs and philanthropic goals. Tax strategy is not about avoiding civic responsibility but about directing more dollars to your chosen missions instead of default government allocation.

Blended families introduce additional layers—stepchildren, former spouses, and late-in-life partnerships—requiring extra vigilance so no one feels disinherited or unfairly favored. A trust can stipulate income to a surviving spouse for life with principal later shifting to biological children, balancing loyalty to both groups. Holding family meetings, or at least communicating intentions individually, mitigates surprise and litigation risk. Transparency can be awkward but pays dividends in family harmony, much as clear grading rubrics prevent grade disputes. If prior divorce decrees dictate life-insurance beneficiaries or pension splits, integrate those obligations into the new estate blueprint rather than assume they vanish.

Your personal library poses both sentimental and practical questions. Students may value heavily annotated texts far more than relatives who prefer digital copies. Decide which materials should go to institutional archives, which to specific individuals, and which to charitable book drives. Rare volumes may require appraisals for tax deduction if donated. Labeling shelves or maintaining a simple spreadsheet avoids posthumous confusion—no executor wants to decipher cryptic marginalia to assess a book's importance. Treat your library like a curated dataset: properly cataloged, it becomes a resource instead of a burden.

Pets are family members to many academics who spend late nights writing with feline or canine companions curled nearby. Include pet-care directives and consider a modest pet trust funding food, vet bills, or placement with a trusted friend. Otherwise, animals may land in shelters despite informal assurances from acquaintances. A pet clause in your will adds perhaps five sentences yet closes a loophole of potential heartbreak. Think of it as a humane footnote to your scholarly life.

Safe storage of documents completes the process. Keep originals in a fireproof home safe or attorney's vault, with digital copies encrypted in cloud storage accessible to executors. Emailing key contacts a "where to find everything" memo prevents scavenger hunts. Update after major life events—marriage, tenure, retirement—and mark your calendar for a five-year review. Estate planning is iterative, like revising a manuscript: output today will need fresh edits tomorrow.

Many universities offer employee assistance programs or alumni networks with free or discounted estate planning resources. Taking advantage is like using library interlibrary loan—available benefits that too few people tap. Attend workshops, ask HR about will-prep benefits, and consult faculty who recently retired for real-world insights. Crowdsourced wisdom saves both money and rookie mistakes. Use academic networks for this most personal professional development.

The emotional payoff of a finished estate plan is peace of mind—knowing that if a sabbatical flight never makes it home, your loved ones won't scramble, your research won't languish, and your values will echo through endowed funds, preserved datasets, and curated archives. Estate planning is less about mortality than stewardship: shepherding intellectual and financial resources so they continue advancing knowledge and supporting communities after you've signed your last attendance sheet. By treating the process like any rigorous scholarly project—mapping objectives, drafting documents, peer-reviewing with professionals, and revising as data change—you transform an uncomfortable chore into an extension of your academic mission. And when your heirs open that neatly organized binder someday, they'll read the final chapter you authored with gratitude instead of guesswork.

Chapter 35: Managing Lifestyle Inflation, Keeping Up with Peers vs. Keeping Wealth Growing

Lifestyle inflation creeps into life the way ivy creeps up a campus wall—slow, steady, and almost charming until you realize the original brickwork is hidden and repairs cost a fortune. The phenomenon begins innocently with a small raise or a promotion, triggering what feels like justified upgrades: a nicer coffee, a slightly bigger apartment, better seats at the conference hotel. These gestures of self-reward are healthy in moderation, yet without guardrails they morph into a perpetual race against ever-shifting expectations. You realize that each time income steps up, expenses sprint to catch up, leaving savings stuck at the same pace—or worse, falling behind. Understanding lifestyle inflation requires naming it, quantifying it, and disentangling genuine joy from reflexive spending motivated by comparison.

Comparison is a powerful academic peer-review force turned inward on personal life. One colleague buys a new electric car, another renovates a kitchen, and suddenly your perfectly functional sedan and laminate counters look shabby by contrast. Social media intensifies this scrutiny by showcasing everyone's highlight reel without the footnotes explaining debt levels or parental subsidies. Remember the replication crisis in psychology? Lifestyle boasts lack replication data too; you see the shiny outcome, not the spreadsheet of trade-offs. A healthy antidote is cultivating financial self-efficacy, recognizing that someone else's purchase neither invalidates your choices nor guarantees their long-term security. Treat peer spending like anecdotal evidence—interesting but insufficient for altering your plan without more rigorous data.

Anchoring can reset expectations so subtly you barely notice. Your graduate-student budget normalized $3 tacos and second-hand furniture, but one faculty paycheck later the anchor shifts to $30 entrees and mid-century modern replicas. Behavioral economists call this the "hedonic treadmill," where each new comfort becomes baseline, requiring fresh novelties to achieve the same psychological reward. Interrupting this loop involves deliberate pauses after income jumps—ideally a three- to six-month waiting period—before locking in new recurring expenses. During the pause, funnel the entire raise into savings or debt payoff, then decide which upgrades truly enhance well-being. Like peer review, delayed gratification weeds out weak justifications.

Financial identities influence spending scripts more than pure math. Some academics see themselves as modest public servants, others as under-recognized high earners deserving belated luxuries. If early career meant scarcity, the first substantial paycheck can unleash pent-up desires. Conduct a values audit: list top five life priorities—research freedom, family time, travel, creative pursuits—and cross-check major expenses against them. If the new designer wardrobe doesn't support any value but absorbs 15percent of take-home pay, reconsider. Aligning spending with core identity produces satisfaction longer than matching an acquaintance's upgrade.

Budgeting often fails because it feels punitive, yet reframed as allocation of limited lab funding, it becomes intellectually familiar. Picture your after-tax income as grant money with line items: fixed costs, variable costs, and high-impact investments like retirement or sabbatical funds. Zero-based budgeting, where every dollar is assigned a role, mirrors how you'd manage a research grant: each expense must justify itself annually rather than rolling over unquestioned. Automation furthers discipline—automatic transfers to index funds and debt payments mean lifestyle cannot inflate until after goals are met. In this framework, leftover discretionary money can be spent guilt-free, knowing it won't cannibalize future wealth.

Tracking actual spending is comparable to data collection in a longitudinal study—imperfections exist, but patterns emerge. Use apps or a simple spreadsheet to categorize expenses monthly, then calculate what percentage of new income went to savings versus lifestyle. A rule of thumb is the 50/30/20 model—needs, wants, savings—but higher earners can push savings toward 30–40percent, especially if tenure or entrepreneurial volatility looms. Reviewing data quarterly reveals trendlines: if travel spending grows by 25percent but happiness remains flat, you have actionable insight. Data-driven reflection replaces vague unease with targeted adjustments.

Debt decisions form another battleground for lifestyle inflation. Luxury car leases, zero-interest furniture financing, and high-limit credit cards disguise spending spikes as manageable monthly bites. The academic mind values long time horizons—apply that to debt by calculating full lifetime interest, not just monthly payments. A $40,000 auto loan at five percent over five years costs an extra $5,300 you could have invested in a diversified index fund. Choosing a reliable used car and investing the difference may not impress neighbors today, but future you will thank present you when compounding delivers a healthy sabbatical fund.

Windfalls and side-income surges invite particular caution. Honoraria, consulting checks, or royalty payments often feel like "found money," leading to equally spontaneous splurges. Pre-commit a policy: fifty percent of windfalls go to long-term goals, thirty percent to mid-term goals like a family trip, and twenty percent to immediate enjoyment. Formalizing percentages before money arrives bypasses emotional decision-making under the dopamine rush of a big payday. It is akin to preregistrations in research—advance planning prevents biased post-hoc rationalizations.

Strategic splurging is not the enemy; unconscious escalation is. Budget for experiences rather than objects, as experiential purchases tend to yield longer satisfaction and fewer maintenance costs. Taking your partner to a Broadway show during an academic conference may cost $200 yet create a lasting memory without raising monthly bills. Conversely, upgrading to a luxury apartment locks you into higher rent plus larger utility costs and renter's insurance premiums. Before any upgrade, ask, "Does this add recurring overhead, and if so, am I still thrilled about it twelve months from now?"

Housing remains the most significant lifestyle decision for most academics, especially in high-cost cities. A common guideline is keeping housing costs under 30percent of gross income, yet pushing closer to 20percent frees cash for investments. Consider commuting trade-offs: a smaller home near campus might offset higher rent by eliminating car expenses and gifting you time. If you anticipate sabbaticals or visiting appointments abroad, renting instead of buying grants flexibility, avoiding transaction costs that erode equity gains. Homeownership can still be a wealth tool, but only when mortgage, maintenance, and property taxes leave room for retirement contributions above employer matches.

Meal choices provide daily micro-battles against lifestyle creep. Lunching off-campus with colleagues could run $15 daily or $3 if you pack. That $12 gap invested monthly at a seven-percent return becomes roughly $18,000 over twenty years. Framing mundane choices as future sabbatical grants brings hidden stakes into focus. Implementing a "three-meal-rule"—restaurant meals limited to three per week—preserves social connection without budget blowouts. Alternatively, schedule intentional splurge nights to enjoy fine dining guilt-free while respecting caps.

Parenthood accelerates lifestyle pressures through peer comparisons around schools, enrichment, and holiday gifting. Resist "best-of-everything" consumption by distinguishing between child needs and parental signaling to other adults. A public magnet school may offer comparable outcomes to private options at a fraction of tuition, especially when savings are reinvested for college. Teach children value by modeling budgeting and trade-offs, turning them from expense drivers into allies in mindful consumption. Family discussions about money nurture financial literacy and lighten future generational burdens.

Vacations can morph from restorative breaks into status showcases, especially with social-media visibility. Setting a travel budget as a fixed percentage of income keeps wanderlust from cannibalizing long-term goals. Off-season trips, travel hacking with points, and home exchanges offer similar experiences at reduced cost. Plan vacations around intellectual curiosity—attend international conferences with family in tow, adding personal days—so professional development subsidizes leisure. Efficiency here parallels grant budgeting—multipurpose trips deliver higher return per dollar.

Clothing and personal aesthetics often track income climb. Adopting a capsule wardrobe—fewer, higher-quality, mix-and-match pieces—reduces impulse shopping while conveying polished professionalism. Shopping with a list, leveraging second-hand platforms, and enforcing a "one-in, one-out" rule curb closet bloat. Remember, Einstein famously wore similar suits to minimize decision fatigue; academic credibility stems more from ideas than designer labels. Redirect clothing savings toward experiences, research assistants, or debt elimination.

Technology upgrades offer another slippery slope. A new laptop for data analysis is justifiable; annual smartphone replacements less so. Extend gadget life cycles by delaying purchases until productivity truly suffers, a method akin to equipment depreciation schedules. When you do buy, target refurbished units with warranties, freeing capital for conference travel or emergency funds. Tech minimalism counters the arms race of visible peripherals without compromising scholarly output.

Friends and extended family may inadvertently encourage lifestyle leapfrogging. Transparent conversations about financial goals invite solidarity instead of competition. Suggest affordable gatherings—potlucks, park outings, board-game nights—that highlight connection over consumption. If peers insist on pricey venues, propose alternatives or set personal spending limits beforehand. Genuine relationships transcend monetary expectations; if not, use the friction as a diagnostic for recalibrating social circles.

Accountability systems anchor new habits. Monthly check-ins with a partner or friend to review spending ratios and celebrate milestone reductions reinforce progress. Some academics form money mastermind groups resembling writing circles, exchanging tactics on frugality and investing. Public goals—such as posting a debt-free countdown on a refrigerator—transform abstract intentions into visible commitments. Positive feedback loops, whether applause for hitting a savings percentage or achieving a no-spend month, fuel momentum.

The ultimate metric for managing lifestyle inflation is the gap between earning and spending, funneled into assets that compound. Aim to grow net worth annually by at least the after-inflation rate plus a personal ambition premium—perhaps ten percent. Track net worth quarterly like you monitor citation counts, using the data to inform adjustments. A widening gap signals healthy resistance to inflationary pressures; a narrowing one serves as an early-warning system requiring intervention.

Your long-term vision should culminate in financial independence—where investment income covers living expenses—allowing you to choose how, not whether, to work. Lifestyle inflation delays this milestone by inflating the target and reducing capacity to save. Consider each spending decision a vote on how soon you want that freedom. Small daily votes compound into decades of results, echoing the aggregate impact of micro-decisions in a longitudinal research program.

In the end, managing lifestyle inflation is an exercise in conscious living. Academics excel at scrutinizing research designs; applying that scrutiny to consumption turns money from master into servant. Choose upgrades that genuinely enrich life and advance values, reject those that merely keep pace with a social media feed, and automate savings so generosity and future security are non-negotiable line items. By staying anchored to purpose, you preserve the best parts of rising income—choice, opportunity, and impact—while sidestepping the treadmill that leaves many high earners gasping at the finish line with little accumulated wealth.

Chapter 36: Insurance Tune-Ups at Every Decade, Coverage Gaps You Didn't Know You Had

Turning twenty feels like switching from a learner's permit to a real driver's license in the adult world, yet most people in this decade still treat insurance like an optional textbook they'll skim before finals. Renters policies often go ignored because new graduates assume the landlord's coverage protects laptops and bicycles, only to discover after a break-in that the landlord is liable for the four walls and not the contents. Car-sharing apps add another twist, as drivers assume platform insurance is fully comprehensive when it may cover only state minimums, leaving users on the hook for damages beyond a modest ceiling. Health insurance via a parent's plan ends at twenty-six, but even before that milestone, lapses happen if human resources forgets to re-enroll dependents after a parent changes jobs. The smart move in your twenties is to conduct a quick inventory—devices, furniture, musical instruments—and price a renters policy that usually costs less per month than a streaming subscription yet saves hundreds or thousands after one mishap.

Your thirties often introduce marriage, a mortgage, or a move to a city where you finally buy real furniture, all of which revamp your risk profile overnight like a syllabus overhaul after new accreditation standards. Homeowners insurance replaces renters, yet many buyers fixate on rebuilding cost without checking if the policy covers sewer-back-up, a surprisingly common and expensive calamity in older neighborhoods.

Dual-income households sometimes forget that both partners should still carry disability insurance, mistakenly thinking two salaries offer redundancy when actually each person's absence would halve household cash flow. First-time parents dive into life insurance but underbuy coverage by calculating replacement income only for the employed spouse, overlooking the economic value of stay-at-home caregiving, which could cost tens of thousands annually if outsourced. A comprehensive tune-up during this decade means updating beneficiary designations, increasing liability limits to match higher net worth, and adding an umbrella policy that shields against lawsuits when playdates or neighborhood gatherings expand your social footprint and your potential liability.

Hitting forty can feel like cruising at altitude—career established, kids in activities, home equity growing—yet turbulence lurks in overlooked coverage caps established a decade earlier when your income was half its current size. Home renovation projects boost property value, but unless you notify your insurer, the rebuild estimate may still reflect pre-addition square footage, leaving you short if a fire levels the place. Those shiny midlife motorcycles or boats parked in the garage might not be explicitly listed, meaning accidents could be denied or reimbursed at minimal "other recreational vehicle" limits. Disability insurance purchased in your early thirties rarely adjusts automatically for inflation or salary increases, so review the monthly benefit now and consider a cost-of-living rider to protect future earnings. This decade is also the moment to verify that teenage drivers are correctly listed on auto policies, as insurers can deny claims for "undisclosed household drivers," turning an already scary fender bender into a financial sinkhole.

Your fifties often bring the highest earning years and the largest college-tuition bills, an ironic overlap that magnifies the stakes of coverage gaps. Empty-nest downsizing may tempt you to trim personal-property limits, but high-value jewelry or newly acquired art could require separate riders because standard policies cap individual items at a few thousand dollars. Travelers who take sabbaticals or bucket-list trips abroad may assume health coverage follows them worldwide, yet many employer plans exclude international medical evacuation, a service that can run six figures without supplemental travel insurance. This decade is also prime time to explore long-term-care insurance while premiums remain relatively affordable and health underwriting more lenient; waiting until symptoms appear is like trying to buy fire insurance while your kitchen is already ablaze. Finally, reassess liability limits if you serve on nonprofit boards—directors-and-officers coverage shields the organization, but personal umbrella coverage adds a second layer of defense if litigation names you individually.

Crossing sixty often coincides with Medicare enrollment, and plenty of academics treat the Part A and Part B sign-up as a tidy bow on medical coverage, not realizing that routine dental, vision, and hearing expenses now fall largely on them. Medigap or Medicare Advantage plans fill those holes differently, and failing to pick the right option in the first enrollment window can lock you into costlier premiums or pre-existing condition exclusions later. Adult children or elderly parents might move in, yet home insurance may not automatically extend liability protection to nonresident relatives or caregivers, so confirm who counts as an "insured" under your policy language. Retirement account balances are largest now, enticing cybercriminals, but few retirees purchase identity-theft insurance or add cyber-fraud riders that reimburse stolen funds when phishing emails mimic familiar institutions. A decade check-up should also update estate-planning documents to ensure life-insurance proceeds and retirement beneficiaries dovetail with trusts and wills, preventing probate hiccups that waste both money and scholarly goodwill.

Seventy-something scholars often assume they've aged out of insurance tune-ups, but longevity changes the math: the average twenty-year retirement now extends well into the nineties, so inflation protection on fixed-payout annuities and long-term-care policies becomes critical. Reread your homeowners deductible, which may be expressed as a percentage of dwelling value rather than a flat amount; rising property prices transform a once-affordable deductible into a budget-busting sum during storms. If you lend classic texts, instruments, or archives to universities or heirs, consider "inland marine" coverage that protects items in transit and on loan—standard homeowners rarely covers property once it leaves premises. Many seniors reduce driving but don't notify insurers, missing discounts for low mileage or defensive-driving certifications that could cut auto premiums by double digits. Finally, check that adult children removed from umbrella policies have secured their own coverage so lawsuits don't boomerang back to the still-wealthy parent who unwittingly remains listed on vehicle titles.

Throughout every decade, umbrella liability stands out as the Swiss Army knife of policies, yet surveys show fewer than fifteen percent of households carry one. Lawyers target deep pockets, and professors' perceived "tenure wealth" can attract litigation even when accidents occur off-duty, such as your dog biting a delivery driver or a social-media post sparking a defamation claim. A one-million-dollar umbrella typically costs less annually than a conference registration fee, yet it safeguards assets, future wages, and even defense costs if allegations prove unfounded. Purchase limits equal to your net worth plus projected retirement savings to avoid catastrophic gaps, and schedule renewals whenever your balance sheet changes meaningfully. Remember that the umbrella requires underlying auto and homeowners policies to carry certain minimums, so coordinate all three rather than buying piecemeal.

Disability insurance remains under-appreciated, especially among younger academics who rely on the assumption that universities offer generous sick leave. Group policies often replace no more than sixty percent of salary and usually exclude consulting or book-royalty income, yet mortgage lenders and student-loan servicers still expect full payments if illness strikes. A supplemental individual policy closes this gap, guarantees portability between institutions, and can include a "future purchase option" to increase benefits without new medical exams. Evaluate contract language—"own occupation" definitions pay even if you can work outside academia, while "any occupation" clauses stop payments once you can perform any work, including a low-pay desk job, potentially derailing a scholar's standard of living. Disability risk peaks higher than many realize: statistical tables show a one-in-four chance of experiencing a long-term disability before retirement age, far eclipsing most people's risk of home fire.

Health-insurance deductibles and out-of-pocket maximums ballooned over the past decade, effectively making many families self-insure the first several thousand dollars of medical costs each year. Pairing a high-deductible plan with a health-savings account addresses the gap by letting you set aside pre-tax dollars that roll over indefinitely and can double as retirement funds after age sixty-five. Failure to build HSA balances while healthy leaves retirees vulnerable to uncovered dental implants, hearing aids, and copays on specialty drugs whose price tags dwarf typical Medicare budgets. Treat HSA contributions as non-negotiable, like mandatory lab-safety protocols, rather than optional savings. If your institution funds only a fraction of the annual limit, top it off yourself and invest the balance rather than keeping it in low-yield cash.

Auto insurance evolves as vehicles integrate expensive sensors and battery packs, pushing repair bills beyond traditional coverage thresholds. Comprehensive and collision limits set in your graduate-school days might not replace a three-year-old electric SUV whose lidar system alone costs four figures. Gap insurance, once dismissed as a dealership upsell, now matters if you finance or lease high-priced vehicles that depreciate faster than loan balances. Usage-based telematics programs can offset premium increases by rewarding careful drivers with rate discounts, yet privacy concerns deter enrollment, so weigh data sharing against savings. As autonomous features grow, verify that policies cover software glitches and hacked vehicle scenarios rather than assuming traditional negligence standards apply.

Homeowners insurance faces climate-related volatility, with insurers hiking premiums or withdrawing from fire-prone and hurricane-coastal markets. Check for "law and ordinance" endorsements covering code-upgrade costs if rebuilding, because outdated wiring replaced after disaster may cost far more than original construction, and standard policies rarely foot the entire bill. Water damage from inside sources like burst pipes now causes more claims than external floods, yet many homeowners still skip optional coverage for sump-pump failure or sewer backups. Installing leak-detection sensors can earn premium discounts that offset device costs, a win-win akin to upgrading lab safety to reduce claims and downtime. Don't overlook personal-property riders for high-tech home offices whose equipment far exceeds the default coverage caps.

Cyber insurance once catered to corporations but now extends to households grappling with ransomware, identity theft, and online scams. Policies reimburse costs for data restoration, legal fees if personal data leaks, and even ransom payments under certain circumstances. Academics who conduct fieldwork abroad with laptops full of sensitive data face heightened exposure; one breach can threaten both finances and professional reputation. Premiums remain modest—often under $100 annually—but coverage varies widely, so examine sublimits for extortion payments and the definition of "covered device" to include tablets and smartphones. As the digital realm overlaps with personal finances, consider cyber insurance the modern alarm system for an online home.

Pet insurance joins the list of frontier protections as veterinary medicine mirrors human health-care inflation, offering MRI scans and chemotherapy for four-legged friends at prices rivaling elective surgery. Monthly premiums offset unexpected $8,000 surgeries that could derail emergency funds or entice medical credit lines charging double-digit interest. Choose policies with lifetime illness limits rather than per-condition caps that reset annually but roll over a low ceiling on chronic needs. Like any insurance, buy while the pet is young to avoid exclusions for pre-existing conditions reminiscent of old-school health policies. For academics who travel frequently, add a boarding-fee rider covering emergency kennel costs if you're hospitalized far from home.

Life-insurance needs fluctuate, yet many people set-and-forget term policies purchased after their first child, ignoring subsequent income jumps, mortgage upgrades, or new dependents like aging parents. Recalculate coverage to replace at least ten years of your current salary plus pay off remaining debts and fund tuition goals. Term-conversion features allow upgrading to permanent coverage without new health exams, valuable if health deteriorates; consider converting a slice before the window closes at age sixty-five or earlier. Conversely, if kids graduate and mortgages shrink, a policy purchased decades ago might exceed need; surrendering or selling it on a life-settlement market could reclaim value instead of letting it lapse. Regular audits ensure life-insurance dollars align with genuine obligations rather than outdated fears.

Legal and professional liability coverage warrants attention for professors embroiled in consulting, expert witness testimony, or outside board service. Universities offer some protection under indemnification policies, but conflicts of interest or side businesses often fall outside scope. Professional -liability (errors-and-omissions) policies cover claims of inaccurate advice, while media-liability riders can shield against copyright or defamation suits for blogs and podcasts. Costs vary by discipline—an engineering consultant pays more than a historian—but the premium is modest relative to potential legal bills. Each new engagement letter should trigger a coverage review, mirroring grant-contract risk assessments that ensure IRB compliance and sponsor indemnity.

Phased retirement or part-time academic roles complicate benefit eligibility, sometimes eliminating employer group life and disability coverage. Purchasing individual policies before reducing hours sidesteps age-based rate jumps and health-status surprises. Medicare enrollment can also disrupt Health Savings Account contributions, so adjust budgeting to compensate for losing that tax-advantaged savings channel. Examine retiree-medical options well ahead of departure; universities occasionally offer supplemental plans cheaper than private Medigap policies, but opt-in deadlines may precede official retirement by a year or more. Treat benefit transitions like grant close-out procedures—failure to meet timelines forfeits resources you spent years building.

Regular insurance tune-ups dovetail with annual financial reviews—tax prep, net-worth calculations, or performance evaluations—creating a habit loop that embeds protection into broader financial wellness. Keep a one-page insurance dashboard listing policy types, coverage limits, premiums, deductibles, and renewal dates, updating it just as you'd maintain a CV. Share the dashboard with trusted family members or estate executors so coverage does its job when you can't advocate. Consider hiring a fee-only insurance consultant every five years to audit gaps objectively, similar to external peer review that strengthens research accuracy. With proactive management, insurance shifts from begrudging expense to confident shield, empowering you to pursue teaching, discovery, and adventure knowing that unseen risks won't dismantle your hard-earned wealth.

In sum, insurance is not a static purchase but a dynamic contract adapting to life's seasons, much like syllabi evolve with new literature and pedagogical trends. Each decade introduces fresh liabilities—new assets, health realities, or technological threats—that render last decade's policy settings obsolete. A thoughtful tune-up asks the same scholarly questions we pose in research: What has changed? What assumptions no longer hold? Where are blind spots? Answering them with periodic adjustments ensures coverage keeps pace with ambition, safeguarding both livelihood and legacy in a world where the only constant is change.

Part V · Late Career, Transitions, and Life After the Last Lecture

Part V · Late Career, Transitions, and Life After the Last Lecture explores the unique financial, emotional, and lifestyle considerations that arise as academics move toward retirement and beyond. This section offers thoughtful guidance on maximizing late-stage income opportunities, preparing for retirement with clarity and confidence, and managing the practicalities of shifting identities—from active professor to emeritus, consultant, mentor, or world traveler. Readers will learn how to assess retirement readiness, time their exits strategically, and navigate healthcare transitions like Medicare enrollment and supplemental coverage. The chapters also address estate planning, long-term care options, giving back through philanthropy, and creating a financial legacy that reflects academic values and personal purpose. This part is not just about winding down—it's about redesigning the next chapter with intention, protecting what you've built, and transitioning from a career of impact to a life of fulfillment. Whether you're five years from retirement or already on the other side of the podium, this section helps ensure that your financial plan honors your journey and sustains your freedom well into the future.

Chapter 37: Full Professor Pay & Perks, Merit Raises, Named Chairs, and Endowed Supplements

Landing the rank of full professor feels a bit like summiting a scholarly mountain: the vista is wide, the air is thinner, and the terrain ahead is less clearly marked than the tenure-track switchbacks you just climbed. Pay typically jumps, yet so do expectations for leadership, mentoring, and institutional citizenship. At most universities, the base salary increase from associate to full is a one-time bump—often five to fifteen percent—followed by smaller annual merit raises that hinge on continued productivity. Because the promotion is meant to recognize sustained excellence, administrators assume you will keep outperforming peers, which means coasting can erode future merit edges quickly. This opening chapter explores how to leverage the new rank into lasting financial advantages rather than a single celebratory pay stub.

Merit raises form the bedrock of post-promotion income growth, but the percentage pool each year is usually modest—sometimes two or three percent of payroll—so the difference between a glowing review and an average one can be measured in hundreds, not thousands, of dollars. To keep merit hikes meaningful, document leadership roles that transcend your own research, like directing a graduate program or chairing accreditation committees. Senior faculty who submit terse annual reports risk "meets expectations" labels that translate into median raises, while those who frame accomplishments within departmental goals often snag top-tier percentages. The lesson is pragmatic: narrative matters as much at full professor as it did in your tenure dossier, even if the stakes shift from job security to incremental income.

Compression and inversion threaten earning potential when junior hires arrive at near-parity salaries after negotiating aggressively in tight labor markets. Institutions sometimes address this gap with "compression adjustments" during budget upticks, but waiting passively can cost years of compounding. Track salary data via Chronicle of Higher Education reports or public-employee databases if you're at a state institution, then schedule a calm, evidence-based chat with your dean if disparities widen beyond reasonable market drift. Frame the conversation around equity and retention rather than personal grievance, showing how salary parity aids morale and mentorship effectiveness. Administrators respond best to solutions grounded in data and departmental health.

Retention offers remain the fastest escalator of senior faculty pay, yet courting outside suitors takes time and moral calculation. Apply for leadership roles, visiting professorships, or targeted searches, not merely to threaten departure but to gauge market value honestly. If an offer emerges, consider total compensation—startup funds, teaching load, cost of living—not just the headline salary. Present any external offer to your dean with transparency, emphasizing alignment with your long-term goals at the home institution if financial adjustments can be made. Beware playing chicken: occasionally administrators call the bluff, and bridging back becomes awkward if funds are unavailable.

Named chairs and professorships transform salary structure by layering stipends—often five to fifty thousand dollars—on top of base pay, sometimes with discretionary research accounts. Eligibility may rely on internal awards, external visibility, or donor preferences for specific fields. Build candid relationships with advancement offices so they know your work when matching donor intent to faculty expertise. If selected, clarify renewal terms—some chairs rotate every three to five years, others are lifetime while employed, and stipends may reset if you assume administrative posts. Use accompanying discretionary funds strategically: seed high-risk projects that generate larger external grants, reinforcing your chair's impact.

Endowed supplements differ from chairs in that they usually attach to administrative titles—department head, program director—or distinguished service recognitions. These stipends can run annually without formal chair branding but still lift total compensation meaningfully. Negotiating stipends when taking on new leadership roles protects against workload creep and provides leverage for future base-salary recalibration. Document the time commitment and outcomes so future negotiations rest on tangible achievements. When stepping down, request that some portion of the stipend roll into base if the role significantly advanced institutional goals beyond its term.

Summer salary remains an underutilized perk at research universities where full professors can pay themselves up to three additional months from grants or contracts. Plan proposals with enough padding to include summer effort lines, and budget future raises by indexing summer rates to projected base increases. For those in teaching-oriented institutions, summer courses may offer modest pay but count toward retirement benefits, so weigh cash today against long-term pension accrual. Sabbaticals complicate summer income because some universities disallow concurrent grant pay, so clarify policies early to avoid clawbacks. Diversify funding sources—federal agencies, foundations, industry contracts—to smooth gaps when grant cycles misalign.

Administrative supplements like department chair stipends or graduate-school fellowships can temporarily outpace named-chair stipends but often fade when the term ends. Negotiate whether a fraction converts to base salary to avoid dramatic dips when you return to regular faculty duties. Factor extra service loads into opportunity cost; scholarly output may slow, hampering eligibility for future merit raises and outside offers. Budget personal finances assuming the supplement ends on schedule, using excess to max retirement contributions rather than inflate fixed expenses. In essence, treat administrative income as a sabbatical grant for your household budget—temporary and mission-specific.

Speaking of retirement, full professors near career zeniths should revisit contribution percentages because IRS limits rise with catch-up provisions after age fifty. Increasing deferrals by even five percent during peak-earning windows compounds significantly, especially when paired with chair stipends or retention raises. Compare traditional versus Roth options if expecting lower taxable income in retirement, and coordinate with spouse accounts to maximize household tax diversification. Consult with HR about 415(c) limits if multiple university plans exist, avoiding accidental over-contributions that trigger penalties. Strategic saving now converts temporary pay perks into lifelong income streams.

Non-salary perks amplify compensation in subtler ways: reduced teaching loads, priority for travel funds, or larger grad-assistant allocations. Quantify these benefits when considering outside offers; two course releases might equal twenty percent of your workload, freeing time for consulting income or book writing. Chronicle accomplishments achieved with each perk to defend them during budget cuts. Remember that perks erode quietly—committee creep can fill freed slots—so guard calendars ruthlessly. Time remains the only nonrenewable currency in academia.

Consulting and expert-witness fees often rise after full-professor promotion because credentials carry courtroom and corporate weight. Adopt rate cards reflecting both market standards and institutional policies capping outside activity. Use separate LLCs for liability protection and tax efficiency, and channel a percentage of fees to professional development or sabbatical self-funding. Disclose engagements transparently to comply with conflict-of-interest rules, and negotiate contract clauses allowing publication of de-identified findings to keep consulting from cannibalizing scholarly output. A healthy consulting portfolio diversifies income and expands industry relevance.

Royalty revenue from textbooks or patents can soar once you're an established authority, but so can associated legal complexities. Audit royalty statements annually, and negotiate escalator clauses keyed to sales thresholds when signing new contracts. If you control ancillary rights, license them strategically—workbook editions, translations, or online courses—while reserving the option to reclaim rights after stipulated periods. Establish a revocable trust to receive royalties if estate-planning objectives include scholarships funded by intellectual property. Vigilant management turns passive income into a legacy engine.

Health benefits rarely change at full rank, yet higher pay may shift you into tiers where premiums or surcharges differ. Investigate high-deductible plans paired with health-savings accounts, which allow triple tax advantages and function as stealth retirement vehicles for healthcare costs. If employer health coverage extends post-retirement only under certain years-of-service thresholds, calculate how long you must remain to qualify, factoring this into decisions about outside offers. Wellness incentives—premium discounts for health screenings or fitness tracking—pile small savings into meaningful sums over decades.

Campus perks extend beyond parking spots. Many universities offer mortgage-assistance programs, tuition remission for children, or subsidized cultural-event tickets. For mid-career professors with college-bound dependents, tuition benefits can rival cumulative merit raises. Clarify eligibility: some programs cover only undergraduate tuition at in-state rates or require a years-of-service vesting period. Include these perks in total-compensation comparisons whenever an external opportunity beckons. A private-sector salary premium may fade when offset by lost tuition remission and academic breaks.

Relocation allowances and spousal-hire accommodations become negotiation chips even for full professors satisfied with their institution. Expressing gentle openness to outside recruitment can prompt discussions about lab renovations, office upgrades, or administrative support that indirectly raise quality of life. When these perks materialize, thank donors and deans publicly, reinforcing goodwill and demonstrating return on investment. Remember that perks carry expectations: a newly endowed chair implies continued scholarly output and visible campus leadership, not a gradual wind-down into early retirement.

Performance metrics evolve at full rank, emphasizing mentorship, diversity leadership, and international reputation. Align efforts with metrics that committees value to sustain merit-raise momentum. For example, mentoring underrepresented doctoral students and securing NSF CAREER grants for them elevates both mentee success and your post-tenure narrative. Document these outcomes meticulously in annual reports, translating intangible contributions into quantifiable impacts. Administrators allocate scarce merit dollars where evidence convinces them of sustained excellence.

Economic shocks—state budget cuts, enrollment declines—can freeze merit pools or furlough salaries even for full professors. Build an emergency fund covering six to twelve months of expenses to cushion these shocks, especially if family obligations or dual-career logistics limit geographic mobility. Diversify income streams—consulting, royalties, investments—so institutional turbulence doesn't imperil household stability. When cuts loom, senior faculty with clear documentation of externally funded research and community impact often fare better in retention prioritization. Strong financial buffers enhance professional courage to advocate against cuts that erode academic quality.

Finally, mindset shapes the difference between fleeting and durable wealth gains at full rank. View every perk—named chair, merit raise, retention offer—not as permission to inflate lifestyle but as capital to secure future autonomy: earlier retirement, sabbatical self-funding, or philanthropic endowments. Automate transfers of incremental income to investment accounts before it hits checking, maintaining spending at pre-promotion levels for at least a year. Celebrate achievements with symbolic treats rather than permanent overhead, perhaps a one-time family trip instead of a bigger mortgage. Such discipline compounds over decades, turning academic distinction into generational security.

Reaching full professor unlocks a menu of pay and perk possibilities wider than any earlier career stage, but harvesting them requires vigilance, negotiation skill, and strategic financial habits. By approaching each raise, chair, or stipend with the same analytical rigor applied to research questions, you convert episodic windfalls into enduring wealth. The result is a career where scholarly freedom, financial stability, and institutional leadership reinforce each other, ensuring that the apex of academic rank becomes a platform, not a plateau, for both personal prosperity and public impact.

Ask ChatGPT

Chapter 38: Phased Retirement Programs, Gradual Exits, Part-Time Teaching, and Benefit Changes

Absolutely. Here's the full book chapter titled *Phased Retirement Programs: Gradual Exits, Part-Time Teaching, and Benefit Changes* written in an educational, friendly tone—like a seasoned mentor talking over coffee:

Phased retirement can feel like merging onto a quieter highway after decades of driving full-speed on the academic interstate. Instead of slamming the brakes with a full stop, you ease into a new rhythm—less noise, fewer meetings, and more control over your time. For many faculty, it's a graceful transition that allows them to keep one foot in the classroom while slowly preparing for life beyond campus. But like any good exit strategy, it's most effective when it's carefully timed and clearly understood. Whether you're contemplating it now or just want to know your options down the road, understanding the mechanics of phased retirement can help you exit on your own terms.

At its core, phased retirement is a formal agreement between a faculty member and their institution that allows a gradual reduction in workload—usually over one to five years—before full retirement. It often involves part-time teaching, reduced administrative duties, or a narrower focus on mentoring and scholarship. Unlike informal arrangements, these programs are usually documented, tied to human resources policies, and may affect your pay, benefits, and retirement contributions. Some universities even offer financial incentives to participate, especially if it helps the department plan transitions or open up positions for new hires. It's not just about working less—it's about intentionally shifting roles while protecting your long-term financial stability.

One of the first things to understand about phased retirement is that it's not guaranteed. Institutions vary widely in whether they offer it, how they structure it, and what faculty must do to qualify. Public universities often have standardized programs that are tied to state retirement systems, while private institutions may handle requests on a case-by-case basis. Eligibility might depend on age, years of service, or vesting status in a pension plan. This means that what works for a colleague at another university may not apply in your situation, so you'll want to have a one-on-one conversation with HR or your department chair early in the planning process.

Let's talk about what a typical phased retirement might look like in practice. Imagine a full professor teaching a 3-2 course load. In the first year of phased retirement, that could drop to 2-1, then 1-1 in year two, and finally just a single class in the final semester. Alongside the lighter load, the professor might keep office hours, mentor a few graduate students, or remain on a dissertation committee. Pay usually decreases proportionally, though some institutions offer pay smoothing or lump sum incentives to maintain stability. Think of it like moving from full-time faculty to a visiting scholar role—with perks and responsibilities adjusted accordingly.

Phased retirement can be a psychological win-win, especially for those who fear the identity loss that often accompanies sudden retirement. If you've built your life around scholarship, teaching, and academic community, walking away overnight can feel like stepping into a vacuum. A phased approach offers continuity, allowing you to wrap up research projects, say goodbye to colleagues and students gradually, and plan for post-academic life. It also gives time to test drive other interests—consulting, writing, volunteering—without having to commit fully just yet. For many, it's a chance to recalibrate before reinventing.

But this transition isn't only emotional—it's financial, too. Once you move into phased status, you're usually no longer eligible for merit raises or leadership stipends, and retirement contributions might shrink if your pay does. In some cases, phased faculty can't contribute to retirement plans at all, especially if they begin drawing from pensions or Social Security. That's why you should map out a timeline that overlaps income needs, healthcare transitions, and pension triggers. It's not enough to reduce your course load—you need to understand how that decision cascades through the rest of your financial life.

Healthcare is one of the most critical—and often confusing—pieces of phased retirement. If you're under 65, you'll need to know whether your employer continues to provide coverage or if you'll need to buy it on your own. If you're over 65, Medicare comes into play, but you'll need to coordinate that with any remaining employer health benefits. Some institutions allow faculty to remain on university plans while phased, others do not. And just because you're working part-time doesn't mean you'll retain full access to campus health centers or mental health services, so double-check what's included.

Another consideration is your pension or defined contribution plan. If you're part of a state retirement system, you may be required to begin drawing your pension once you reduce your hours below a certain threshold. That might sound appealing, but it also triggers tax consequences and permanently locks in your monthly benefit amount. You'll want to run projections to see whether it's better to defer that income for a few more years or start collecting it now. Some faculty choose to supplement phased retirement income with savings or outside consulting, giving themselves a smoother financial glide path.

Speaking of consulting, phased retirement can be the perfect gateway into this kind of work. Once your university obligations shrink, you may have more time and mental bandwidth for side projects. Just be sure to review your institution's policies around outside work, especially if you're still drawing a paycheck or using university resources. Some schools limit the number of consulting days even in phased retirement. Others may ask you to report income earned during the phased period for conflict-of-interest purposes. Transparency is your best protection.

One often overlooked opportunity is legacy planning. As you wind down your teaching load and start thinking about your academic footprint, consider how you might use the phased years to mentor junior faculty, codify your research, or donate to campus initiatives. Some professors write final books or create archives of their work. Others endow scholarships, fund student travel, or leave behind teaching materials for future instructors. Phased retirement can be a capstone moment—the final chapter of your academic story—so use it to wrap up your career with purpose and pride.

Departments benefit from phased retirement, too. It gives them time to plan for your exit, adjust course offerings, and recruit replacements. In some cases, departments receive partial salary savings that can be reallocated toward adjuncts or new hires. But clarity is key: make sure everyone understands what you will and will not be doing during the phased period. If you don't want to supervise theses or attend faculty meetings, spell that out in your agreement. This avoids burnout and ensures your final years feel like a privilege, not a burden.

One of the best ways to prepare for phased retirement is to start envisioning your post-academic life early. What will your days look like when you no longer have a teaching schedule? Will you travel, volunteer, write, or consult? The more specific your vision, the easier it is to structure your phased years to support it. If you're planning to relocate, use this time to downsize or explore new regions. If you want to launch a new chapter—whether it's a business, creative pursuit, or lifestyle change—start laying the groundwork now.

Sometimes faculty hesitate to enter phased retirement because they fear losing relevance. They worry about being sidelined in departmental decisions, excluded from research grants, or seen as disengaged. While some of that is inevitable as you shift out of full-time roles, there are ways to remain influential. Stay active in mentoring, offer guest lectures, or continue to publish on a manageable schedule. Let colleagues know how they can still involve you. Relevance doesn't have to end with your title—it can evolve along with your role.

If your institution doesn't offer phased retirement, or if their program feels too rigid, you may be able to negotiate your own version. Start with your department chair and propose a reduced teaching load for reduced pay. Emphasize how this creates room for mentoring or institutional memory. You might also explore grant-funded teaching, short-term contracts, or part-time roles after full retirement. The key is to frame it as a win-win—your needs are met, and the department gains predictability and experience during the transition.

Timing matters in phased retirement. If you phase too early, you might leave money or impact on the table. Too late, and you risk burnout or a rushed exit. Consider your energy, health, personal finances, and academic pipeline. Do you still have meaningful projects you want to finish? Is your body telling you it's time to slow down? Talk to your financial advisor, your family, and your mentors to triangulate the right window for starting the transition. Ideally, you'll leave on a high note—with momentum, dignity, and peace of mind.

A phased retirement agreement is a binding contract, so read the fine print. What happens if your health declines mid-phase? Can you accelerate your exit? Will your benefits adjust if the university budget tightens? Be clear on what's flexible and what's locked in. You may want to have a lawyer or advisor review the document, especially if you're relying on this income to bridge into full retirement. A little foresight here prevents misunderstandings later.

Finally, phased retirement is not just about what you're leaving—it's about what you're building next. Think of it as a runway, not a ramp. You're not stepping down so much as stepping into a new phase of freedom, purpose, and reinvention. By easing out of academia thoughtfully, you preserve the best parts of your identity while creating space for new adventures. Whether you teach one class a year, lead a writing group, or finally take that cooking course you always skipped during grading season, the next chapter is yours to author. Let it be a good one.

Chapter 39: Don't Roll It Yet, When State Retirement Plans Are Better Left Alone

For many faculty members and public employees, retirement planning starts with a familiar message: "Roll your old accounts into an IRA to have more control and better investment choices." While that advice often makes sense for people in the private sector, it can backfire badly for those with retirement plans that include special state-backed guarantees or protection. Before you click "transfer" on your pension or defined contribution plan, it's important to understand exactly what you'd be giving up. In some cases, the benefits attached to your plan are far more valuable than the flexibility or control you gain by moving it into an IRA. The smartest retirees aren't always the ones with the fanciest brokerage account—they're the ones who know what not to touch.

Let's start with the basics. Many states offer retirement plans for their public employees—including professors, teachers, and government workers—that are different from the 401(k) you may have heard about in the private sector. These can take the form of defined benefit pensions, hybrid plans, or defined contribution accounts with special perks like guaranteed interest rates or creditor protection. Often, these state-sponsored plans are backed by legislation that gives participants rights to certain payout structures, inflation protection, or tax advantages that IRAs don't offer. The catch is that if you roll the money into an IRA, you may lose those rights permanently. It's like trading in a vintage car for a new one without realizing the old one was a collector's item.

Take the example of a professor in a state with a defined contribution plan that comes with a guaranteed annuity option. This professor may have spent 25 years contributing to a plan where, upon retirement, they can convert their balance into a lifetime income stream backed by the state. If that professor rolls the funds into an IRA before retirement, the annuity option disappears forever. What seemed like a simple administrative step becomes a costly mistake. That guaranteed payout—backed by the state, not the markets—can offer peace of mind no mutual fund will ever replicate. The state isn't trying to trick you into staying; it's actually offering you a benefit that only a long-term public servant can unlock.

Now think about inflation protection. Some pension systems offer cost-of-living adjustments (COLAs) that help your income rise over time to keep pace with inflation. If you opt into the state plan and take distributions through it, your checks may automatically increase every year. But if you move your funds into an IRA and take withdrawals on your own, you're responsible for making sure your portfolio keeps up with inflation. That might sound manageable, but imagine trying to self-manage withdrawals during a long market downturn while inflation rises. You're suddenly wearing the hat of investment manager, pension administrator, and economist—all at once, with your own money on the line.

There's also the issue of legal protection. Many state retirement plans come with strong creditor protections that shield your funds from lawsuits or bankruptcy claims. While IRAs do have some federal protections, they vary by state and aren't always as robust. For professors or public employees with complex family situations or legal exposure—say, from owning rental properties, running a side business, or simply living in a litigious society—those protections can be worth their weight in gold. You might never expect to need them, but you also never plan for a car accident, lawsuit, or medical event that could upend your financial world. When something bad happens, you'll want your retirement funds locked behind legal doors, not sitting in an account that's easier to tap.

Another often overlooked factor is access to retiree healthcare benefits. In some states, continued participation in a state retirement system allows access to group retiree health plans—either subsidized or at lower premiums than private options. But if you roll your money into an IRA and "exit" the system, you may no longer qualify. This can be particularly impactful if you retire before Medicare kicks in at age 65. Private health insurance in your early 60s is no small bill, and group coverage—even if not fully subsidized—can be a lifeline. That benefit alone might be more valuable than getting to choose between two more mutual funds in your IRA.

Timing also matters. If you're within a few years of retirement and already vested in a state plan, you're likely nearing the point where your account becomes eligible for enhanced benefits. Sometimes that means a higher annuity payout, lower administrative fees, or greater access to retiree perks. If you move your money too early, you may miss out on these cumulative benefits. It's like leaving a concert before the encore—you did all the work, sat through the main event, and then missed the best part. A bit of patience and planning can turn a good retirement into a great one.

Consider also how withdrawal rules differ. State retirement systems often allow partial or phased distributions with built-in support, while IRAs require you to manage your own withdrawal schedule and taxes. With an IRA, if you mess up a required minimum distribution (RMD), you could face steep penalties. State systems often offer more hand-holding, simpler rules, and automatic features that make retirement income more predictable and less stressful. For academics used to order and structure, this can be a welcome continuation of the system they've trusted their entire career.

Now let's address a common myth: that investment choices in state plans are always inferior. While it's true that some plans have limited fund menus or higher expense ratios, others offer institutional-grade options that are hard to replicate in retail IRAs. These might include access to low-fee index funds, target-date funds with better glide paths, or pooled investments with economies of scale. And even if the fund options seem limited, the trade-off might be worth it if the plan offers guaranteed income, longevity insurance, or professional oversight. Don't mistake simplicity for inferiority—sometimes, fewer options means fewer chances to make mistakes.

There's also something to be said about behavioral finance—the psychology of money. Rolling your funds into an IRA puts the entire balance in front of you, ready to tap at any time. That accessibility can be dangerous, especially in emotional moments like market downturns, family emergencies, or periods of uncertainty. Keeping your money in a more structured state plan can act as a buffer, preventing knee-jerk decisions that undermine long-term goals. In this sense, the constraints are actually a form of protection, like seatbelts in a car. They don't restrict your freedom—they help you survive a crash.

Let's not forget about the administrative ease. When you stay within your state's retirement system, much of the heavy lifting is handled for you. Taxes are withheld properly, paperwork is streamlined, and you're likely to receive a monthly check on autopilot. With an IRA, especially a self-directed one, you may need to manage withdrawals, estimate taxes, coordinate with a financial advisor, and field year-end reporting yourself. For someone who has spent a career deep in research or teaching, managing a financial operation in retirement may not feel like the best use of time or energy. Simplifying your financial life can be one of the most underrated forms of retirement wealth.

There are, of course, situations where rolling over to an IRA does make sense. If you're moving to a state that doesn't recognize your former plan's tax benefits, or if your plan has unusually high fees and poor performance, then yes, a rollover may be wise. Or maybe you have multiple retirement accounts and want to consolidate for easier estate planning. The point isn't that IRAs are bad—it's that they aren't always better. Like any financial move, it depends on your goals, your situation, and the unique structure of the plan you're leaving behind.

This is why it's crucial to get advice from someone who understands the fine print of your specific plan. Many financial advisors are trained primarily on private-sector retirement tools, and may not know the implications of exiting a state system. Ask questions, request plan documents, and insist that any recommendation to roll over includes a written analysis of what benefits you're giving up. A good advisor should respect your questions, not rush you toward a decision. You've worked too long to gamble with your nest egg because of someone else's cookie-cutter advice.

Think also about legacy and survivorship benefits. Some state retirement systems offer robust spousal or beneficiary benefits that continue after your death. These might include continued income for a surviving spouse, access to health coverage, or life insurance tied to the retirement system. IRAs can be customized for beneficiaries, but they don't always provide the same level of continuity or support. If leaving a stable income stream for a spouse is part of your plan, you need to know which option offers the better terms—and that's not always the IRA.

Taxes, too, can be more complicated than they seem. Some state retirement systems offer partial tax exemptions on distributions, especially if you're a resident retiree. Others provide tiered benefits that reduce taxable income after a certain age. IRAs, on the other hand, are governed by federal tax rules with fewer local perks. Over a 25-year retirement, those small state-level benefits can add up to tens of thousands of dollars. Don't underestimate the value of tax simplicity and savings.

In the end, rolling over your retirement account into an IRA is like opening a door that closes behind you. Sometimes it's the right path—but once you step through, it can be hard to go back. Before you move your money, ask yourself what protections, benefits, and support systems you're leaving behind. Talk to HR. Talk to a specialist. Talk to your spouse. And most importantly, talk to yourself about what kind of retirement you want to have—not just financially, but emotionally and logistically.

Remember, the best financial decisions aren't always the flashiest ones. Sometimes, keeping things where they are—stable, familiar, protected—is the wisest move of all. Especially when that move was designed for people just like you: long-serving public employees who've earned more than just a paycheck. You've earned a retirement system that works for you—not against you. Don't give that up without making absolutely sure you understand what's at stake.

Chapter 40: Leaving for Administration, Financial Trade-Offs of Becoming Dean, Provost, or President

Stepping across the threshold from faculty life into upper administration is a little like moving from the orchestra to the conductor's podium: the view is wider, the baton heavier, and every miscue echoes far beyond your own section. Many professors eye the dean's suite because it promises a meaningful bump in salary, influence over institutional direction, and a fresh intellectual challenge once the familiar rhythms of teaching and research feel routine. Yet the financial trade-offs of becoming a dean, provost, or president are more nuanced than a simple pay-raise calculation; they ripple through retirement trajectories, consulting freedom, family schedules, and even long-term scholarly identity. I have watched colleagues leap enthusiastically into administration only to discover hidden costs—extra tax exposure, fading summer grant income, and the slow erosion of tenure protections if they stay too long away from the classroom. Others have thrived, parlaying administrative stipends into accelerated saving plans while preserving their academic muscle with one strategic seminar a year. The difference is rarely about luck; it is about understanding the full ledger—credits and debits—before signing the appointment letter.

Start with base salary, the most visible incentive dangled before a newly minted dean. A transition from full professor to entry-level dean can mean a 20-to-40-percent increase, with provosts and presidents often doubling previous faculty pay. That headline figure feels life-changing at first glance, but remember it typically arrives as a 12-month contract rather than the 9- or 10-month pay cycle most faculty enjoy. The extra summer pay you once cobbled together from grants, overload courses, or consulting? It is now presumed baked into the annual figure—and, in many cases, prohibited or heavily restricted under conflict-of-interest rules. So while your biweekly paycheck is bigger, your side-income flexibility shrinks. Calculate your former twelve-month income—base plus summer—and compare it with the administrative offer before assuming the promotion truly multiplies your earning power.

Benefits packages also morph. Administrators are often classified as "exempt" or "executive" staff, which can shift retirement contributions from state pension formulas to capped defined-contribution plans. If you spent fifteen years accruing a formula-driven benefit pegged to your highest salary, jumping into an executive tier could freeze that calculation at the moment of departure. The new plan may or may not offer matching contributions at a similar rate. Speak with HR to understand whether your administrative years count toward pension service credit or require a separate 403(b) structure. A dean I coached discovered too late that her five years in administration contributed zero to her state pension multiplier, costing her thousands annually in retirement income despite the larger paycheck she enjoyed while in office.

Healthcare perks can improve—executive physicals, spousal travel allowances, or supplemental long-term-disability policies—but they can also complicate transitions back to faculty ranks. Some universities fund top administrators' premiums at a higher percentage, a benefit that evaporates once you step down, causing sudden out-of-pocket hikes. If you plan only a short administrative stint, bank the differential rather than inflating lifestyle; your future self will need that buffer when premiums snap back. At the presidential level, you may gain access to a university-owned house with utilities covered, which sounds wonderful until you realize imputed-income rules treat some of that value as taxable. A colleague moved into the president's residence and saw her W-2 spike by tens of thousands in taxable perks, nudging her into a higher federal bracket and triggering unexpected estimated-tax payments.

Leadership roles frequently come with discretionary budgets—a dean's fund or presidential account used for donor cultivation, faculty retention, or program pilots. While these resources expand professional influence, they create a psychological trap: spending university money feels less painful than personal funds, and the line between institutional entertainment and private lifestyle can blur. Meticulous documentation and clear internal controls protect against scrutiny, especially when public-records requests or board audits examine expense reports. Remember, donor dinners at upscale restaurants accrue imputed benefit only if personal family members attend, but auditors may raise eyebrows at repeated spousal participation. Keep personal and institutional transactions so separate that any third party could audit the books without confusion.

The opportunity cost of lost research productivity is harder to quantify but equally real. Administrators often sacrifice laboratory momentum or book-writing time, which can shrink future royalty streams and diminish eligibility for external grants. If you rely on summer salary from federal awards, check agency policies: many grants disallow principal investigators who allocate more than 50percent effort to administration. Deans sometimes maintain a token grad student or small project, yet labs thrive on the principal's availability; prolonged absences can lead to talent attrition and reputational drift. Before accepting, map the research pipeline and decide whether to pause, delegate to a trusted collaborator, or shift into entirely new scholarly territory such as higher-education policy—just don't cling blindly to old projects and watch them whither.

Tax planning must shift too. Higher pay may push you beyond contribution limits for Roth IRAs, trigger the 0.9-percent Medicare surtax on wages over $200,000, and expose you to the 3.8-percent net-investment-income tax on side ventures. Use expanded cash flow to maximize 403(b) and 457(b) deferrals, investigate backdoor Roth conversions, and consider donor-advised-fund bunching strategies while itemized deductions still exceed the standard threshold. Also examine whether relocation from a faculty housing neighborhood to the president's residence changes state-tax domicile: crossing a state line, even temporarily, can create multi-state filing complexities you never needed to solve as a professor.

Work-life balance tips dramatically. Evening rehearsals for the university orchestra or weekend soccer games for your kids may conflict with trustee retreats and alumni dinners. Spousal considerations escalate; partners unaccustomed to public visibility may resent constant scrutiny at campus events. Some institutions offer coaching for administrative couples, but emotional strain remains a hidden cost rarely factored into salary negotiations. One provost friend joked that her raise barely covered the vacations she purchased to make up for lost family dinners. Budget for intentional decompression or marital-counseling sessions just as you would for conference travel.

The length of service is its own financial variable. A brief administrative stint—say, three to five years—provides a salary boost without catastrophic detachment from scholarship, but long incumbencies can erode teaching credentials and make reintegration awkward. Some contracts include a "sabbatical back" clause granting paid leave upon return to faculty ranks to revive research agendas. If your offer lacks this, negotiate it; you'll need that runway to publish or redesign courses before student evaluations compare you unfavorably to peers who never left the classroom.

Golden parachutes and deferred-compensation plans sweeten top-tier leadership offers. A president might receive a five-hundred-thousand-dollar retention bonus payable after five years of service or an annuity funded over her term. These vehicles often vest on specific dates and may carry noncompete clauses or clawbacks tied to performance metrics like fundraising targets. Evaluate worst-case scenarios: what if a budget crisis forces your resignation in year four? Forfeit clauses could wipe out anticipated windfalls, altering lifetime earnings projections. Diversify savings aggressively rather than banking on a single deferred-comp bucket.

Professional liability increases with rank. Faculty rarely face personal litigation, but deans, provosts, and presidents get named in suits ranging from TitleIX disputes to vendor contract breaches. Institutional indemnification exists, yet an umbrella insurance policy remains prudent, especially if state-law immunities are limited. Directors-and-officers coverage typically protects corporate trustees, not administrators, so verify whether your role is included. If not, secure supplemental coverage just as physicians carry malpractice insurance. Legal fees can erode personal assets even when claims lack merit.

Geographic mobility often accompanies administrative ambition. Climbing from dean to provost to president may require moves every five to seven years, uprooting partners' careers and resetting home-equity trajectories. Relocation packages cover initial costs but not long-term housing-market risks; selling during a downturn can erase gains. Evaluate whether each move's salary bump offsets potential real-estate volatility, children's school disruptions, and partner income sacrifice. A dual-academic household might negotiate spousal appointments, but in industry fields, trailing spouses could face limited local opportunities, imposing hidden opportunity costs.

Community obligations escalate too. Town-gown relationships, alumni councils, and civic boards expect leadership to attend galas and serve on committees—unpaid time that might once have gone to paid consulting. While these roles expand influence, they dilute bandwidth for revenue-producing side work. Set boundaries early: allocate certain evenings per week to family or personal projects, and decline invitations outside strategic priorities. A yes-to-everything stance impresses few and exhausts many.

On the upside, administrators access donor networks that can evolve into post-retirement board seats or consulting roles paying stipends. Cultivate relationships authentically—not merely as stepping stones—by expressing genuine curiosity about donors' industries and expertise. Document projects you spearhead—new interdisciplinary centers, scholarship funds—so future search committees see measurable impact. An administrative resume brimming with outcomes can command lucrative interim-leadership gigs or corporate directorships later, diversifying retirement-era income.

Exit strategies should be plotted from day one. Decide whether your long game is to climb the administrative ladder, return happily to faculty, or pivot to nonprofit leadership. Financial preparations differ: a lifelong administrator might prioritize portable retirement savings and executive-level disability insurance, whereas a temporary dean may focus on maintaining research credentials and reestablishing grant pipelines. Update your written financial plan annually, stress-testing scenarios like forced resignation or health crises. Flexibility—liquid emergency funds, multiple income streams—trumps any single-track assumption.

When negotiating an offer, think beyond salary and office size. Ask for continued tuition benefits for dependents, housing allowances that convert to cash if you stay in your current home, and guaranteed research or professional-development funds even in administrative roles. Clarify faculty rank and tenure rights upon return, including office space and startup resources. Stipulate periodic compensation reviews tied to external salary surveys of peer institutions to prevent lagging pay if budget freezes delay across-the-board increases. Every clause you secure upfront reduces future friction.

Remember that prestige is not a retirement plan. Headlines announcing your deanship won't pay Medicare premiums at 70. Use the income spike to boost savings rates, pay down high-interest debt, and pad your health-savings account. Avoid lifestyle inflation that locks you into administrative work longer than desired; keep fixed expenses tethered to your prior professor salary. When you eventually step down, your budget will flex gracefully rather than plunge.

Finally, keep a sliver of your former academic identity alive. Teach an occasional honors seminar, publish editorials on higher-ed policy, or mentor doctoral candidates. Not only does this maintain intellectual joy; it fortifies your résumé for a smooth reentry if administrative life loses appeal. Financially, adjunct-level teaching after tenure may pay peanuts, but the professional continuity safeguards against the existential cost of feeling untethered once the administrative spotlight dims. In the long run, the most successful deans, provosts, and presidents are those who balance stewardship of institutional resources with stewardship of their own financial and intellectual well-being. The baton is worth holding—just be sure you're ready for its weight and have planned for the day you pass it on.

Chapter 41: Changing Universities Mid-Career, Vesting Rules, Portability, and Relocation Math

Changing universities mid-career feels a little like transplanting a mature oak: your roots are deep, your canopy wide, and any move requires careful digging around delicate systems you can't afford to sever. What tempts many professors to uproot is a tantalizing mix of fresh colleagues, upgraded labs, or simply a salary bump that finally catches up with market realities. Yet underneath those visible perks lie layers of fine print—retirement vesting schedules, benefit portability rules, and relocation costs—that can turn a dream offer into a long-term financial stumble if ignored. Think of the negotiation process as a grant proposal for the next chapter of your life: every assumption must be tested, and every hidden cost surfaced, before you click "accept." Done thoughtfully, a mid-career move can accelerate your research and wealth; rushed, it can leave you scrambling to rebuild what you already had.

Start with vesting, the backstage clock governing how much of your employer's retirement contributions actually belong to you. State pensions often require five to ten years of service before benefits become portable, while university 403(b) matches may vest immediately or phase in gradually. If you leave one semester shy of the cliff vesting date, you might forfeit thousands in future annuity payments—money you effectively earned but never get to spend. Run the numbers: calculate the present value of unvested benefits and weigh it against the raise and resources on the table at the new institution. Sometimes the wisest path is to negotiate a spring-semester start after crossing the vesting threshold in December, pocketing tenure-track momentum and pension rights in one decisive move.

Portability isn't just about retirement dollars; it includes sick leave, sabbatical credit, and even years-of-service calculations for future merit raises. Some universities accept full service credit from prior institutions, meaning you'll reach eligibility for paid leave sooner, while others reset the clock to zero. Clarify whether your accumulated sabbatical time can travel with you or will be cashed out at a modest hourly rate that undervalues its strategic worth. If you're nearing sabbatical eligibility, negotiate a one-year delay in relocation or request that the new university honor your earned credit as part of the package. That concession could be worth more than a signing bonus if it protects an uninterrupted research year down the line.

Relocation allowances often headline offer letters, but the devil lurks in reimbursable categories and tax treatment. Federal rules now generally treat moving reimbursements as taxable income unless you're in the military, so a $10,000 allowance might net only $7,000 after withholding. Ask whether the institution gross-ups the payment to offset taxes; many will if you frame it as standard practice. Itemize big-ticket costs—real-estate commissions, interim housing, lab-equipment shipping—and get them written into the agreement instead of relying on a capped lump sum. A well-structured relocation budget can preserve emergency savings and ease early months when dual housing costs overlap.

Cost-of-living differentials complicate salary comparisons more than most candidates realize. Moving from a Midwest college town to a coastal metropolis might raise your paycheck by 20percent yet cut purchasing power in half once housing, childcare, and taxes catch up. Use reputable calculators that factor regional price indices, not just headline income figures, and adjust offer negotiations accordingly. If the new salary won't cover comparable living standards, bargain for mortgage-assistance programs, subsidized faculty housing, or a tuition-remission boost for dependent children. Remember: real wealth is measured in discretionary dollars left after life's essentials—not in the pre-tax number HR prints on your contract.

Spousal and partner employment ranks among the trickiest financial variables in a mid-career move. Universities increasingly market dual-career support, but programs range from genuine job placement to vague goodwill letters with no budget. Ask for concrete commitments: interview timelines, bridge funding, or at least coordinated introductions across campus. Each forfeited partner paycheck subtracts from the apparent salary gain, so calculate household net change, not individual income bump. Couples who treat the move as a joint enterprise, including negotiating start-up for both careers, report far less relocation regret.

Homeownership multiplies both risks and opportunities when switching institutions. If you sell in a soft market, closing costs and price declines can erase equity gains; conversely, retaining a rental property can diversify retirement income but add landlord headaches from afar. Model scenarios: one where you sell and reinvest, one where you rent it out, and one where you keep it vacant until you're sure the new job sticks. Factor in capital-gains exclusions, rental management fees, and state tax residency rules. A relocation offer that includes a down-payment loan or temporary housing can buy time to make a deliberate decision rather than a fire-sale rush.

Start-up packages shine brightest for lab scientists but matter across disciplines. Humanities scholars may negotiate archival travel funds, while social scientists seek data-purchase budgets. Pin down not just dollar amounts but disbursement timing and allowable uses: a $200,000 start-up spread over five years may feel abundant yet hamper the up-front equipment buys you need. Parallel-track large expenditures with grant-writing timelines so you're not caught between spending deadlines and external review cycles. Treat start-up negotiations as designing an experiment—list critical resources first, then argue budget needs logically.

Promotion pathways vary: some institutions treat mid-career hires as lateral moves requiring fresh dossiers; others grant tenure on arrival but delay eligibility for full professor until local criteria are met. Understand review calendars, publication expectations, and external-funding thresholds before committing. If the new university demands grant portfolios triple your current level, secure bridge support or reduced teaching for the ramp-up phase. Ambiguity can be as dangerous as outright denial, so push for written clarification of expectations within the offer letter or faculty handbook reference.

Speaking of teaching, course loads can surprise if you only glance at published norms. A "2-2" load on paper can morph into extra advising, new-program developments, or blend undergraduate and graduate seminars requiring double prep. Verify whether released time for administrative roles you're expected to fill—graduate director, diversity liaison—actually reduces classroom hours or merely stacks on top. Each unanticipated section dilutes research capacity despite a flashier title. Ask current faculty privately about hidden teaching obligations; their stories illuminate labyrinths HR brochures overlook.

Grants administration and indirect-cost recovery differ widely, affecting net funds available for your lab. Check overhead rates, return-to-PI percentages, and internal seed-grant opportunities. A lower salary supplemented by generous overhead return can beat a higher salary drained by high university tax on grants. Transparent budget models help project multi-year cash flows, especially if you depend on external funding for student stipends or summer salary. Institutions serious about research will share these figures readily; reluctance signals bureaucratic hurdles later.

Healthcare plans are rarely identical. Compare premiums, deductibles, out-of-pocket maximums, and network breadth. If you or a family member has ongoing medical needs, coverage gaps can dwarf salary increases. Ask whether the university contributes to health-savings accounts, offers on-site clinics, or negotiates lower drug costs through specialty pharmacies. Secure plan documents before signing anything; glossy summaries often omit exclusions critical to chronic-care management.

Child-education benefits deserve a separate audit. Some institutions extend tuition exchanges with hundreds of colleges, while others confine remission to the home campus. Evaluate the likelihood your children will attend partner schools or prefer private universities outside the network.

Tuition assistance usually vests after a few years of employment; if kids near college age, align job start with vesting dates to maximize value. A colleague once chose a slightly lower-paying offer solely because its tuition-exchange roster included her son's dream conservatory, saving roughly $200,000 over four years.

Culture carries financial weight in ways spreadsheets miss. Departments with collegial norms share graduate teaching assistants and lab space generously, reducing your budget pressures; competitive climates force each faculty member to duplicate resources. Visit campus, sit in common areas, and note interactions. Ask junior faculty about workload fairness and resource allocation. If you sense turf wars, include extra start-up or staff lines in negotiations to buffer against institutional scarcity.

State taxes may rise or fall. A move from no-income-tax Florida to high-tax California can offset half your salary jump. Also consider property and sales taxes, plus retirement-income taxation if you plan to stay post-career. Investigate reciprocity agreements if you'll live in one state and work in another. A relocation allowance that covers moving vans won't fix a lifetime of higher tax drain, so incorporate net-of-tax calculations into your decision matrix.

Immigration or visa status complications arise for international scholars. Changing employers may reset green-card timelines or jeopardize H-1B cap exemptions. Secure immigration counsel before accepting to confirm portability of your current status and anticipate processing delays. Institutions promising legal support should fund premium processing fees where possible. Visa uncertainty can stall research travel, sabbaticals, and family planning, so integrate these risks into your financial and professional assessments.

Professional reputation faces reboot risks: new colleagues evaluate you from scratch, and citation networks may shift if you move far from disciplinary hubs. To mitigate, schedule colloquia, join local consortia, and leverage institutional press to announce your arrival. Visibility maintains grant reviewer familiarity, indirectly bolstering funding odds and, hence, income stability. Relocation math isn't just dollars—intellectual capital must also recalibrate.

Moving mid-career can boost happiness if geographic fit improves lifestyle. Shorter commutes, cultural amenities, or proximity to family convert into non-monetary dividends. Quantify saved time as value: an hour reclaimed daily equates to six workweeks a year—an invisible raise. Conversely, losing a support network can increase childcare or eldercare costs, eroding gains. Map logistical routes—schools, hospitals, grocery stores—before relocating, treating life-admin time as part of compensation.

Finally, trust your gut but verify with numbers. Create a side-by-side spreadsheet comparing current and prospective positions across salary, benefits, cost of living, taxes, and intangible perks. Assign weights reflecting personal priorities—research facilities, family needs, professional growth. Share the model with a mentor or financial advisor to uncover blind spots. A deliberate approach transforms the uncertainty of mid-career mobility into a strategic leap that accelerates both finance and fulfillment, ensuring the transplanted oak not only survives but flourishes in richer soil.

Ask ChatGPT

Chapter 42: Bridge Jobs & Encore Careers, Consulting Firms, Policy Institutes, and Think Tanks

Bridge jobs and encore careers serve as intellectual footholds between the familiar cliffs of academia and the wide valley of traditional retirement, letting you climb down gradually rather than leaping into emptiness. Consulting firms, policy institutes, and think tanks all court seasoned scholars because they need rigorous analysis, credible voices, and storytelling skills that resonate with decision-makers who don't speak in footnotes. For retiring professors or mid-career professionals hungering for fresh purpose, these organizations offer a second act that preserves mental agility while introducing new networks and revenue streams. Picture them as academic sabbaticals turned outward: the reading and writing continue, but the audience shifts from peer reviewers to legislators, corporate boards, or philanthropic foundations eager for actionable insight. That pivot entails new rhythms—shorter deadlines, cross-disciplinary teams, and client feedback cycles that replace journal referee reports—yet the core skill set remains: frame a problem, test evidence, and communicate findings clearly. When approached thoughtfully, bridge jobs become both an income buffer and a laboratory for personal reinvention.

The first step in targeting an encore role is clarifying your professional narrative so nonacademic employers quickly see relevance. Hiring managers at consulting firms, for example, won't parse your curriculum-vitae entries about departmental service, but they will value a record of solving complex problems under tight grant deadlines or presenting findings to skeptical audiences. Translate "principal investigator on an NSF grant" into "led multimillion-dollar, multi-stakeholder research projects on time and under budget." If you chaired a search committee, say "directed full-cycle talent recruitment and onboarding." This reframing resembles translating a dense scholarly article into an op-ed; the findings stay intact, but jargon yields to accessible language. A polished narrative also anticipates the question, "Why leave academia?" framing it as running toward new impact rather than escaping old frustrations.

Consulting firms come in flavors as varied as coffeehouse roasts, ranging from the global giants that parachute teams into Fortune500 boardrooms to boutique specialists who design surveys for nonprofit coalitions. Large firms typically run a pyramid model: partners sell work, senior directors manage projects, and analysts crunch data. Mid-career academics often slot in as "subject-matter experts," parachuting in for specific engagements while training junior staff on methodology. Compensation can dwarf faculty salaries—sometimes $200 an hour or more for part-time expertise—yet schedules can spike unexpectedly when client fires erupt. Negotiating a retainer or project-based fee, instead of billing by the hour, protects intellectual property and ensures you're paid for phone calls, prep time, and travel days.

Boutique consultancies may align more closely with scholarly temperaments, emphasizing depth over volume. These firms often allow remote work, flexible hours, and creative freedom to design research protocols rather than retrofit findings into preexisting templates. However, budgets are leaner; your hourly rate may hover closer to $125, and marketing your services becomes partly your responsibility. Think of it as writing grant proposals without the internal overhead: you must network, pitch, and sometimes co-author white papers to attract business. The upside is autonomy—you choose assignments that resonate with your values, shaping a portfolio that feels like an extension of your scholarly mission rather than a detour.

Policy institutes often sit at universities' edges or operate independently with philanthropic backing. Here the agenda is overtly public-facing: brief legislators before votes, testify in hearings, and craft op-eds that translate technical nuance into policy levers. Many institutes offer "senior fellow" appointments, paying stipends ranging from $30,000 to $80,000 for part-time contributions over a year. Instead of faculty meetings, you attend coalition roundtables and public forums. Metrics shift from journal impact factors to citations in legislative memos or media interviews. For academics craving broader societal influence, this feedback loop can be exhilarating, but it demands comfort with rapid response—publishing a policy brief within weeks, not semesters.

Think tanks resemble policy institutes yet often operate on national or international stages, with a heavier emphasis on fundraising and donor relations. Researchers split time between original studies and grant cultivation, pitching foundations on pressing issues where evidence can shape strategy. As a scholar, you may relish the interdisciplinary collaborations—economists, sociologists, and public-health experts hashing out solutions around the same table—but navigating think-tank politics requires soft skills in coalition building and brand positioning. Compensation here varies widely: entry-level research directors might earn $90,000, while senior fellows with marquee reputations can negotiate six-figure packages, travel budgets, and their own staff. The biggest perk is platform: policy briefs published under a respected think tank's banner travel quickly across capitals and boardrooms.

Financially, bridge jobs differ from tenure-track income streams in predictability and benefits. Most consulting and fellowship roles classify you as an independent contractor, meaning no automatic tax withholding, retirement match, or health insurance. You'll need to set aside roughly 30percent of gross income for quarterly taxes and consider establishing an LLC to separate business and personal finances. Health coverage may come through a spouse, COBRA, or marketplace plan, and retirement savings shift to SEP-IRAs or Solo401(k)s with higher contribution limits but no employer match. Factor these gaps into rate negotiations: an hourly fee that seems generous can shrink fast after self-employment tax. On the upside, business deductions—home office, professional development, travel—can lower taxable income.

Time management becomes the new sabbatical grant; without departmental structures, your calendar can either bloom with autonomy or choke with overcommitment. Establish working hours, project buffers, and a pipeline tracker to avoid feast-or-famine cycles common in consulting. Many encore professionals adopt a "three-bucket" model: one marquee project for income stability, one passion project aligned with values, and one exploratory engagement testing new skills. Calendaring weekly "CEO time" to review finances, marketing, and strategic goals prevents months from slipping by in reactive mode. Think of it as your own faculty development day, except you are both the dean and department chair.

Networking fuels encore careers, but professors sometimes mistake conference circuits for broader professional ecosystems. Instead of disciplinary societies, attend industry meetups, policy forums, and chamber-of-commerce breakfasts. LinkedIn becomes more valuable than Academia.edu; updating your profile with clear consulting deliverables attracts recruiters searching keywords like "program evaluation" or "data-driven policy analysis." Build a concise portfolio—case studies, media clips, testimonials—and share it proactively when introductions arise. Just as a strong teaching statement sells your pedagogy to hiring committees, a compelling capability statement sells your expertise to clients.

Illustrate impact with stories. Tell potential clients about the time your statistical model saved a nonprofit six figures in misallocated funds or how your curriculum redesign boosted completion rates by 20percent. Clients buy outcomes, not résumés. Frame each example with a clear before-and-after metric and a brief explanation of your process. This storytelling mirrors grant-writing's significance-innovation-approach triad, repackaged for private-sector ears. When done well, it converts academic accomplishments into concrete value propositions.

Risk tolerance shapes the structure of your encore transition. Some professors jump out entirely, but most phase gradually—one course release to free consulting time, a sabbatical test year, or early-retirement agreements allowing part-time teaching. Each model carries distinct tax and benefit implications; consult HR to avoid forfeiting retiree health coverage by dropping below certain workloads too soon. A phased approach also tests cultural fit: you might discover policy advocacy feels like committee work on steroids and pivot back to pure scholarship. Treat the transition as hypothesis testing: small, reversible experiments beat sweeping, irreversible changes.

Intellectual property rules shift outside academia. Consulting contracts often claim deliverables and underlying data unless negotiated otherwise. Read clauses on "work made for hire" and carve out rights to use anonymized findings in future publications. Some policy institutes allow dual-publishing agreements, letting you place extended studies in peer-reviewed journals. Protect your academic brand while respecting the client's confidentiality needs; trust grows when both sides are clear on boundaries. Remember, reputation is your most liquid asset in an encore career—guard it as diligently as tenure.

Interdisciplinary agility becomes essential. A think-tank economist might collaborate with climate scientists, requiring quick uptake of unfamiliar literature. Lean on your scholarly muscle: ramping up on new fields is second nature after years of comprehensive exam prep. Yet be humble; "expert" status carries weight in public discourse, and overreaching erodes credibility. Balance curiosity with prudence, verifying claims and citing sources even when the audience doesn't demand Chicago style. Reliability is why organizations hire career academics in the first place.

Metrics of success evolve. Accolades may come as contract renewals, op-ed bylines, or invitations to brief legislative committees rather than journal acceptance letters. Set personal key performance indicators: income targets, policy citations, or media reach. Track them monthly, celebrating wins with the same gusto you once reserved for tenure approval. Skipping this step risks drifting into perpetual busyness without strategic growth; you left the syllabus treadmill for autonomy, so measure progress on your own terms.

Work-life balance can improve if you design engagements deliberately. Consulting from home reduces commuting, and project-based work allows off-season travel or caregiving flexibility. Yet boundary erosion lurks when your home office doubles as client HQ. Schedule tech-free evenings, enforce email curfews, and designate a space solely for work. Your encore career should enrich life, not devour it. Guard personal time the way you used to guard research blocks against administrative creep.

Mentorship opportunities flourish in bridge careers. Junior analysts or policy fellows crave methodological rigor and career guidance you can supply. Offer brown-bag seminars on causal inference or effective briefing writing; this cements your value to the organization and satisfies the teaching itch many professors miss. Coaching gigs also diversify income, especially if you package workshops for multiple clients. Remember, the pedagogy skills honed over decades are portable assets.

Geography broadens or contracts depending on your field. Remote work exploded post-pandemic, enabling participation in D.C. think tanks from a cabin in Maine, yet in-person networking still dominates high-stakes policy influence. Budget for periodic travel if you live outside power corridors. Conversely, relocating closer to clients can cut travel costs and open local consulting gigs, but weigh housing expenses and family ties. Real-estate choices become strategic business decisions rather than mere lifestyle preferences.

Exit strategy matters. Whether you plan a three-year consulting sprint or a decade-long second act, outline financial milestones that signal it's time to taper. Maybe it's funding grandkids' 529s, paying off a mortgage, or hitting a target retirement portfolio value. When you reach the goal, reassess workload and gradually hand off clients to protégés. Sunset with intention, leaving behind a knowledge legacy through publications, toolkits, or open-source datasets.

In the final analysis, bridge jobs and encore careers in consulting, policy institutes, and think tanks convert a lifetime of scholarly expertise into fresh relevance, income, and purpose. The path rewards those who approach it as they would any rigorous project: define objectives, gather data, assess risks, and iterate. Done right, your encore can feel less like retirement and more like tenure 2.0—fewer committee meetings, more autonomy, and a direct line from ideas to impact. The world still needs your insights; you just need to deliver them through new channels. Design the chapter thoughtfully, and it can be the most satisfying one in your professional story.

Chapter 43: Social Security & Medicare Timing for Professors, Coordination with University Health Plans

Deciding when to claim Social Security is a bit like choosing the optimal moment to submit a journal article: rush it and you leave citation potential on the table, wait too long and someone else may publish first—or in this case, you may spend years living on cash reserves you wish you still had. For professors, the stakes feel higher because our income trajectories typically peak later than many careers, and we often hold onto university health coverage longer than friends in private industry. Social Security benefits rise roughly eight percent for every year you delay claiming after full retirement age, up to seventy. That delayed-retirement credit can dwarf the modest annual raises you're used to negotiating, but only if you can cover expenses meanwhile through teaching stipends, consulting, or pension payouts. Before making a decision, map your cash-flow needs semester by semester and decide which funding source—Social Security, TIAA withdrawals, or part-time teaching—fills the gap most efficiently.

Medicare timing is equally strategic, and it begins with understanding the alphabet soup of PartsA,B,C, andD. PartA, which covers hospital stays, is usually premium-free if you've paid into the system for ten years, so most professors sign up at sixty-five even if they keep working. PartB, on the other hand, charges a monthly premium and could duplicate services you already get through a university plan. Delaying PartB is permitted without penalty if you are covered by "creditable" employer insurance, but the moment that coverage ends you have an eight-month special enrollment window to avoid lifelong surcharges. Think of it as the add-drop period for a course: miss it and you're stuck with financial consequences far longer than the misstep seemed to last.

University health plans complicate the picture because their generosity varies wildly. Some institutions allow retirees to remain on group coverage until Medicare becomes primary, while others shift costs to a retiree plan that can be double or triple PartB premiums. If your university requires you to pay full freight for retiree insurance, enrolling in PartB immediately at sixty-five may actually save you money. Conversely, if your university offers a high-quality plan at subsidized rates and mandates that it remains primary until you drop below halftime employment, delaying PartB keeps more cash in your pocket. The only way to know is to request your university's retiree health booklet and compare not just premiums but deductibles, prescription tiers, and network doctors.

Once you enroll in any part of Medicare, contributing to a Health Savings Account must stop because IRS rules prohibit pre-tax contributions while enrolled. Professors who rely on HSA contributions to lower taxable income should plan for a contribution cutoff the month before Medicare coverage starts. The HSA itself remains usable for qualified expenses, including future PartB premiums, so the account doesn't lose value—it just stops growing from new deposits. One strategy is to front-load the final year's contribution in January if you plan to sign up for Medicare mid-year, maximizing the tax deduction before the window closes. Treat that final deposit like making sure grades are submitted before the registrar's deadline: miss it and the door slams shut.

Income matters for Medicare premiums because PartB and PartD surcharges—called IRMAA—kick in when your modified adjusted gross income crosses preset thresholds. For professors who consult, write textbooks, or draw royalties, a single lucrative year two years before Medicare enrollment can raise premiums hundreds of dollars monthly. If possible, shift income into years outside the two-year look-back or defer royalties through a small business entity taxed in a lower bracket. Alternatively, consider one-time deductions such as charitable lump sums via a donor-advised fund during high-income years to keep MAGI beneath the trigger lines. Think of IRMAA brackets as grant-budget ceilings: plan your spending carefully, or you'll pay a steep overhead charge.

Coordinating spousal benefits adds another layer. If both partners are professors but only one keeps employer health coverage past sixty-five, the uncovered spouse generally enrolls in PartA and PartB immediately. If both stay employed, each can delay PartB until dropping below the required workload. However, your university's HR may insist that spouses join Medicare sooner, depending on plan design, so verify rules rather than assume parallel timelines. If one spouse claims Social Security early and the other delays, remember that Medicare premiums will be deducted from monthly Social Security checks, altering net cash flow between household members. Running a combined budget projection ensures no surprises when automatic premium withholding begins.

Another decision point arrives at full retirement age—currently sixty-six and some months—when you can claim Social Security without reducing benefits if you continue working. Many professors delay anyway because of the eight-percent credit, but claiming now while teaching halftime could produce a hybrid income that allows a step-down lifestyle without tapping investments. The trade-off is lower lifetime survivor benefits for a younger spouse, so weigh personal health, family longevity, and pension options before locking in. It's similar to accepting a half-year sabbatical: appealing short-term but possibly reducing long-term research momentum.

Speaking of pensions, if you contributed to a state retirement system that doesn't withhold Social Security taxes, the Windfall Elimination Provision may cut your Social Security benefit. The reduction tops out at a few hundred dollars but can surprise retirees counting on the full payout. The Government Pension Offset may also reduce spousal benefits. Consult the Social Security Administration's calculators early to stress-test numbers, and consider a financial advisor who specializes in public-sector academics to navigate the labyrinth. Forewarned, you can adjust savings rates ahead of retirement instead of scrambling later.

Many universities offer 403(b) and 457(b) plans in addition to pensions. Required Minimum Distributions from these plans now begin at age seventy-three, but if you remain employed and own less than five percent of the institution, you can often delay RMDs on the 403(b). That delay pairs nicely with postponing Social Security: two levers that keep taxable income low while you're still insured through work. Once you fully retire, RMDs, Social Security, and Medicare premiums can stack into a tax torpedo, so planning withdrawals strategically before Medicare kicks in can smooth lifetime taxes. Imagine assembling a jigsaw puzzle: fit the edges first—RMD and Medicare deadlines—then shape income streams in the middle.

Prescription coverage under PartD is easy to overlook when you're healthy at sixty-five. Late-enrollment penalties never vanish, so even if you don't take medication, consider a low-cost PartD plan unless your university retiree plan remains primary for drugs. If your campus coverage is "creditable," you can delay PartD without penalty, but you'll need proof when you finally enroll. Keep the certificate like you keep your tenure letter: in both hard copy and digital form. Losing it triggers arguments with insurance companies that feel eerily similar to reconciling missing grant receipts.

Dental and vision are not included in original Medicare, and university retiree plans may drop these benefits or charge separate premiums. Budget out-of-pocket dental care or purchase stand-alone coverage, weighing premium costs against likely procedures. For academics who logged decades grading papers in dim libraries, cataract surgery and prescription lenses are almost inevitable costs to plan for. The best practice is an earmarked Health Savings Account or a brokerage sweep fund dedicated to medical extras, separate from core living expenses. A little segregation now prevents future raids on travel savings when dental implants come calling.

If you decide to claim Social Security at seventy, remember to apply for Medicare at sixty-five even if you delay benefits. Enrolling in PartA is straightforward online and establishes your right to future PartB without penalty. If you accidentally skip enrollment and lack employer coverage, late penalties can inflate PartB premiums by ten percent for every twelve-month delay—an avoidable expense that lingers like unpaid library fines. Set calendar alerts two months before you turn sixty-five, and loop in your spouse so deadlines don't slip through the academic term's chaos.

Health-saving strategies evolve once Medicare begins. You can still reimburse out-of-pocket medical costs from your existing HSA, and after age sixty-five you can also pull HSA funds for nonmedical expenses at ordinary-income tax rates without the ten-percent penalty. Coordinate withdrawals with income levels to avoid IRMAA surcharges. For example, pay Medicare premiums directly from the HSA to reduce adjusted gross income, effectively getting a tax deduction you couldn't claim otherwise. It's like retroactively lowering tuition expenses by using scholarship credits—legal, but only if you know the rules.

International faculty members face unique hurdles. If you spent years abroad and didn't pay into Social Security, you may not have the forty quarters needed to qualify, but spousal benefits could still apply. Some countries have totalization agreements with the U.S., allowing work credits to combine for eligibility. Meanwhile, Medicare coverage stops at the border except in rare emergencies, so carrying expatriate health insurance becomes mandatory if you plan long stays overseas. Factor these costs when comparing foreign retirement locales; cheaper housing can be offset by pricey private health premiums.

A common pitfall is assuming you can time everything perfectly; life intervenes. Health changes might push you into retirement sooner, or administrative shake-ups could curtail phased-retirement plans. Build flexibility by keeping six months of cash reserves, preserving access to lines of credit, and maintaining licensure for consulting work. Delaying Social Security and Medicare PartB is less stressful when you have multiple fallback options. Think of it as diversifying your curriculum: if one course cancels for low enrollment, your teaching load and paycheck remain secure.

Don't underestimate the psychological shift from university health plans to Medicare. Suddenly you're choosing among dozens of Medigap or Medicare Advantage options, each with its own formulary, network, and star rating. Approaching this process like course selection helps: list deal-breakers, compare syllabi (plan brochures), and seek peer reviews. Some states have free SHIP counselors—akin to academic advisors—who guide you through choices without sales pressure. Use them; the service is already funded and can prevent costly mistakes.

Finally, revisit your decisions annually. Premiums, IRMAA thresholds, and university plan costs change, as do your health needs. Set an autumn ritual after midterm grading: review Medicare plan notices during open enrollment, estimate next year's income, and tweak Social Security strategies if life events warrant. Continuous review mirrors effective teaching—syllabi evolve, and so should retirement tactics. By staying proactive, you ensure that Social Security, Medicare, and university benefits harmonize like a well-conducted orchestra instead of clashing in financial dissonance.

In the grand scheme, coordinating Social Security and Medicare with university health plans isn't a one-time calculation; it's an ongoing research project with annual data points. Approach it with the same curiosity and diligence you bring to scholarship, and the payoff will be a retirement as intellectually satisfying as it is financially secure.

Chapter 44: Annuities, TIAA, and Lifetime Income, Converting 403(b) Balances into Paychecks

Annuities often sound as mysterious to professors as quantum mechanics does to first-year undergraduates, yet the concept is wonderfully simple when you strip away jargon: you hand over a lump sum and an insurance company—often TIAA in higher-ed circles—promises to pay you a steady paycheck for life. That paycheck is called "lifetime income," and its value lies in removing one of retirement's biggest stressors: the fear of outliving your savings. Instead of staring at a fluctuating 403(b) balance and wondering how much you can safely withdraw each year, you receive a predetermined monthly deposit, rather like the university payroll you knew for decades. The company absorbs market volatility and longevity risk, letting you budget confidently for groceries, travel, and spontaneous book purchases. Think of annuitization as trading the uncertainty of a co-op apartment's variable assessments for the predictability of a fixed mortgage payment—less excitement perhaps, but far fewer sleepless nights.

TIAA has long been the annuity giant for academics, partly because Andrew Carnegie's foundation established it in 1918 with the explicit mission of giving teachers dignified retirements. When you contributed to your 403(b) over the years, chances are at least some of those dollars went into either TIAA Traditional, which behaves like a fixed annuity, or CREF accounts, which invest in equities and bonds. The big decision as you approach retirement is whether to keep those balances in liquid mutual funds you manage, roll them to an IRA, or convert some portion into a lifetime annuity stream. Each pathway has pros and cons, but mixing them is often the secret sauce: guaranteed payments for essential expenses and flexible investments for discretionary dreams. Picture a two-bucket system—one faucet always running to cover utilities and prescriptions, the other bucket sloshing around to fund cruises or grandkids' college gifts depending on market tides.

TIAA offers several flavors of lifetime-income options, the most iconic being "Traditional," which credits a guaranteed interest rate plus potential additional amounts each year based on performance. Once you annuitize, payments arrive on the first of every month forever, adjusted by periodic increases thanks to that surplus performance. Another option is converting CREF or mutual fund balances into a "life annuity" where payments can rise or fall annually with market results. Think of Traditional as a slow-cooker stew—steady, predictable—and CREF annuitization as a stir-fry: potentially zesty but sensitive to heat levels. Many retiring professors choose a combination, ensuring a base level of stable income with some exposure to growth for inflation protection.

The timing of annuitization matters because TIAA uses "payout interest rates" that can change monthly, similar to mortgage rates. When prevailing rates rise, new annuitants lock in larger initial payments; when rates fall, payouts shrink. People nearing retirement sometimes ladder their annuitizations, converting a slice each year over five years to average out interest-rate risk. That ladder mimics dollar-cost averaging from your accumulation days, except now you're spreading decisions across time to hedge against locking everything in at a low-rate trough. The key takeaway is not to let fear of picking the perfect month paralyze you; spreading the decision itself can reduce regret.

Another twist is the choice between single-life and joint-life annuities. Single-life maximizes the check while you're alive but stops at your death; joint-life continues payments to a spouse, typically at 50 to 100percent of the original amount, for as long as either of you lives. Selecting joint-life is like buying extra insurance on your family car—there's a cost in reduced monthly benefit, but it keeps your partner from walking if the financial engine fails. If your spouse has his or her own pension or a robust Social Security benefit, you might lean toward a higher single-life payout. Yet many couples sleep better knowing an income floor continues no matter who goes first, so weigh peace of mind along with arithmetic.

Professors also face the "refund" decision. A life-only annuity ceases at death, but a "ten-year or twenty-year guaranteed period" option promises that if you die early, remaining payments through that period go to beneficiaries. Like rider upgrades on an airline ticket, each guarantee lowers your monthly check a notch. Financially, a healthy non-smoker in their mid-sixties may get more value from the larger payment of life-only, but risk-averse retirees sometimes pay for the guarantee. Just remember that once you add refund features, you're shifting some longevity risk back onto yourself, which defeats part of the purpose. Run sample quotes with and without guarantees to see the trade-off in real dollars.

Critics often warn that annuities lock up capital, which is true to an extent: money you exchange for lifetime income is generally illiquid. However, TIAA Traditional has some flexibility through its "Transfer Payout Annuity," allowing gradual moves back to liquid funds if circumstances change. Still, you should only annuitize amounts earmarked for foundational spending—housing, food, insurance—while keeping an emergency fund and investment account for surprises. Consider Social Security and any defined-benefit pension first, then fill the remaining essential-expense gap with an annuity. Treat discretionary goals separately, funded by remaining mutual funds that can grow or shrink without jeopardizing light and heat.

One big advantage of TIAA's system is its non-profit heritage, which historically translated into lower expense ratios on annuity payouts than many commercial insurers. While not immune to corporate evolution, TIAA still spends less on commissions because most higher-ed plans involve no brokers. Lower costs mean higher checks for you. That said, always compare: independent insurance marketplaces now offer immediate annuities that sometimes beat TIAA for pure payout if you sacrifice growth-sharing features. Shop around like you would for airfares before a conference, but remember that credit strength and administrative simplicity also matter.

Taxes on annuity payments follow "exclusion-ratio" rules: part of each check is treated as a return of your after-tax basis and part as taxable ordinary income. If all your 403(b) contributions were pre-tax, then nearly the entire payment is taxable. Understanding this helps you plan withholding so April doesn't bring an unpleasant tuition-bill-sized surprise. Roth 403(b) balances, if annuitized, generate tax-free payments—a compelling reason to diversify contribution types during working years. Coordinate annuity income with Social Security timing; stacking them in the same tax year could nudge you into the Medicare surcharge bracket. A tax-wise withdrawal plan is like good syllabus design: get it right upfront and the semester—read: retirement—flows smoothly.

Inflation is the dragon lurking outside every annuity castle. TIAA Traditional historically increases payments via "additional amounts," but these are not guaranteed and lag when markets dip. One hedge is to annuitize only a portion now and let a remaining pool of equities grow untouched for a decade, then annuitize that chunk later at higher payout rates thanks to age and hopefully market appreciation. Another hedge is buying Treasury-inflation-protected securities or I-Bonds in a separate bucket. No single product defeats inflation alone, so craft a diversified strategy and revisit annually.

Behavioral finance research shows retirees with guaranteed income streams report higher happiness and lower anxiety than those relying solely on portfolio withdrawals, even when both groups have similar net worth. The mental accounting benefit—knowing rent and groceries are covered—frees you to enjoy discretionary spending without guilt or fear. Anecdotally, professors tell me that after annuitizing they stop checking the S&P ticker every morning and instead check the symphony schedule. That psychological return is hard to quantify but real.

DIY withdrawals from a 403(b) remain an option, of course. The 4-percent rule—the notion you can withdraw four percent of your initial balance annually, adjusting for inflation—works decently in back tests, but remember those tests assume nerves of steel during bear markets. If watching your balance drop twenty percent while continuing fixed withdrawals sounds unsettling, an annuity can offload that stress. Hybrid approaches exist: allocate enough to cover basics via TIAA Traditional, then apply the 4-percent rule to the rest. This barbell strategy balances certainty and flexibility, giving you optionality if market returns outpace projections.

Sequence-of-returns risk is the academic term for the boating principle "try not to hit rough seas right after setting sail." If a market downturn hits early in retirement, portfolio withdrawals cause disproportionate damage. Annuitizing early sidesteps that hazard by converting part of your portfolio into checks immune to market shocks. Even a partial annuitization acts like an anchor, stabilizing the vessel so rough markets don't capsize your lifestyle. Wait too long and a market crash might force annuitizing at depressed balance levels, securing a permanently smaller paycheck.

One underappreciated benefit of TIAA lifetime income is longevity pooling. Not everyone in your cohort will live to ninety-five, but the ones who do receive income funded partly by those who pass earlier. This risk-sharing is impossible to replicate with individual portfolios unless you oversave by trying to plan for worst-case lifespan. Economists call that "mortality credits," and they amount to free return you can't get elsewhere. In essence, annuities let you insure against running out of money cheaper than self-insurance.

Estate considerations give some faculty pause: annuitized funds generally don't pass to heirs unless you purchased refund options. If legacy goals top your priority list, carve out separate investment accounts earmarked for heirs while annuitizing only what you need for lifetime security. Remember, Social Security benefits also cease at death, yet most advisors still recommend delaying for higher survivor income. Balancing personal financial independence with inheritance motives mirrors balancing teaching and research loads; both matter, but security of the present program must come first.

Implementing lifetime income through TIAA is paperwork-friendly. You can annuitize online or with a phone call, choosing start date, payment frequency, and withholding. Expect a short window—about thirty days—to reverse the decision, known as a "free look" period. After that, you're locked in. Double-check beneficiary designations and banking details so the first payment arrives without hiccups. It's oddly reminiscent of submitting final grades: you verify each student, hit submit, and breathe a sigh of relief when the confirmation email arrives.

After annuitization, monitor annual statements to track additional interest credits and ensure tax withholdings remain appropriate. TIAA posts rate announcements each March, and bumps often appear in July payments. Use these statements as prompts for a yearly household budget review, updating spending categories and fine-tuning charitable giving or travel plans. Lifetime income simplifies the macro picture, but micro-budgets still deserve your scholarly attention.

In closing, converting a portion of your 403(b) balance into guaranteed lifetime income through TIAA or similar providers can transform an abstract nest egg into a palpable, steady paycheck. The process requires decisions about timing, joint benefits, refund guarantees, and portfolio balance, but each lever can be understood with the analytical mind you've honed over years of research. Approach it like any scholarly project: gather data, consult peer-reviewed resources, iterate scenarios, and then commit. Once implemented, you'll join the ranks of retirees who spend their days engaged in curiosity and community rather than calculator gymnastics. Annuities are not magic, but for the right slice of your portfolio they can be the faithful teaching assistant that keeps class running smoothly while you finally take that sabbatical of a lifetime—this time, on your own schedule.

Chapter 45: Legacy on Campus, Endowments, Scholarships, and Ethical Wills

Many academics reach a turning point later in their careers when they begin reassessing what they really need—physically, emotionally, and financially—from the space they call home. For years, the larger house made sense: kids were at home, commute mattered, and hosting graduate students or colleagues over dinner required elbow room. But once the children move out and faculty life becomes more flexible, that three-bedroom house in a pricey neighborhood can start to feel more like a storage unit than a sanctuary. Downsizing isn't about giving up, it's about recalibrating—to reclaim time, reduce stress, and often, unlock financial freedom for new pursuits like travel, sabbaticals, or part-time living abroad. It's less about square footage and more about aligning your living situation with the lifestyle you actually want.

Consider the case of Ellen, a psychology professor who spent 30 years at a Midwest university. As she approached retirement, she realized her charming but aging home was consuming more energy and cash than she cared to admit. Between the upkeep, property taxes, and underutilized space, she felt like she was maintaining a museum to her past, not preparing for her future. After talking with a financial advisor and a few former colleagues who had already downsized, she sold her house, purchased a modern condo downtown, and pocketed nearly $180,000 in equity. That cushion now supports her travel fund and provides breathing room for unexpected costs—proof that downsizing can be an emotional and financial liberation rolled into one.

Of course, downsizing isn't always easy. The emotions tied to a long-time home can be thick and tangled—every corner, photo, and creaky step contains decades of life. It helps to approach the decision in phases. Start by imagining your "next chapter" rather than focusing on what you're leaving behind. Then think in terms of functionality: Are you still using that basement guest room? Do you still need a yard? Downsizing doesn't mean compromising comfort. It means choosing a space that fits your current life, not the one you lived 15 years ago.

Not every move needs to be a downsize. Some professors discover that their real dream is a second home—one near family, in a favorite vacation spot, or simply in a place with better weather or walkability. These aren't always "retirement homes" in the classic sense. Think of them more as lifestyle hubs—places you can spend summers writing or winters avoiding snow, that also appreciate in value or generate rental income. A second home can double as a sabbatical base, a family gathering place, or a part-time rental that offsets the mortgage when you're not using it. It's not for everyone, but with careful planning, it can work surprisingly well.

James and Carol, a married couple teaching at different universities in New York and Pennsylvania, bought a small lake cottage in upstate New York when their daughter started college. The home wasn't fancy—two bedrooms, one bath—but it was on the water and only 90 minutes from both campuses. They now spend summer weekends there, write papers on the screened porch, and let their daughter use it for quiet study breaks. During off-season months, they rent it on a short-term vacation platform, generating enough income to cover maintenance and taxes. It's more than a second property—it's a second chapter.

If you're considering a second home, it's critical to run the numbers with full transparency. Think beyond the mortgage to include maintenance, taxes, HOA dues, insurance (especially if it's near water or in a wildfire zone), and travel costs. Also, consider whether you'll be managing it or hiring someone local to do so—particularly if you plan to rent it out. Some faculty enjoy the logistics of owning and managing a property; others find it a time-sink that detracts from research and relaxation. Know your own tolerance before jumping in.

For some professors, the allure of international living—especially during sabbaticals—is irresistible. Spending a semester or even a year in a global city can breathe new life into both personal and academic growth. But the logistics matter. Do you maintain your primary residence while abroad or rent it out? Will you need to sublet or swap homes with another academic? Will your university health insurance cover you overseas? These are the sorts of questions that often get overlooked in the early excitement of planning a sabbatical in Florence or Tokyo.

An example worth learning from is Dr. Renu, a literature professor who spent her sabbatical year in Lisbon. She rented out her U.S. condo to a visiting scholar from Brazil, used the rental income to cover her Portuguese apartment, and relied on travel insurance to fill in healthcare coverage gaps abroad. She said the key was starting early—nearly 18 months before her departure—to coordinate housing, visas, university paperwork, and financial contingencies. The result? A low-stress, high-reward experience that sparked new research ideas and reignited her enthusiasm for teaching.

Sabbaticals abroad can also spark interest in more permanent global relocation—especially as retirement nears. Many professors find that certain countries offer affordable, culturally rich living with excellent healthcare and robust expat communities. Portugal, Costa Rica, Mexico, and parts of Southeast Asia often top the list. Some universities even allow phased retirement while living abroad, especially if you're teaching online or providing occasional consulting. Just make sure you understand how your pension or Social Security payments will be taxed under international agreements.

Deciding between downsizing, a second home, or international living isn't a one-and-done choice. These options can evolve over time or even coexist. One year, you may rent out your home and travel; the next, you may spend summers at the cottage; later, you may consolidate into a condo and simplify everything. The point isn't to get it "right" the first time—

it's to stay flexible and curious. The academic lifestyle, with its built-in seasonal rhythms and sabbatical opportunities, offers more latitude than most careers. Use that flexibility wisely.

Selling a home can also free up capital for other financial goals, like funding grandkids' college accounts, starting a charitable fund, or paying off lingering debts. Just be cautious of the tax consequences if the home appreciated significantly. Fortunately, primary residences enjoy favorable capital gains exclusions—up to $250,000 per owner, if you meet IRS guidelines. Still, a quick meeting with a tax advisor before listing the house can save you from unpleasant surprises later.

If a move involves downsizing into a retirement community or continuing-care facility, ask specific questions about costs, refundable deposits, contract types, and healthcare escalation. These communities offer peace of mind and social interaction, but they also vary widely in price and quality. Visit more than once. Ask to have lunch with residents. And talk to your financial planner before signing a six-figure contract with unclear refund terms. As with tenure, it's better to understand the long game upfront.

Technology also plays a growing role in making transitions smoother. Smart home monitoring allows you to track a second property's condition while away. Digital mail services can scan and forward letters to wherever you are. And expense tracking apps make it easier to monitor rental income, maintenance costs, and tax deductions. The modern professor can live across time zones without losing track of the budget or missing a bill.

Some scholars fall into the trap of thinking that their housing decisions must match their academic status. But there's no shame in scaling down to something simpler, more affordable, or more fun. After all, what's the point of tenure, flexibility, and financial planning if not to enjoy the fruits of your work? You earned your options—now it's time to exercise them with purpose. Whether that's fewer square feet, more beach sunsets, or longer global stays, the only wrong move is the one made out of fear or habit.

In blending professional goals with personal aspirations, housing becomes more than shelter. It becomes a vehicle for freedom, rest, and growth. That old saying "location, location, location" is as much about mindset as it is about zip code. What location best matches the season of life you're in? Where can you think deeply, rest fully, and live with greater ease? These aren't just real estate questions—they're questions about how you want to spend your most valuable currency: time.

For faculty with the good fortune of financial flexibility, the question becomes not "Can I afford to make this change?" but rather, "Can I afford not to?" Are you clinging to a house that ties up your time and money? Are you curious about a new rhythm that a smaller space or second home could support? Are you ready for new scenery after decades of the same campus view? These are good questions to ask—not because something is wrong, but because something new might be even better.

Ultimately, housing choices are deeply personal—but they're also deeply powerful. Downsizing can unlock liquidity, lower stress, and fund a vibrant next chapter. A second home can provide joy, flexibility, and even financial return. Sabbaticals abroad can widen your worldview while strengthening your academic relevance. The common thread is intentionality. Make your decisions deliberately, aligned with your values, not based on default assumptions or external expectations.

Downsizing, owning a second home, and traveling globally as a professor aren't just lifestyle upgrades—they're strategic financial and emotional decisions that can shape the quality of your retirement years. You don't need to have every detail figured out now, but start the conversations, run the numbers, and let yourself dream a bit. The same critical thinking you applied to your research and teaching can—and should—apply here too. You've shaped young minds. Now shape a life that inspires your own.

Chapter 46: Downsizing, Second Homes, and Global Sabbaticals, Real-World Case Studies

Many academics reach a turning point later in their careers when they begin reassessing what they really need—physically, emotionally, and financially—from the space they call home. For years, the larger house made sense: kids were at home, commute mattered, and hosting graduate students or colleagues over dinner required elbow room. But once the children move out and faculty life becomes more flexible, that three-bedroom house in a pricey neighborhood can start to feel more like a storage unit than a sanctuary. Downsizing isn't about giving up, it's about recalibrating—to reclaim time, reduce stress, and often, unlock financial freedom for new pursuits like travel, sabbaticals, or part-time living abroad. It's less about square footage and more about aligning your living situation with the lifestyle you actually want.

Consider the case of Ellen, a psychology professor who spent 30 years at a Midwest university. As she approached retirement, she realized her charming but aging home was consuming more energy and cash than she cared to admit. Between the upkeep, property taxes, and underutilized space, she felt like she was maintaining a museum to her past, not preparing for her future. After talking with a financial advisor and a few former colleagues who had already downsized, she sold her house, purchased a modern condo downtown, and pocketed nearly $180,000 in equity. That cushion now supports her travel fund and provides breathing room for unexpected costs—proof that downsizing can be an emotional and financial liberation rolled into one.

Of course, downsizing isn't always easy. The emotions tied to a long-time home can be thick and tangled—every corner, photo, and creaky step contains decades of life. It helps to approach the decision in phases. Start by imagining your "next chapter" rather than focusing on what you're leaving behind. Then think in terms of functionality: Are you still using that basement guest room? Do you still need a yard? Downsizing doesn't mean compromising comfort. It means choosing a space that fits your current life, not the one you lived 15 years ago.

Not every move needs to be a downsize. Some professors discover that their real dream is a second home—one near family, in a favorite vacation spot, or simply in a place with better weather or walkability. These aren't always "retirement homes" in the classic sense. Think of them more as lifestyle hubs—places you can spend summers writing or winters avoiding snow, that also appreciate in value or generate rental income. A second home can double as a sabbatical base, a family gathering place, or a part-time rental that offsets the mortgage when you're not using it. It's not for everyone, but with careful planning, it can work surprisingly well.

James and Carol, a married couple teaching at different universities in New York and Pennsylvania, bought a small lake cottage in upstate New York when their daughter started college. The home wasn't fancy—two bedrooms, one bath—but it was on the water and only 90 minutes from both campuses. They now spend summer weekends there, write papers on the screened porch, and let their daughter use it for quiet study breaks. During off-season months, they rent it on a short-term vacation platform, generating enough income to cover maintenance and taxes. It's more than a second property—it's a second chapter.

If you're considering a second home, it's critical to run the numbers with full transparency. Think beyond the mortgage to include maintenance, taxes, HOA dues, insurance (especially if it's near water or in a wildfire zone), and travel costs. Also, consider whether you'll be managing it or hiring someone local to do so—particularly if you plan to rent it out. Some faculty enjoy the logistics of owning and managing a property; others find it a time-sink that detracts from research and relaxation. Know your own tolerance before jumping in.

For some professors, the allure of international living—especially during sabbaticals—is irresistible. Spending a semester or even a year in a global city can breathe new life into both personal and academic growth. But the logistics matter. Do you maintain your primary residence while abroad or rent it out? Will you need to sublet or swap homes with another academic? Will your university health insurance cover you overseas? These are the sorts of questions that often get overlooked in the early excitement of planning a sabbatical in Florence or Tokyo.

An example worth learning from is Dr. Renu, a literature professor who spent her sabbatical year in Lisbon. She rented out her U.S. condo to a visiting scholar from Brazil, used the rental income to cover her Portuguese apartment, and relied on travel insurance to fill in healthcare coverage gaps abroad. She said the key was starting early—nearly 18 months before her departure—to coordinate housing, visas, university paperwork, and financial contingencies. The result? A low-stress, high-reward experience that sparked new research ideas and reignited her enthusiasm for teaching.

Sabbaticals abroad can also spark interest in more permanent global relocation—especially as retirement nears. Many professors find that certain countries offer affordable, culturally rich living with excellent healthcare and robust expat communities. Portugal, Costa Rica, Mexico, and parts of Southeast Asia often top the list. Some universities even allow phased retirement while living abroad, especially if you're teaching online or providing occasional consulting. Just make sure you understand how your pension or Social Security payments will be taxed under international agreements.

Deciding between downsizing, a second home, or international living isn't a one-and-done choice. These options can evolve over time or even coexist. One year, you may rent out your home and travel; the next, you may spend summers at the cottage; later, you may consolidate into a condo and simplify everything. The point isn't to get it "right" the first time—

it's to stay flexible and curious. The academic lifestyle, with its built-in seasonal rhythms and sabbatical opportunities, offers more latitude than most careers. Use that flexibility wisely.

Selling a home can also free up capital for other financial goals, like funding grandkids' college accounts, starting a charitable fund, or paying off lingering debts. Just be cautious of the tax consequences if the home appreciated significantly. Fortunately, primary residences enjoy favorable capital gains exclusions—up to $250,000 per owner, if you meet IRS guidelines. Still, a quick meeting with a tax advisor before listing the house can save you from unpleasant surprises later.

If a move involves downsizing into a retirement community or continuing-care facility, ask specific questions about costs, refundable deposits, contract types, and healthcare escalation. These communities offer peace of mind and social interaction, but they also vary widely in price and quality. Visit more than once. Ask to have lunch with residents. And talk to your financial planner before signing a six-figure contract with unclear refund terms. As with tenure, it's better to understand the long game upfront.

Technology also plays a growing role in making transitions smoother. Smart home monitoring allows you to track a second property's condition while away. Digital mail services can scan and forward letters to wherever you are. And expense tracking apps make it easier to monitor rental income, maintenance costs, and tax deductions. The modern professor can live across time zones without losing track of the budget or missing a bill.

Some scholars fall into the trap of thinking that their housing decisions must match their academic status. But there's no shame in scaling down to something simpler, more affordable, or more fun. After all, what's the point of tenure, flexibility, and financial planning if not to enjoy the fruits of your work? You earned your options—now it's time to exercise them with purpose. Whether that's fewer square feet, more beach sunsets, or longer global stays, the only wrong move is the one made out of fear or habit.

In blending professional goals with personal aspirations, housing becomes more than shelter. It becomes a vehicle for freedom, rest, and growth. That old saying "location, location, location" is as much about mindset as it is about zip code. What location best matches the season of life you're in? Where can you think deeply, rest fully, and live with greater ease? These aren't just real estate questions—they're questions about how you want to spend your most valuable currency: time.

For faculty with the good fortune of financial flexibility, the question becomes not "Can I afford to make this change?" but rather, "Can I afford not to?" Are you clinging to a house that ties up your time and money? Are you curious about a new rhythm that a smaller space or second home could support? Are you ready for new scenery after decades of the same campus view? These are good questions to ask—not because something is wrong, but because something new might be even better.

Ultimately, housing choices are deeply personal—but they're also deeply powerful. Downsizing can unlock liquidity, lower stress, and fund a vibrant next chapter. A second home can provide joy, flexibility, and even financial return. Sabbaticals abroad can widen your worldview while strengthening your academic relevance. The common thread is intentionality. Make your decisions deliberately, aligned with your values, not based on default assumptions or external expectations.

Downsizing, owning a second home, and traveling globally as a professor aren't just lifestyle upgrades—they're strategic financial and emotional decisions that can shape the quality of your retirement years. You don't need to have every detail figured out now, but start the conversations, run the numbers, and let yourself dream a bit. The same critical thinking you applied to your research and teaching can—and should—apply here too. You've shaped young minds. Now shape a life that inspires your own.

Chapter 47: Retirement Rehearsal & Final Exit, Psychological Prep, Financial Checklists, Saying Goodbye Confidently

Retirement begins long before the farewell reception and the final click of the classroom lights, and the most successful exits start with a rehearsal period that feels less like waiting in the wings and more like stepping onto a practice stage. Picture a dress rehearsal where you test lighting cues, stage directions, and even your costume so opening night holds no surprises; a retirement rehearsal works the same way, letting you practice living on a reduced income, experiment with new daily routines, and address any psychological jitters in advance. Professors often overlook that the emotional cadence of academic life—lectures, office hours, committee meetings—has set their internal metronome for decades, so eliminating that structure cold turkey can feel like wandering off beat. By simulating "future Fridays" or taking a mini-sabbatical, you can sense whether hobbies fill the day or whether boredom creeps in, and adjust accordingly. Think of it as conducting a pilot study before launching a full research project: you identify flaws early, tweak variables, and proceed with confidence rather than blind optimism.

One straightforward rehearsal technique is to live for three months on the budget you expect in retirement while still collecting your regular paycheck, funneling the surplus into a separate savings account. This forced-scarcity experiment helps reveal hidden expenses—subscriptions you forgot, spontaneous coffee runs, or travel costs you didn't include—that could derail a carefully drafted retirement spreadsheet. If groceries and entertainment come in under target, you gain reassurance; if costs blow past estimates, you still have time to refine the plan without jeopardizing real bills. Document each surprise and brainstorm sustainable fixes rather than short-term cuts; canceling streaming services might work now, but if you love films, plan a cheaper alternative like the public library's digital portal. By treating your spending data like lab results—objective feedback—you can calibrate rather than guess.

Social rehearsal matters, too. Schedule a "practice month" free of campus commitments, then observe which relationships and activities naturally fill your calendar. Some professors discover that colleagues quickly shift focus to new hires, leaving them feeling adrift; others relish unstructured mornings filled with tennis games or grandchild visits. Identifying potential loneliness early gives you time to cultivate outside networks—choral groups, volunteer tutoring, language classes—before the university ID expires. Remember, social voids often lead retirees to reverse decisions prematurely, returning part-time not for money but for camaraderie. Building multiple relational pillars reduces that temptation and broadens life's stage.

Psychologically, identity rehearsal is crucial. Write a brief paragraph finishing the sentence "I am..." without referencing your academic title—no "professor," "chair," or "researcher." Many find the page suddenly sparse, revealing how deeply they equate worth with vocation. That exercise can feel uncomfortable, but it opens space to add descriptors untethered from institutional validation: gardener, mentor, jazz enthusiast, traveler, community advocate. Reading that new self-portrait daily trains the brain to uncouple status from self-esteem, smoothing the emotional landing when the title disappears from email signatures. It's cognitive restructuring, plain and simple.

Next comes the financial checklist, the scaffolding that keeps rehearsal from becoming improvisation. Confirm you have at least six months of liquid cash in a high-yield savings account for unexpected repairs or medical copays—investment portfolios fluctuate, but refrigerators still break. Double-check that required minimum distributions, Social

Security timing, and pension start dates coordinate so income doesn't dip unexpectedly. Review healthcare coverage during gaps, especially if you retire before Medicare eligibility; a subsidized COBRA bridge or Affordable Care Act plan may be necessary. Update estate documents—wills, powers of attorney, beneficiary designations—because life changes and law libraries seldom keep hours past first bell. Finally, map out debt: a mortgage isn't automatically bad in retirement, but know the rate, balance, and payoff plan so surprises don't sneak in like uninvited collaborators to a grant proposal.

Another checklist area is tax planning. Estimate your post-retirement bracket by adding all income streams—pension, annuities, Social Security, consulting—and subtracting standard or itemized deductions. This projection can reveal whether Roth conversions make sense in early retirement low-income years or whether charitable bunching through a donor-advised fund can maintain itemization. Don't forget that up to 85percent of Social Security can be taxable depending on provisional income; a well-timed withdrawal strategy can minimize that bite. Consider meeting with a CPA who understands higher-ed retirement nuances like 403(b) rollover options and required minimum distributions from multiple accounts. Think of it as peer review for your tax manuscript: a second set of eyes catches errors before publication—also known as April15.

Health is your most valuable asset, yet many retirement plans treat it as an afterthought behind income flows and travel dreams. Schedule baseline screenings—cardiac, vision, hearing—so you understand current status and potential costs. If you anticipate long-term-care needs, price insurance or research hybrid annuity-LTC products before rates jump with age or diagnoses. Build a wellness routine into your rehearsal year: test gym classes, walking clubs, or meditation apps until you find ones you'll stick with. These habits become automatic in the new routine, reinforcing both physical stamina and social connection. Neglecting this pillar can unravel even the soundest financial plan.

Emotional closure is another rehearsal component many skip until the farewell luncheon, when they realize tears and anxieties surface amid the cheesecake. Start months earlier by listing professional loose ends:

unfinished manuscripts, mentees needing letters, departmental archives to organize. Tackle one each week, celebrating progress visibly—perhaps a checklist on a whiteboard. This systematic closure mimics the satisfaction students feel when each assignment disappears from the syllabus, replacing dread with accomplishment. It also prevents last-minute all-nighters that could mar your exit narrative.

Mentorship handoffs are a delicate but essential chore. Identify people who can inherit major roles you've played—whether shepherding the undergraduate journal or managing the departmental colloquium. Offer them shadowing opportunities while you still draw salary, easing the learning curve and signaling trust. Not only does this protect institutional memory; it lessens your own guilt, knowing programs won't collapse post-departure. Future you will relish sipping coffee without worrying whether someone printed flyers for next week's lecture series. Like preparing a successor for a research lab, it ensures continuity and upholds your legacy.

Saying goodbye confidently also involves communicating intentions clearly to stakeholders—students, advisees, donors, collaborators—long before the final semester. Craft an email template explaining your timeline, continuing availability for limited advice, and referrals for new contacts. Broadcasting this plan early prevents misinterpretations and curtails last-minute requests. It's professional courtesy wrapped in boundary-setting, making the departure feel organized rather than abrupt. Faculty who keep quiet often end up overwhelmed by frantic demands once rumors swirl.

During the official countdown semester, test-drive new leisure pursuits aggressively. If you think you'll write poetry, join a workshop now; if woodworking beckons, enroll in a weekend class. Experiencing these activities pre-retirement helps gauge genuine interest versus romanticized imagination. You may discover ceramics beats oil painting, saving hundreds on brushes later. Moreover, sharing new hobbies with colleagues can reshape their perception of you beyond academia, smoothing the social path post-exit.

Financial rehearsal also includes downsizing or relocating practice. Spend a week in the target city or apartment size, tracking daily routines and costs. Can you adapt to a smaller kitchen? Does the coastal humidity aggravate allergies? Real-world trials expose issues brochures omit. They also provide data to negotiate better lease terms or contractor quotes. Call it ethnographic research on your future life.

Plan a mini-"retired budget" week with your partner to test joint schedules and spending. Cook at home, share chores, and allocate hours for individual solitude, mimicking the rhythm you'll share daily. Friction points—like too much togetherness in a small space—surface quickly but harmlessly. You can then design conflict-avoidance systems, from separate hobby corners to designated errand days. It's marital regression testing: fix bugs before the software, otherwise known as retirement, goes live.

A farewell tour of favorite campus spots—library stacks, hidden gardens, coffee nooks—offers emotional closure and sparks gratitude. Capture photos, maybe compose a brief journal entry for each location, turning memories into artifacts you can revisit. This ritual transfers nostalgia into documented gratitude rather than lingering ache. It's akin to archiving data before closing a grant: you preserve value for future reference and move on uncluttered.

Celebrate milestones as they occur: the last undergraduate lecture, final committee vote, final grade submission. Each ceremony trains your psyche that transition is incremental, not a single cliff. Colleagues and students appreciate these markers, too; they know when to say thanks without feeling they're intruding. Short, sincere acknowledgments beat one overwhelming party where you struggle to remember names.

In final financial preparations, create a rhythm for monitoring accounts post-retirement: perhaps the first Monday of each month you review investment performance, the second Wednesday you reconcile checking, and quarterly you assess withdrawal rates. Regular but limited check-ins prevent obsessive market watching while ensuring you remain on course. Consider consolidating accounts to reduce paperwork, but keep enough separation between spending and investment buckets to avoid accidental overspending. Automation—direct deposit of annuity checks to checking, scheduled transfers to savings—reduces cognitive load, freeing bandwidth for pursuits beyond spreadsheets.

On your actual last day, arrive with one light task list and one symbolic item to leave behind—maybe a reference book younger colleagues will cherish or a framed photo of your first cohort. Physical gestures anchor intangible transitions. After handing in keys and parking pass, pause at the exit door, deeply inhale, and recognize that silence replacing hallway chatter. That quiet is not absence; it's space for your next chapter. Take a step forward, not backward, and let the automatic doors close on their own.

The first official week of retirement should feature at least one pre-planned event each day—breakfast with friends, a morning hike, a volunteer shift—to fend off post-commencement letdown. Structure breeds confidence, and after decades of syllabi dictating life, blank calendars can intimidate. Soon spontaneity will feel liberating, but initial scaffolding provides steady footing. It's like moving from strict lab protocols to exploratory research; the shift is invigorating once initial guardrails exist.

Three months in, schedule a reflection check. Journal successes, surprises, and lingering anxieties. Adjust budgets, hobbies, or social commitments accordingly. View this as peer review of your personal retirement manuscript, ensuring coherence and impact. Over time, the revisions grow smaller, and confidence replaces rehearsal. Eventually, you realize the performance has begun and you're not just ready—you're thriving.

By approaching retirement as a rehearsal followed by a well-staged final exit, you gain mastery over both the numbers and the emotions. Psychological readiness dovetails with financial preparedness, and saying goodbye becomes less about loss and more about intentional evolution. Like concluding a seminal research project, you close the notebook satisfied, knowing the work is complete and the legacy secure. Now new questions beckon, and the lab lights—this time, perhaps, a sunny garden or a bustling art studio—are yours to switch on each morning.

Chapter 48: The Next Chapter Is Yours, Closing Reflections and Financial Confidence for the Road Ahead

There's something bittersweet about reaching the final pages of a book like this. On one hand, we've covered a great deal of ground—from salary structures to retirement strategies, from student loans to estate planning, from credit cards to cultural values. On the other, your journey is just beginning. That's the beauty of financial literacy—it doesn't end with knowledge. It begins when you start making different choices because of that knowledge. If this book has done its job, you now see your money life with more clarity, more confidence, and more control.

By now, you've probably realized that personal finance is less about spreadsheets and more about self-awareness. It's about naming your goals, understanding your trade-offs, and aligning your actions with your values. No two lives are identical, which means no two financial paths will be either. What works for one family or colleague might feel completely wrong for your circumstances, and that's not failure—it's wisdom. Knowing what's not for you is just as powerful as knowing what is.

Along the way, I hope you've found more than facts—you've found frameworks. Not just what to do with your 403(b), but how to think about risk. Not just which insurance to buy, but how to evaluate what peace of mind is worth. Not just how to pay for your child's education, but how to define what kind of future you want to build with your resources. That deeper thinking is what will sustain you long after you've put this book back on the shelf.

And let's be honest—money can be overwhelming. It touches everything. It intersects with our emotions, our identities, our relationships, and our aspirations. That's why financial literacy isn't just about understanding investments or budgets—it's about understanding yourself. What fears drive you? What stories have you inherited? What beliefs are you ready to rewrite? Financial clarity isn't just a skill—it's a kind of emotional liberation.

You might still have doubts or lingering questions. That's perfectly normal. No book can answer every single financial scenario. But hopefully, you now have the language to ask better questions—and the courage to seek help when needed. Whether from a trusted advisor, a peer, or a new resource, continuing this journey with curiosity will serve you well. Progress in personal finance is rarely a straight line; it's more like a long hike with a few switchbacks.

You've likely noticed that we never focused on perfection. We didn't chase the "ideal" retirement age or obsess over squeezing every last tax deduction. That's because your financial life isn't a performance—it's a process. You can recover from mistakes, course-correct from bad advice, and start fresh at any age. Whether you're 28 or 68, the next smart step is the one you take with intention.

Maybe the biggest shift you'll experience after reading this book isn't in your net worth—but in your mindset. That moment when you stop avoiding the tough money conversations. When you finally open the statements you used to ignore. When you sit down and talk openly with your spouse, your kids, or your financial planner. That mindset shift is the real victory. Everything else flows from that.

And don't forget to celebrate. Celebrate your first emergency fund, your first paid-off credit card, your first Roth IRA contribution. Celebrate reviewing your will, setting boundaries with family, or finally understanding how Medicare works. These aren't small wins—they're the building blocks of a financially resilient life. Too often we wait until we "arrive" to feel proud. But in reality, the journey is full of milestones that deserve recognition.

If you ever feel discouraged, come back to your "why." Why are you working this hard? Why are you budgeting? Why are you trying to build wealth in the first place? Maybe it's to give your kids a better start. Maybe it's to travel more, retire earlier, or live without financial fear. Whatever your "why" is, keep it front and center. It will sustain you when the numbers feel flat or the progress feels slow.

Also, remember that generosity is a part of abundance. When your finances are in order, you can give without resentment. You can help others without hurting your own stability. Whether through time, money, mentorship, or service, your financial literacy can become a ripple effect. You never know who's watching, learning, or being inspired by your example. You might be the spark for someone else's journey.

This book wasn't written to turn you into a financial expert—it was written to help you take control. To help you feel less shame, less confusion, and less isolation around money. To help you navigate life's transitions—from job changes to retirements—with more foresight and less stress. To help you ask smarter questions, avoid common traps, and know when to say yes—or no—with clarity.

The road ahead will still have twists. Life will still surprise you. But you're now walking it with your eyes open, your tools sharpened, and your mindset aligned with your goals. That matters. That makes you dangerous in all the best ways—less reactive, more strategic, and more resilient.

So, what now? Close the book. Take a breath. And then take action. Not everything at once. Just one thing. Review a statement. Update your beneficiaries. Talk to your partner. Set up the calendar reminder for your next financial review. The small moves matter, because they add up. And they remind you that you are the author of your next chapter.

This isn't goodbye—it's a baton pass. The information is yours now. The questions are yours to explore. The power is yours to wield. Go build a financial life that reflects your brilliance, your values, and your future.

You've got this. And the next chapter of your money story? It's going to be your best one yet.

Disclaimer

Financial Literacy for Professors was written to educate, empower, and encourage faculty, researchers, administrators, and academic professionals—at every stage of their careers—to take control of their financial lives. The ideas and frameworks in these pages draw on my MBA training, industry credentials, and more than two decades of advising people who live and work in higher-education settings. Still, it's important to be clear about what this book is—and what it is not.

Educational Purpose Only

1. All material in this book is offered for general educational and informational purposes.
2. Its goal is to introduce professors—adjunct or tenured, early-career or emeritus—to core financial concepts, strategic tools, and the unique opportunities and pitfalls that come with academic compensation, benefits, and career rhythms.
3. Although you will find frameworks, case studies, and real-world examples here, they are not a substitute for individualized advice. Your goals, compensation mix (nine-month salary, summer grants, overloads, stipends), retirement plans, tax profile, and risk tolerance are yours alone.
4. Always consult qualified professionals before making major financial, legal, or career decisions.

No Legal Advice

1. Faculty routinely sign contracts, negotiate intellectual-property

clauses, review grant agreements, and consider consulting or start-up ventures. Nothing in this book constitutes legal counsel.
2. If you are drafting or revising employment contracts, setting up an LLC for consulting income, protecting intellectual property, managing outside-income disclosures, or structuring estate documents, seek a licensed attorney experienced in higher-education or small-business law.
3. Regulations differ by state, institution, and individual circumstance. You are responsible for remaining in compliance.

No Financial or Investment Advice

1. While this book discusses salary negotiation, retirement planning, investment allocation, and phased-retirement strategies, it does so from an educational standpoint.
2. I am not acting here as your Certified Financial Planner™, Registered Investment Adviser, or broker-dealer.
3. Before reallocating investments, annuitizing TIAA balances, rolling over retirement accounts, or adjusting withdrawal strategies, work with a credentialed advisor who understands university plans and your personal objectives.

No Accounting or Tax Advice

1. Taxes matter deeply to academics who juggle W-2 income, 1099 consulting fees, fellowship stipends, and grant funding—but this book is not authored by a CPA or Enrolled Agent.
2. Discussions of deductions, estimated payments, or multi-state teaching income are illustrative only.
3. If you:

- Teach or consult in multiple states or abroad
- Receive fellowship stipends or sabbatical housing allowances

- Need guidance on self-employment tax for side gigs
- Plan charitable gifts of appreciated securities or set up a donor-advised fund

work with a qualified tax professional to optimize and comply with current law.

No Guarantees or Promises

Reading this book will not guarantee tenure, investment gains, debt freedom, or a stress-free retirement. Financial literacy, like scholarship, is an ongoing discipline that requires study, reflection, and action. Examples in these pages illustrate possibilities, not promises. Outcomes depend on your decisions, market forces, institutional policies, and sometimes luck.

Limitation of Liability

By reading this book you agree that Pat Brown, MBA, and associated brands—including FinancialLiteracyForProfessors.com—are not liable for financial losses, legal disputes, tax penalties, or career consequences resulting from actions you take (or don't take) based on this content. You bear full responsibility for your financial, legal, and professional choices.

Build Your Professional Team

Every professor—whether lecturing, leading a lab, chairing a department, or transitioning to emeritus status—benefits from a trusted circle of experts:

*A fee-only financial advisor

*A knowledgeable CPA or EA

*An attorney versed in employment and estate matters

*An insurance specialist familiar with academic benefit gaps

This book is meant to complement, not replace, that team. If you don't have one yet, consider this your nudge to start assembling it. You devote immense energy to research and teaching; your financial future deserves the same rigor and intentional design.

You've shaped minds and advanced knowledge. Now let's make sure your money works just as intelligently.

Learn More and Stay Connected

Financial Literacy For Professors was created with one goal in mind: to help faculty, researchers, and academic professionals navigate the financial landscape of higher education with clarity, confidence, and control. But this book is just the beginning.

To dive deeper, ask questions, access bonus materials, or connect with the author and his team, please visit:

Website: www.FinancialLiteracyForProfessors.com

This official platform is designed exclusively for professors, academic professionals, and those who support them. There, you'll find tools and resources tailored to the unique financial challenges and opportunities of university life, including:

- Budget templates designed for 9-month and 12-month pay schedules
- Tax planning guides for grants, sabbaticals, and side income
- Retirement planning tips across 403(b), 457(b), and state pension systems
- Practical checklists for relocation, sabbatical prep, and benefit elections
- Timely blog articles addressing real questions from real faculty
- Access to workshops, speaking events, and educational webinars

Whether you're negotiating a new offer, evaluating an early retirement option, or simply trying to organize your financial life more intentionally, this platform is here to help you stay informed, organized, and empowered at every stage of your academic journey.

Email Contact: info@financialliteracyforprofessors.com

If you have questions, want to invite Pat Brown to speak at your institution, or are interested in partnership opportunities, please reach out directly. This inbox is monitored by Pat's team and is especially open to inquiries from faculty associations, HR offices, professional development coordinators, and university leaders seeking to expand financial education offerings on campus.

Who We Serve

Financial Literacy For Professors is written for the realities of academic life. We support:

- Tenure-track and tenured faculty navigating complex compensation and benefits
- Adjuncts and lecturers balancing multiple income sources and retirement gaps
- Mid-career professors seeking to build wealth while juggling family needs
- Administrators and academic leaders weighing the financial impact of transitions
- Financial advisors, CPAs, and campus HR teams looking for professor-specific resources

What's Next

The financial landscape for professors is changing. From growing administrative demands to evolving retirement structures, from managing student loan debt to supporting children or aging parents, today's academics face a more complex set of financial decisions than ever before.

That's why this book is just one piece of a larger mission. Through the *Financial Literacy For Professors* platform, we're building a nationwide movement—one that empowers faculty not just to teach and research, but to plan, protect, and prosper. A movement that values clarity over complexity, planning over panic, and education over guesswork.

You're Part of That Movement

If you're reading this, you care. You're taking ownership of your financial future—and that makes you part of a growing community of academic professionals committed to doing things smarter, earlier, and with more intention.

We're excited to continue this journey with you—in faculty lounges, department retreats, professional development days, and one-on-one conversations. From early-career postdocs to emeritus professors, you have a seat at this table.

Stay Informed. Stay Equipped. Stay Empowered.

Visit www.FinancialLiteracyForProfessors.com today to subscribe for updates, download new resources, or share your story with our team. You can also email us directly at **info@financialliteracyforprofessors.com** to ask a question, request a resource, or begin a meaningful conversation.

Financial literacy isn't just for Wall Street. It's for the classroom. It's for faculty. It's for anyone who wants their career in higher education to translate into long-term financial wellness.

Important Dates

Below is a concise "academic-year calendar" of the most common U.S. tax, investing, and benefits deadlines that trip up—or empower—college faculty. Treat it as a living checklist: confirm exact dates each year (they may shift to the next business day when they fall on weekends or holidays) and add any state-specific or campus-specific items your HR office publishes.

JANUARY

*Jan1– New payroll year starts. 403(b), 457(b), and 401(a) salary-deferral limits reset; update your contribution percentages before the month's first payroll run if you plan to max out.

*Jan15– Fourth-quarter estimated-tax payment (IRS Form1040-ES) for the prior tax year, required if you have consulting, book royalties, or summer income not fully withheld through payroll.

*By Jan31– Expect W-2, 1099-NEC/MISC, 1099-DIV/INT, 1099-R, and (if you have a health-savings account) Form5498-SA; reconcile them against your own records.

FEBRUARY

*Mid-Feb– Most institutions release prior-year 1095-C (proof of employer health coverage). Keep for your records; you no longer mail it with your return, but tax preparers sometimes ask.

*LateFeb– TIAA and other retirement vendors post annual statements. Verify year-end balances, investment mix, and that contributions hit the IRS limits.

MARCH

*Mar31– Deadline for e-filing Form1099 with the IRS if you paid independent contractors (e.g., research assistants you hired personally) during the prior year.

*Planning reminder – If you'll turn 73 this calendar year, map out first Required Minimum Distribution (RMD) strategy; you can delay the *first* RMD until April1 of next year, but that means taking two in one year.

APRIL

*Apr1– Final date to take the prior-year RMD if last year was your first RMD year and you delayed.

*Apr15(or next business day) –

- Federal and most state tax returns are due
- Last day to make prior-year Traditional or Roth IRA contributions
- First-quarter estimated-tax payment for current tax year

*Campus note – Many universities require summer-salary paperwork and grant-based overload requests by mid-to-late April. Mark departmental cutoffs.

MAY

*Early May– Review spring-semester overload or extra-service pay stubs to be sure extra withholdings are adequate; adjust FormW-4 if summer funding will spike income.

JUNE

*Jun15– Second-quarter estimated-tax payment.

- Also the automatic federal filing deadline if you've been on a sabbatical abroad (at least outside the U.S. on Apr15); attach a statement to your return.

*Mid-Jun– Some campuses open online enrollment for fall parking permits and Flexible Spending Accounts (FSAs) tied to the academic year—mark reminders if those affect your paycheck.

JULY

*Jul31– If you run a side LLC paying other people (e.g., editing services), Form941 (quarterly payroll tax) is due. Most professors won't need this but note it if applicable.

*Planning reminder – Check year-to-date retirement contributions; if only on nine-month pay, ensure fall deductions will hit the annual maximum.

AUGUST

*Mid-Aug– Many institutions freeze changes to fall payroll schedules. Verify that your deferral percentages, HSA amounts, and charitable payroll deductions are correct before the term starts.

SEPTEMBER

*Sep15–

- Third-quarter estimated-tax payment
- Final deadline for prior-year calendar-year S-corps/partnership returns if you consult through an entity

*LateSep– TIAA and Fidelity typically publish next-year contribution-limit reminders; build them into course-release negotiations or chair stipends now.

OCTOBER

*Oct1– Most universities release open-enrollment materials (health, dental, vision, life, FSA, HSA) for the next calendar year. Block time to read the booklet, especially if you're considering retirement-phase coverage shifts.

*Oct15–

- Extended federal and state individual tax returns due
- Last day to re-characterize prior-year Roth IRA conversions

NOVEMBER

*Early Nov– Open-enrollment deadline at many campuses (often stays open ~2weeks). Missing it means default coverage for another year.

*Mid-Nov– Start charitable-giving and tax-loss-harvest reviews; custodians can be overloaded in December.

DECEMBER

*Dec1– Finalize any Roth conversions, donor-advised-fund gifts, or 529 plan contributions if using payroll year-end bonuses; wire cutoffs come earlier than you think.

*Dec15– Last-day campus deadlines for year-end 403(b)/457(b) catch-up elections and unused FSA claims (some plans run grace periods—verify).

*Dec31–

- Charitable donations must be postmarked or initiated to count for the tax year
- Last chance to reach the IRS elective-deferral limit ($23,000 in 2025, plus $7,500 catch-up if age50+)
- Deadline to complete RMDs for the year (if age73+ or from inherited accounts)
- HSA qualified-distribution deadline if your plan forfeits unused funds (many roll over, but some campus-sponsored HSAs may differ)

AGE-BASED MILESTONES

*Age50– Eligible for catch-up contributions in 403(b), 457(b), and IRA plans.

*Age55– Separation-from-service rule may allow penalty-free withdrawals from your 403(b) tied to that employer.

*Age59½ – 10percent early-withdrawal penalty on IRAs/403(b)s disappears.

*Age62– Earliest Social Security retirement benefit eligibility.

*Age65– Medicare enrollment window opens (three months before, the month of, and three months after birthday).

*Age73– RMDs begin (unless still working and eligible for the "still-in-service" exception on your 403(b)).

ANNUAL "BIG-PICTURE" REMINDERS

1. **Early January** – Set or review financial goals for the year; adjust monthly auto-transfers to emergency savings or brokerage.
2. **Post-Spring Commencement** – Mid-year check on spending, with-

holding, and retirement contribution pace.

3. **Late Summer** – Evaluate fall teaching loads, grant income, or administrative stipends; update estimated-tax projections.
4. **December First Week** – Final strategic tax moves: bunch deductions, harvest losses, or finalize generous Roth conversions.

Keep this calendar handy—tape it inside a cabinet door, bookmark it digitally, or share it with a trusted accountability partner. Your future self, grading fewer papers and stressing less over deadlines, will thank you.

Questions to Ask a Financial Advisor (For Professors and Academic Professionals)

1. Are you a fiduciary 100% of the time?
2. Do you have experience working with university faculty, administrators, or professionals in education?
3. How do you get paid—fee-only, fee-based, or commission-based?
4. Can you help me make the most of my university retirement plan options like 403(b), 457(b), and pension plans?
5. Will you coordinate with my CPA, estate attorney, or other professionals as part of my planning team?
6. What is your investment philosophy, and how do you tailor it to clients nearing or entering retirement?
7. How do you advise clients preparing for phased retirement, sabbaticals, or encore careers after academia?
8. Can you assist with planning around big financial moments—like sabbaticals, home purchases, or supporting family members?
9. Are you familiar with university benefit plans, including healthcare options, HSA/FSA accounts, and group life insurance?
10. Do you offer financial modeling or retirement scenario planning so I can see outcomes clearly?

Questions to Ask a CPA (Certified Public Accountant)

1. Do you have experience working with university faculty, especially those with consulting, research, or speaking income?

2. Do you offer year-round tax planning or only provide tax return preparation services?
3. Can you advise me on tax-efficient charitable giving strategies, including donor-advised funds?
4. Are you familiar with multi-state taxation for professors who earn income in multiple states or countries?
5. Can you help with education-related deductions, 529 plans, or student loan strategies?
6. Will you represent me if I get audited by the IRS or state tax authority?
7. Can you consult on income from rental properties, book royalties, or intellectual property?
8. How do you approach tax strategy for those with fluctuating income from grants or outside speaking?
9. What software or systems do you use to track complex income and deductions?
10. Can you explain my withholding and estimated tax payment obligations clearly?

Questions to Ask an Estate Planning Attorney

1. Do you have experience helping university professionals with estate planning, including TIAA annuities or pensions?
2. What are the core documents I should have—will, trust, powers of attorney, healthcare directives?
3. Can you assist with charitable giving as part of my estate plan (such as charitable trusts or bequests to a university)?
4. Are you knowledgeable about state-specific probate or estate laws that could affect my assets?
5. How do you handle digital assets or academic research materials as part of estate planning?
6. Should I consider a revocable living trust or other advanced estate strategies based on my net worth and goals?
7. Can you help protect my assets through proper titling and legal

structures?

8. Do you advise on succession planning for faculty who own consulting practices or publishing businesses?
9. How often should I update my estate plan based on job changes, retirement, or major life events?
10. Will you collaborate with my financial advisor and CPA to ensure everything is coordinated?

Questions to Ask Your University's HR or Benefits Office

1. Can I contribute to both the 403(b) and 457(b) plans to maximize my retirement savings?
2. What are the rules and deadlines for the university's retiree medical benefits or healthcare subsidies?
3. What happens to my benefits if I take a sabbatical, reduce hours, or enter phased retirement?
4. Does the university offer any group long-term care or supplemental insurance options?
5. How do I change or update my beneficiary designations across retirement accounts and insurance policies?
6. Are there differences between investment providers like TIAA, Fidelity, and Vanguard within the retirement plan?
7. Does the university offer financial education workshops or meetings with retirement representatives?
8. How can I access my plan documents and compare fees or fund performance within my retirement accounts?
9. If I leave the university, what happens to my pension or vested benefits?
10. Are there any retiree perks or continued access to university services after separation?

Questions to Ask a Business Attorney (For Professors with Consulting or Side Income)

1. Do you have experience with academics who earn money from consulting, publishing, speaking, or intellectual property?
2. Should I form an LLC or S-Corp to protect my side income activities?
3. Can you review my contracts for consulting engagements, publishing deals, or speaking gigs?
4. Do I need liability insurance or special contract language to protect myself when working outside the university?
5. Are you familiar with licensing rights for professors' educational materials, software, or course content?
6. Can you help with negotiating research agreements or private grant contracts?
7. Do you offer flat-rate pricing for standard contracts or ongoing legal support?
8. Can you advise on succession planning for a personal brand, business, or intellectual property I've created?
9. Do I need to disclose outside income to the university, and can you help me do it properly?
10. Can you help me protect my academic work if I retire or move to another institution?

Bonus: Questions for Other Key Professionals

Insurance Agent

1. Are you independent or tied to a specific insurance company?
2. Can you review my life, disability, umbrella, and long-term care policies to see if they still fit my needs?
3. Should I consider supplemental insurance for gaps in my university's offerings?
4. Can you advise me on the pros and cons of term versus permanent life insurance based on my retirement timeline?
5. What type of coverage is appropriate if I plan to consult after retirement?

Real Estate Advisor

1. Can you help me evaluate downsizing, relocating, or purchasing a second home before or during retirement?
2. Do you have experience advising university professionals who move for sabbaticals or post-retirement lifestyles?
3. Are you familiar with tax strategies like 1031 exchanges or home-sale exclusions?
4. Can you help with rental income analysis if I want to turn my current home into a rental after retirement?
5. Do you understand how a real estate decision fits into a broader retirement income plan?

Career Coach or Transition Consultant

1. Can you help me plan for a second-act career, such as consulting, writing, or nonprofit work?
2. Do you offer support for professors transitioning out of academia or preparing for phased retirement?
3. Can you model the financial and lifestyle implications of leaving academia early?
4. Are there opportunities to serve on nonprofit boards, think tanks, or alumni programs?
5. Do you offer values-based planning to help align post-career goals with my financial situation?

Final Thought

You've spent a career asking hard questions in pursuit of truth. Apply the same discernment when building your financial team. Your finances are no less worthy of critical thinking than your research, teaching, or mentorship. When you ask the right questions, you don't just gather information—you gain confidence, clarity, and control. Financial literacy for professors means knowing how to choose wisely, collaborate intentionally, and build a future that reflects your values. Keep asking. Keep learning. And never stop advocating for your future self.

Wealth Manager's Coordination

At the higher rungs of academia, managing money is not a side errand you squeeze in between grading and committee meetings—it is an enterprise of its own. Once grants, royalties, consulting income, endowed-chair stipends, and multiple retirement plans start stacking up, personal finance for a senior professor begins to resemble the complexity of a small family office. Turning that tangle into a coherent strategy requires more than a casual chat with HR. A first-rate wealth manager for academics must become the chief architect and conductor of a finely tuned ecosystem—coordinating estate planning, tax strategy, insurance coverage, investment policy, charitable giving, and retirement cash-flow design. Done well, that orchestration converts complexity into clarity, risk into resilience, and a distinguished career into an enduring legacy.

Estate planning is the foundation. Coordinating wills, trusts, and beneficiary designations ensures that book royalties, TIAA annuities, and family property transition smoothly to heirs while minimizing estate taxes and shielding assets from potential claims. Tools like revocable living trusts, qualified terminable interest property (QTIP) trusts, and charitable remainder trusts (CRTs) have become standard—not exotic—in the financial playbook for professors with substantial intellectual-property income or real-estate holdings. Real-life scenario: a retired literature scholar placed global translation rights to her best-selling textbook into a testamentary CRT, providing lifetime income for her spouse and an eventual endowment for first-generation students. Action step: schedule a comprehensive estate-plan review to verify that your documents reflect current tax law, university contract language, and your legacy goals.

Accounting and tax coordination sit at the nerve center of academic wealth. Sabbatical housing allowances, international conference honoraria, multi-state adjunct gigs, and grant stipends all layer unique tax consequences on top of W-2 wages. Seamless collaboration among your wealth manager, CPA, and estate attorney is essential to keep withholdings accurate and after-tax results optimized. Pros: greater cash-flow predictability and audit protection. Cons: continuous vigilance and a truly interdisciplinary team. Action step: assemble a tax team fluent in higher-education nuances—such as foreign-earned income exclusions, accountable-plan reimbursements, and self-employment tax on consulting fees—and insist on mid-year strategy meetings, not just April fire drills.

Insurance often hides in plain sight. Standard group coverage from the university rarely protects a lifetime of accumulated manuscripts, rare books, or growing consulting liability. Home, auto, umbrella, professional-liability, cyber, and long-term-care policies must be customized to your risk profile. Real-life scenario: an economics professor's laptop, containing decades of unpublished data, was stolen abroad. A specialty rider reimbursed both the hardware and the costly data-recovery process. Action step: conduct an annual insurance audit—itemizing personal assets, professional exposures, and travel patterns—to close coverage gaps before they become headlines.

Investment management for academics must be both disciplined and flexible. TIAA Traditional may provide guaranteed income, but it seldom hedges inflation alone. Direct indexing, low-cost index funds, real-estate investment trusts (REITs), and charitable gift annuities can complement university plans and reduce overall tax drag. Increasingly, professors channel portions of consulting income into diversified brokerage or donor-advised-fund (DAF) portfolios rather than overloading additional 403(b) contributions. Action step: craft a written investment policy statement (IPS) that marries TIAA's benefits with broader diversification and a clear rebalancing schedule.

Trading and execution demand sophistication once outside income grows. Selling a large block of university stock received as part of a tech-transfer royalty agreement or liquidating a concentrated position in a legacy mutual fund can trigger outsized taxes or market impact. Continuous tax-loss harvesting on taxable accounts is vital, particularly in volatile markets. Real-life scenario: a professor's family foundation partnered with an institutional trading desk to unwind a seven-figure royalty-stock position over several quarters, harvesting losses along the way and re-directing proceeds to an endowment. Action step: engage a trading specialist who can execute large transactions silently and tax-efficiently.

Liquidity and retirement cash-flow planning are non-negotiable. Whether you're shifting to phased retirement, launching a consulting practice, or planning a sabbatical-home purchase, preparation must begin years in advance. Liquidity isn't just a safety cushion—it's strategic capital for new research, family support, or philanthropic ventures. Real-life scenario: a biology chair arranged a line of credit secured by brokerage assets two years before stepping down, ensuring smooth cash flow while awaiting delayed grant reimbursements. Action step: map out five- and ten-year liquidity needs, then align retirement-account withdrawals, annuitizations, and taxable-account strategies accordingly.

Philanthropy often becomes a capstone for professors who have spent careers advancing knowledge. Donor-advised funds, charitable remainder trusts, and planned gifts to alma maters can lock in tax deductions, provide income streams, and cement your academic legacy. Aligning charitable intentions with estate and investment plans maintains coherence. Action step: articulate a clear giving mission, then integrate philanthropic vehicles—whether a DAF or a scholarship endowment—into your overall financial strategy.

Remember, academic finances evolve. Grants dry up, royalties spike, tax laws shift, and family needs change. A wealth manager who acts as quarterback ensures every specialty advisor stays in sync. Real-life scenario: A distinguished historian coordinated estate planning, international tax issues, investment oversight, and charitable giving through one lead advisor—preserving family harmony and maximizing philanthropic impact. Action step: demand fully integrated advice; if your current team operates in silos, re-engineer the structure or appoint a lead professional to orchestrate collaboration.

The call to action is clear: insist on coordination, not fragmentation. The goals—wealth preservation, strategic growth, risk management, tax efficiency, family unity, and enduring impact—are fully attainable. But they require a skilled conductor guiding the orchestra of estate, tax, insurance, investment, liquidity, and philanthropy. For professors whose expertise has generated substantial wealth or influence, mastery lies in seamless integration—a symphony of strategy poised to last for generations.

While this book serves an educational purpose, deep, personalized support can accelerate results. If you need help building or refining this level of coordination, I would be honored to assist. With extensive experience serving professors, academic leaders, and multi-generational faculty families, I bring the discretion, expertise, and holistic vision required to turn complexity into clarity. Reach out anytime; together we can ensure your financial achievements amplify the legacy of your life's work.

Final Word

Need Help? Start Here

This book exists because financial education is one of the most powerful tools a professor can have. Whether you're early in your academic journey, navigating mid-career choices, or preparing for retirement, understanding how money works can help you make informed decisions, reduce stress, and build lasting security for yourself and your loved ones.

But just like teaching, research, or mentoring students, financial success doesn't happen by accident. It takes structure. It takes planning. It takes the willingness to ask thoughtful questions, consider trade-offs, and seek guidance when things feel unclear. You don't need to be a financial expert—you just need a mindset of curiosity and a framework to follow.

Use this book as a guide, not a prescription. Let it prompt reflection and smart action. Let it serve as a trusted reference as your career evolves. But remember, no book—this one included—can replace the value of personalized advice. Keep asking questions, keep reading carefully, and don't hesitate to reach out to professionals who understand your world.

Trusted Resources

If you're ready to take the next step or want to talk through what you've read, connect with someone who works specifically with academic professionals—someone who understands university compensation models, retirement plans like TIAA or 403(b)s, sabbatical funding, consulting income, and the unique financial puzzles professors often face.

Pat Brown, MBA

Wealth advisor. Financial literacy advocate. Former Division I athlete.

Advisor to professors, researchers, administrators, and high-performing professionals across the country.

Website: www.financialliteracyforprofessors.com
Email: info@financialliteracyforprofessors.com
LinkedIn: linkedin.com/in/patrickbrownmba

Join Our Newsletter

Stay up-to-date with practical strategies, financial reminders, and timely insights tailored for academic professionals.

Subscribe at www.financialliteracyforprofessors.com and receive actionable content in your inbox—designed specifically for the academic lifestyle.

Final Word: Use This. Don't Shelf It.

The ideas in this book are here to be put to work. Come back to them as your life and career evolve. Share them with a colleague, a graduate student, or your department. Adapt what fits. Question what doesn't. Use this book to start building the kind of financial clarity that supports both your mission and your peace of mind.

This is your playbook—not just for your career, but for your life.

Professionally, personally, and financially.

Stay thoughtful. Stay proactive. And keep designing a future that supports the life you've worked so hard to build.

Ask ChatGPT

Made in the USA
Monee, IL
04 November 2026

67387592R00193